THE

INFANT SYSTEM,

FOR

DEVELOPING THE INTELLECTUAL AND MORAL POWERS OF ALL CHILDREN,

FROM

ONE TO SEVEN YEARS OF AGE.

BY

SAMUEL WILDERSPIN.

SIXTH EDITION, REVISED THROUGHOUT.

"Whoso shall receive one such little child in my name, receiveth me."
Matt. xviii. 5.
"Take heed that ye despise not one of these little ones."
Matt. xviii. 10.

LONDON:

SIMPKIN AND MARSHALL,

STATIONERS' HALL COURT.

1834.

LONDON

PRINTED BY J. S. HODSON, CROSS STREET, HATTON GARDEN.

PREFACE.

———

In again presenting this volume to the world, and especially in doing so under the distinguished patronage of our beloved Queen I trust I feel thankful to God for the favour with which the Infant System has been received, and for all the aid I have enjoyed in my course of labour. Had the measures I originated for the development of the Infant mind, and the improvement of the moral character been sanctioned at first, as many now think they should have been, their progress would, undoubtedly, have been far greater;

a 3

but when I consider what has been accomplished under the divine benediction, amid greater difficulties than ever beset the path of an individual similarly occupied, I know not how to express **the gratitude** of which I am conscious. It seems proper and even necessary to remark, that the system explained in this volume, is the result of many years of labour. Thousands of children have been attentively observed, and for the necessities that arose in their instruction, provision has been made. Others have doubtless reached some of the conclusions at which I have arrived, but this is only another instance of the coincidence in judgment and effort, often discoverable in persons far apart; for, with the exception of the elliptical plan, devised by Dr. Gilchrist, I am not aware that I owe an idea or contrivance to any individual whatever. Nearly sixteen thousand children have been now under my own care, in various parts of the United Kingdom, whose age has not exceeded six years; myself, my daughter, and my agents, have organized many score of schools, and thus I have had opportunities of studying the infant mind and heart, such as none of my contemporaries have ever possessed.

Still I am aware I have much to learn. I am far less satisfied with my knowledge, and far less confident now than I was in the earlier part of my course; but should I have the pleasure to labour for years to come, I trust I shall have much more to communicate on the subject.

Two editions of this work in its former state have been printed in German; and it has also been reprinted in America. I have, however, felt it due to the friends of education, to make this volume as complete as possible, and as my constant engagements are unfavourable to such efforts, a friend has kindly undertaken to make the alterations and additions I have suggested, which I hope will render it more acceptable and useful.

Alpha House, Alstone, Cheltenham,
        November, 1833.

A FEW TESTIMONIALS TO THE INFANT SYSTEM.

———

"It is said that we are aiming at carrying education too far; that we are drawing it out to an extravagant length, and that, not satisfied with dispensing education to children who have attained what in former times was thought a proper age, we are now anxious to educate mere infants, incapable of receiving benefit from such instruction. This objection may be answered in two ways. In the first place, it should be observed, that the objection comes from those very persons who object to education being given to children when they arrive at a more advanced period, on the ground that their parents then begin to find them useful in labour, and consequently cannot spare so much of their time as might be requisite: surely, then, the education of the children should commence at that time when their labour can be of no value to their parents. But the other answer, in my opinion, is still more decisive: it is found even at the early age of seven or eight, that children are not void of those propensities, which are the forerunners of vice, and I can give no better illustration of this, than the fact of a child only eight years old, being convicted of a capital offence at our tribunals of justice; when, therefore, I find that at this early period of life, these habits of vice are formed, it seems to me that we ought to begin still earlier to store their minds with such tastes, and to instruct them in such a manner as to exclude the admission of those practices that lead to such early crime and depravity. A Noble Friend has most justly stated, that it is not with the experiences of yesterday that we come armed to the contest: it is not a speculation that we are bringing forward to your notice, but an experiment."---*The Lord Chancellor.*

"In leaving poor children to the care of their parents, neglect is the least that happens; it too frequently occurs that they are turned over to delegates, where they meet with the worst treatment; so that we do not in fact come so much into contact with the parents themselves as with these delegates, who are so utterly unfit for the office they undertake. Infant Schools, however, have completely succeeded, not only in the negative plan they had in view, of keeping the children out of vice and mischief, but even to the extent of engrafting in their minds at that early age those principles of virtue, which capacitated them for receiving a further stage of instruction at a more advanced school, and finally, as they approached manhood, to be ripened into the noblest sentiments of probity and integrity."--- *The Marquis of Lansdowne.*

"I am a zealous friend, upon conviction, to Infant Schools for the children of the poor. No person who has not himself watched them, can form an adequate notion of what these institutions, when judiciously conducted, may effect in forming the tempers and habits of young children; in giving them, not so much actual knowledge, as that which at their age is more important, the habit and faculty of acquiring it; and in correcting those moral defects which neglect or injudicious treatment would soon confirm and render incurable. The early age at which children are taken out of our National Schools, is an additional reason for commencing a regular and systematic discipline of their minds and wills, as soon as they are capable of profiting by it; and that is at the very earliest opening of the understanding, and at the first manifestation of a corrupt nature in the shape of a childish petulance and waywardness."--- *The Bishop of London.*

"The claims of this Institution were of such a nature, that they required no recommendation but a full statement of them. The foundation of its happy results had been pointed out to exist in the principles of policy, and of religion paramount to all policy---a religion that appealed to every feeling of human nature. He would recommend this charity, as one less attended with perplexity in its operations or doubt as to its utility, than many, which, though established with the best possible motives, frequently failed in effecting the good proposed; but in this the most acute opponent could not discover any mischief that would arise from its success."--- *Sir James Mackintosh.*

"I have always thought that that man would be the greatest benefactor to his country who did most for the suppression of crime;

this, I am sorry to say, our legislature have neglected in a great degree, while they have readily employed themselves in providing for its punishment. Those acquainted with our prisons must know that those found to have sunk deepest into vice and crime were persons who had never received any education, moral or religious. In the Refuge for the Destitute, an exact account was kept, and it was found that of the great mass of culprits sent there by the magistrates on account of their youth, two-thirds were the children of parents who had no opportunity of educating them. By this institution they would at once promote virtue and prevent vice."---*Dr. Lushington.*

" The real fact is, that the character of all mankind is formed very early---much earlier than might be supposed : at the age of two or three years, dispositions were found in children of a description the most objectionable. In these schools the principles of mutual kindness and assistance were carried as far as could well be conceived, and it was most delightful to regard the conduct of the children towards each other. Instead of opposition, they displayed mutual good-will, inculcated to the greatest degree, so as to destroy in the minds of the children that selfishness which was the bane of our nature. Such effects appeared almost to realize the golden age, for the children appeared always happy, and never so happy as when attending the schools."--- *W. Smith, Esq. M.P.*

" I feel, having witnessed the happy effects produced by these schools, a warm zeal in support of such institutions. We cannot begin too soon to impress religious principles on the minds of the young : it is an affecting consideration, that while great statesmen have been busied in their closets on some fine scheme or speculation, they have neglected those salutary principles which the Almighty had given to mankind. It is remarkable how eagerly the young mind receives the histories of the Bible, and how well they are fitted to work on their dispositions ; and when I consider the miserable state of the poor, I cannot but feel that the rich are in some degree, the authors of it, in having neglected to afford them the means of education."— *W. Wilberforce, Esq.*

"I am much delighted with what I have seen and heard. I confess I entertained doubts of the practicability of the Infant School System, but these doubts have this day been removed. If in *one month* so much can be done, what might not be expected from further training? I now doubt no longer, and anticipate from the extension of such schools a vast improvement in the morals and religion of the humble classes. I conclude with moving a vote of thanks to Mr. Wilderspin."—*Lord Chief Justice Clerk.*

" Sir John Sinclair rose, and, addressing Mr. Wilderspin, said, that he was astonished with the results of five weeks training in these perfect infants. He had never seen a greater prodigy. He too had had his prejudices—his doubts of the possibility of infant training, but these doubts had now vanished, and for ever. The arrangements for bodily exercise, connected with mental and moral improvement, especially delighted him. He was amused as well as instructed by the well-applied admixture of diverting expedients to keep the children alive and alert. It was 'seria mixta jocis,' but there was practical sense in the seemingly most frivolous part of the plan. He trusted that the time was not far distant when there would be many such institutions. He called on all present to join him in returning cordial thanks to Mr. Wilderspin."—*Scotsman.*

" The grand secret of the improvement found to be derived from these establishments, is their constant tendency to remove evil example and misery from the little creatures during almost the whole of their waking hours. Consider how a child belonging to one of these passes his day. As soon as he is up, the indispensable condition, and the only one of his admission to the school, that of clean face and hands, is enforced, and the mother, in order to be relieved of the care of him during the day, is obliged to have him washed. He then leaves the abode of filth and intemperance, and squalid poverty, and ill-temper, for a clean, airy place, pleasant in summer, warm and dry in winter ; and where he sees no face that is not lighted up with the smile of kindness towards him. His whole day is passed in amusing exercises, or interesting instruction; and he returns at evening-tide fatigued and ready for his bed, so that the scenes passing at his comfortless home make a slight impression on his mind or his spirits."—*Edinburgh Review.*

CONTENTS.

CHAPTER I.

JUVENILE DELINQUENCY.

CHAPTER II.

CAUSES OF EARLY CRIME.

CHAPTER III.

REMEDY FOR EXISTING EVILS.

CHAPTER IV.

PRINCIPLES OF INFANT EDUCATION.

b

CHAPTER X.

LANGUAGE.

CHAPTER X.*

ARITHMETIC.

CHAPTER XI.

FORM, POSITION, AND SIZE.

CHAPTER XII.

GEOGRAPHY.

CHAPTER XIII.

PICTURES AND CONVERSATION.

CHAPTER XIV.

TEACHING BY OBJECTS.

CHAPTER XV.

EXERCISE.

CHAPTER XVI.

MUSIC.

CHAPTER XVII.

GRAMMAR.

CHAPTER XVIII.

THE ELLIPTICAL PLAN.

CHAPTER XIX.

REMARKS ON NATIONAL, BRITISH AND FOREIGN SOCIETY'S, AND SUNDAY SCHOOLS.

CHAPTER XX.

HINTS ON NURSERY EDUCATION.

Plan for an Infant School, City, Ground & Masters House

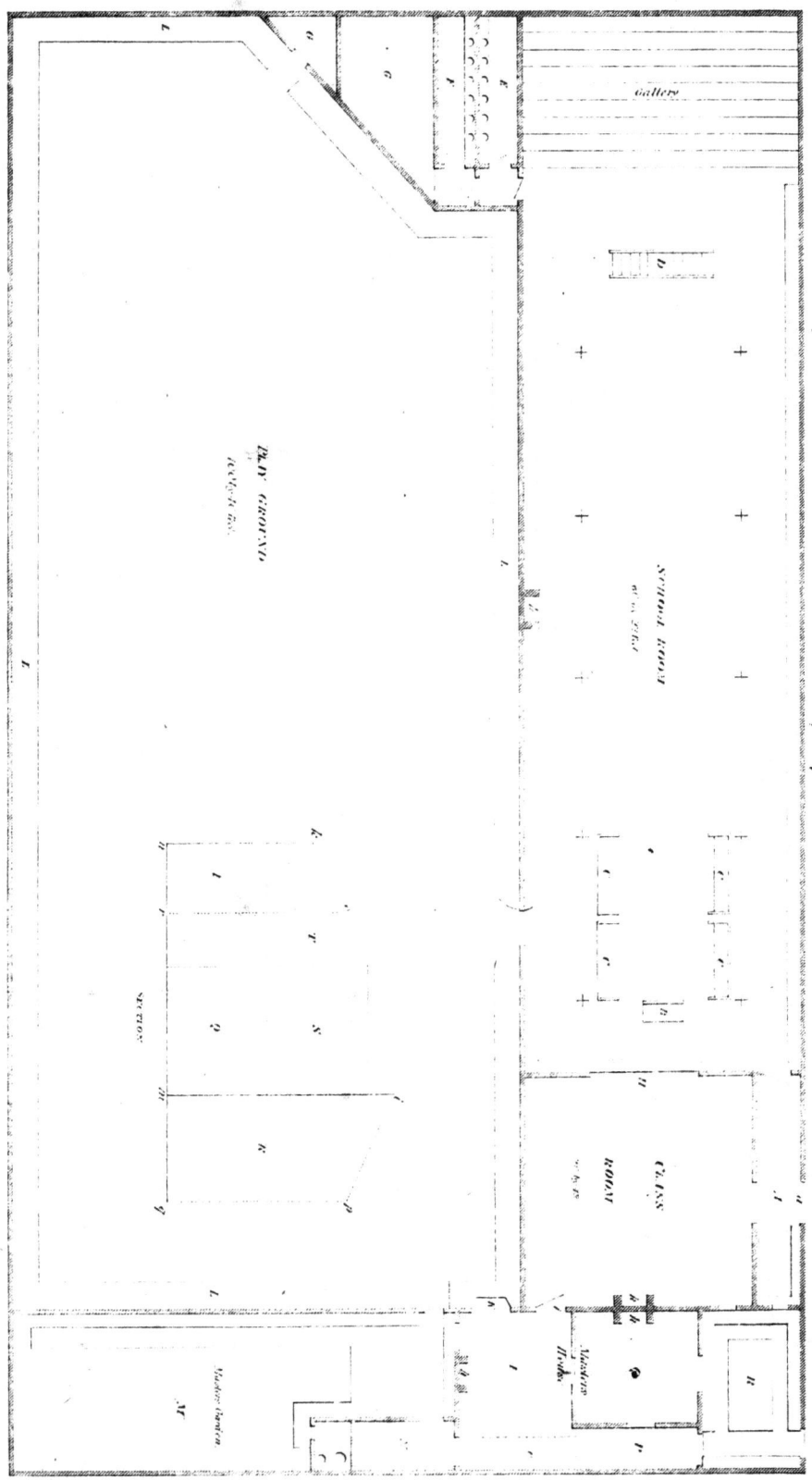

Gallery

SCHOOL ROOM
60 × 25½

PLAN GROUND
60 × 25½

CLASS ROOM

SECTION

Masters Garden

Masters House

THE

INFANT SYSTEM.

CHAPTER I.

JUVENILE DELINQUENCY.

" An uneducated, unemployed poor, not only must be liable to fall into a variety of temptations, but they will, at times, unavoidably prove restless, dissatisfied, perverse, and seditious: nor is this all, even their most useful and valuable qualities, for want of regular and good habits, and a proper bias and direction from early religious instruction, frequently become dangerous and hurtful to society; their patience degenerates into sullenness, their perseverance into obstinacy, their strength and courage into brutal ferocity."

THE BISHOP OF NORWICH.

IT has long been a subject of regret as well as of astonishment to the reflecting and benevolent, that notwithstanding the numerous institutions which exist in this country for the education and improvement of the poor, and in defiance of the endeavours of

B

our magistracy and police establishment, crime should rather increase than diminish. Many persons have been induced to conclude from this fact that our Sunday, Parochial, and National Schools, as well as our Bible Societies, and institutions of a similar nature, are of no use whatever. Absurd as the inference is, I have known more than one or two persons draw it; not considering, that although these means may be insufficient to counteract the cause of crime, or to prevent all its evil effects, yet, nevertheless, they must certainly check its progress;—that if there be many offenders, despite of these institutions, there would, doubtless, be many more were they not in existence; and hence to revile or neglect them is unworthy of good sense or good feeling.

It is not my purpose in the present chapter to dwell on the commission of crime generally, but on juvenile delinquency in particular; and on this only so far as regards the case of young children. I will, therefore, make public a collection of facts, some of which were obtained at considerable personal hazard and inconvenience, which will place it in a clear yet painful light.

It is said, that in the year 1819, the number of boys, in London alone, who procured a considerable part of their subsistence by pocket-picking and thieving in every possible form, was estimated at from eleven to fifteen hundred. One man who lived in Wentworth-street, near Spitalfields, had forty boys in training to steal and pick pockets, who were paid for their exertions with a part of the plunder; fortunately, however, for the public, this notable tutor of thieves was himself convicted of theft and transported. This system of tutorage is by no means uncommon, nor is it confined to the male sex. I remember reading some time back in the Police Reports, of a woman who had entrapped *eight or ten children* from their parents, had trained them up, and sent them out thieving; nor was it until one of these infantile depredators was taken in the act of stealing, that this was made known, and the children restored to their homes. Here we see eight or ten children, probably from the neglect of their parents, enticed away no doubt by the promise of a few cakes, or of some other trifling reward, and in imminent danger of becoming confirmed thieves, from which they were rescued by this providential discovery of their situation; and we know not how many children may have been led to evil practices in like manner.

I will give another instance which occurred at the office at Queen Square.—A female, apparently not more than nineteen years of age, named Jane Smith, and a child just turned of five years old, named Mary Ann Ranniford, were put to the bar, before Edward Markland, Esq., the magistrate, charged with circulating counterfeit coin in Westminster and the county of Surrey to a vast extent.

It appeared that the elder prisoner had long been known to be a common utterer of base coin, in which she dealt very largely with those individuals who are agents in London to the manufacturers of the spurious commodity at Birmingham. She has been once or twice before charged with the offence, and therefore she became so notorious that she was necessitated to leave off putting the bad money away herself; but so determined was she to keep up the traffic, that she was in the habit of employing children of tender years to pass the counterfeit money. On one occasion two Bow-street officers observed her at her old trade, in company with the child Ranniford. The officers kept a strict eye upon her movements, and saw her several times pass something to the little girl; and she, by the direction of her instructor, went into different shops (such as hosiers, where she purchased balls of worsted, pastry-cooks, tobacconists, and fruiterers), where she passed the bad money, and received in return goods and change. On the other side of the bridge, the patroles saw the prisoner Smith deliver something to the child, and point out the shop of Mr. Isaacs, a fruiterer, in Bridge Street, Westminster. The child went in, and asked for a juicy lemon, and gave a counterfeit shilling in payment. Mrs. Isaacs had no suspicion from the tender age of the utterer, and its respectable appearance, that the money was bad, and was about to give change, when one of the officers entered and took the deluded child into custody, whilst his companion secured the elder prisoner (Smith), and on searching her pockets he found twelve bad shillings, some parcels of snuff, several balls of cotton and worsted, and other trifling articles, which the child had purchased in the course of the day. The officers who had secured them learned from the child that her parents lived in Cross Street, East Lane, Walworth, and that Smith had taken her out for a walk. The patrol instantly communicated the circumstance to the child's parents, who are hard-working honest people, and their feelings on hearing that their infant had been seduced into the commission of such a crime, can be more easily conceived than described. They stated that the woman Smith had formerly lived in the same street, and was frequently giving half-pence and cakes to the child, who would, in consequence, follow her anywhere. Some time since, she removed to Lock's Square, Lock's Fields, and they (the parents) had not seen her for some time. On the day referred to the child was playing in the street, and not finding her come home they became alarmed, and went every where, broken-hearted, in quest of her, but they could hear no tidings of her till the sad news was brought them by the officers. The poor mother was now in attendance, and her feelings were dreadfully affected, and excited the commiseration of all present.

The prisoner Smith made no defence, and held her head down during the examination. The child stood by her, and took no notice of the proceedings, and they were both fully committed for trial. The mother on seeing her infant consigned to prison, became quite frantic, and wept hysterically, and had it not been for the gaoler, she would have inflicted some violence upon the woman Smith for seducing her infant.

Facts of this kind are sufficient to shew the utility, indeed I may say, the necessity of providing some means, more efficient than those at present in existence, for the protection and improvement of the infant poor; that they may not thus fall into the hands of evil and designing wretches, who make a living by encouraging the children of the poor to commit crimes, of the produce of which they themselves take the greatest part.

The younger the children are, the better they suit

the purpose of such miscreants ; because, if children are detected in any dishonest act, they know well, that few persons will do more than give the child or children a tap on the head, and send them about their business. The tenth part of the crimes committed by these juvenile offenders never comes under public view, because should any person be robbed by a child, and detect him in the act, he is silenced by the by-standers with this remark,—"Oh ! he is but a child, let him go this time, perhaps the poor thing has done it from necessity, being in want of bread." Thus the delinquent is almost sure to escape, and, instead of being punished, is not unfrequently rewarded for the adventure, as was the case in the following instance.

Having had occasion to walk through Shoreditch some time since, I saw a number of persons collected together round a little boy, who, it appeared, had stolen a brass weight from the shop of a grocer. The shopman stated that three boys came into the shop for half-an-ounce of candied horehound, and that while he was getting down the glass which contained it, one of them contrived to purloin the weight in question. Having some suspicion of the boys, from the circumstance of having recently lost a number of brass weights, he kept his eyes on them, when he saw one put his hand into a box that was on the counter, take out the largest weight, and then run out of the shop, followed by the other two. The boy who stole it, slipped the weight into the hand of one of the others ; but the shopman, having observed this manœuvre, followed the boy who had the weight, who, being the youngest of the three, could not run very fast ; he, finding himself closely pursued, threw the weight into the road, and when he was taken, declared it was not he who took it. The man wished to take the child back to the shop, in order that his master might do with him as he thought proper, but the by-standers, with a charitable *zeal* which evinced little *knowledge*, prevented him; one man in particular seemed to interest himself much in the boy's behalf, stating that he knew the child very well, and that he had neither father nor mother. The child immediately took up this plea, and added that he had had no victuals all day. The individual before mentioned then gave him a penny, and his example was followed by many more, till I think the boy had obtained nearly a shilling. I put several questions to him, but was checked by this fellow, who told me, that as I had given the child nothing, I had no right to ask so much; and, after a great deal of abuse, he ended by telling me, that if I did not "take myself off," he would " give me something for myself."

Feeling, however, a great desire to sift further into the matter, I feigned to withdraw, but kept my eye upon the boy, and followed him for nearly two hours, until I saw him join two other boys, one of whom I had not seen before, and who had a bag with something very heavy in it, which, I have every reason to believe, were weights, or something which they had obtained in a similar manner. Wishing to ascertain the fact, I approached them, but they no sooner perceived me, than the little fellow who had been the principal actor in the affair, called out, *" Nose, Nose,"* —a signal-word, no doubt, agreed upon amongst them,—when they all ran down some obscure alleys. I followed, but was knocked down, as if by accident,

by two ill-looking fellows, who continued to detain
me with apologies till the boys had got safely away.
I have little doubt that this was an instance of that
organized system of depredation of which I have
before spoken, and that the man who took so active
a part at the first was at the bottom of the business ;
—and, in fact, the tutor and employer of the preda-
tory urchins.   His activity in preventing the boy
from being taken back to the shop—his anxiety to
promote a subscription for the boy,—and, lastly, his
threat of personal violence if I interfered in the matter, by continuing to question the child,—all these
circumstances confirm me in the opinion.

It is only by the knowledge of this fact—the association of infant offenders with those of maturer and
hardened habits—that we can account for such cases
as the following.—On the 17th of July, 1823, a
child *only seven years old*, was brought before the
magistrate at Lambeth Street office, charged with
frequently robbing his mother, and was ordered to be
locked up all night in the gaol-room.   In the evening, however, when his mother returned, he forced
his way out of the room, and behaved with such
violence that the attendants were obliged to iron both
his hands and legs !   There can be no doubt that
this child had been for a long time under the instruction and evil influence of some old and hardened
offender; he must, indeed, have undergone much
training before he could have arrived at such a pitch
of hardihood, as to make it necessary to handcuff and
fetter a child of so tender an age; and to enable him
to hold even the magistrates, officers, and his own
parent, at defiance.

The following cases afford further proof of the same lamentable truth; the first is extracted from a morning paper of the 20th of September, 1824. "A little boy, not more than *six years of age*, was brought before the Lord Mayor at the Mansion House, on Saturday, the 18th instant, having been found in a warehouse, where he had secreted himself for the purpose of thieving. At a late hour on Friday night, a watchman was going his round, when, on trying a warehouse in which there was much valuable property, to see whether it was safe, he heard the little prisoner cry. The persons who had the care of the warehouse were roused, and he was taken out. In his fright he acknowledged that a man had taken him from his mother, and induced him, upon a promise of reward, to steal into the warehouse; upon a concerted signal, he was to act as directed by the fellow on the outside; but becoming terrified at being confined so long in the dark, he had cried out and discovered himself. His mother came forward, and received a good character as the wife of a hard-working man. The Lord Mayor gave her son up to her, with an injunction to act carefully and strictly with him. There was reason to believe, he said, that several considerable robberies had been recently committed by means of children like the prisoner, who stole in and remained concealed until midnight, when they gave admission to the robbers. The police should have their eyes upon him."

The other instance is from a report of one of the sessions in London :—

"William Hart, an urchin *seven years of age*, was indicted for stealing twenty-two shillings in money, numbered, from the person of Mary Conner. The prosecutrix stated, that on the day named in the indictment, she took twenty-five shillings to get something out of pledge, but as there was a crowd in Mary-le-bone, assembled to witness a fight, she was induced to join the mob. While standing there she felt something move in her pocket, and putting her hand outside her clothes, she laid hold of what proved to be the hand of the prisoner, which she held until she had given him a slap on the face, and then she let him go; but on feeling in her pocket she discovered that the theft had actually been committed and that only three shillings were left. A constable took the urchin into custody, and accused him of robbing her of twenty-two shillings. The prisoner said, 'I have twenty-two shillings in my pocket, but it is my mother's money; she gets so drunk she gives me her money to take care of.' The officer stated to the same effect as the prosecutrix, and added, that *in a secret pocket in his jacket he found fourteen shillings and sixpence. It was the practice of gangs of pickpockets to have a child like this to commit the robbery, and hand the plunder to them.* Witness went to his parents, who said he had been absent seven weeks, and they would have nothing to do with him. Mr. Baron Garrow, in feeling terms, lamented that a child of such tender years should be so depraved. He added, 'I suppose, gentlemen, I need only to ask you to deliver your verdict.' His lordship then observed, that he would consult with his learned brother as to the best manner of disposing of the prisoner. They at length decided, that although it might seem harsh, the court would record against him fourteen years' transportation, and, no doubt, government would place him in some school; if he behaved well there, the sentence might not be carried into full effect."

I remember a query being once put to me by a person who visited the Spitalfields Infant School at the time it was under my management: "How can you account for the fact, that notwithstanding there are so many old and experienced thieves detected, convicted, and sent out of the country every session, we cannot perceive any diminution of the numbers of such characters; but that others seem always to supply their places?" The foregoing instances of the systematized instruction of young delinquents by old adepts in the art of pilfering affords, I think, a satisfactory answer to the interrogatory.

The dexterity of experienced thieves shews, that no small degree of care and attention is bestowed on their tuition. The first task of novices, I have been informed, is to go in companies of threes or fours, through the respectable streets and squares of the metropolis, and with an old knife, or a similar instrument, to wrench off the brass-work usually placed over the key-holes of the area-gates, &c. which they sell at the marine store shops; and they are said sometimes to realize three or four shillings a day, by this means. Wishing to be satisfied on the point, I have walked round many of the squares in town, and in more than a solitary experiment, have found that *not one gate in ten* had any brass-work over the key-hole; it had moreover been evidently wrenched off,—a small piece of the brass still remaining on many of the gates. Having practised this branch of the profession a considerable time, and become adepts in its execution, the next step, I have been informed, is to steal the handles and brass knockers from doors, which is done by taking out the screw with a small screw-driver : these are disposed of in the same manner as the former things, till the young pilferers are progressively qualified for stealing brass weights, &c. and at length, become expert thieves.

The following fact will shew what extensive depredations young children are capable of committing. I have inserted the whole as it appeared in the public papers :—" *Union Hall; Shop Lifting.*—Yesterday, two little girls, sisters, very neatly dressed, *one nine,* and the *other seven years of age,* were put to the bar, charged by Mr. Cornell, linen-draper, of High Street, Newington, with having stolen a piece of printed calico, from the counter of his shop.

"Mr. Cornell stated, the children came to his shop, yesterday morning ; that while he was engaged with his customers at the further end of the shop, he happened to cast his eyes where the prisoners were, and observed the eldest roll up a large piece of printed calico, and put it into a basket, which her little sister carried : the witness immediately advanced to her, and asked if she had taken any thing from off the counter ; but she positively asserted that she had not. However, on searching her basket, the calico was found ; together with a piece of muslin, which Mr. Cornell identified as belonging to him, and to have been taken in the above way. Mr. Allen questioned the eldest girl about the robbery, but she positively denied any knowledge as to how, or in what manner, the calico and muslin had got into her basket, frequently appealing to her little sister to confirm the truth of what she declared. When asked if she had ever been charged with any offence, she replied, 'O yes, sir, some time back I was accused of stealing a watch from a house, but I did not do it.' The magistrate observed, that the father should be made acquainted with the circumstance, and, in the mean time, gave the gaoler instructions that the two little delinquents should be taken care of.

"Hall, the officer, stated that he had information that there was a quantity of goods, which had been stolen by the prisoners, concealed in a certain desk in the house of the father; and that a great deal of stolen property would, in all probability, be found there, if a search-warrant were granted, as the two unfortunate children were believed to be most extensive depredators.

"Mr. Allen immediately granted the warrant; and Hall, accompanied by Mr. Cornell, proceeded to the residence of the father of the children, who is an auctioneer and appraiser, at 12, Lyon street, Newington.

"Hall returned in half an hour with the father in his custody, and produced a great quantity of black silk handkerchiefs, which he had found on the premises; but the desk, which had been spoken of by his informers as containing stolen property, he had found quite empty. The father, when questioned by the witness as to whether he had any duplicates of property in his possession, positively denied that fact. At the office he was searched, and about fifty duplicates were found in his pockets, most of which were for silk handkerchiefs and shawls. There were also a few rings, for the possession of which the prisoner could not satisfactorily account. He was asked why he had assured the officer he had no duplicates? He replied, that he had not said so; but Mr. Cornell, who was present during the search, averred that the prisoner had most positively declared that he had not a pawnbroker's duplicate in his possession.

"Mr. Watt, a linen-draper, of Harper Street, Kent Road, stated, that he attended in consequence of seeing the police reports in the newspapers, describing the two children; he immediately recognised the two little girls as having frequently called at his shop for trifling articles; and added, that he had been robbed of a variety of silk handkerchiefs and shawls, and he had no doubt but that the prisoners were the thieves. It was their practice, he said, to go into a shop, and call for a quarter of a yard of muslin, and while the shopkeeper was engaged, the eldest would very dexterously slip whatever article was nearest to her to her little sister, who was trained to the business, and would thrust the stolen property into a basket which she always carried for that purpose. Mr. Watt identified the silk handkerchiefs as his property, and said that they had been stolen in the above manner by the prisoners.

"The father was asked where he had got the handkerchiefs? He replied, that he had bought them from a pedlar for half-a crown a piece at his door. However, his eldest daughter contradicted him by acknowledging that her sister had stolen them from the shop of Mr. Watt. He became dreadfully agitated, and then said—'What could I say? Surely I was not to criminate my own children!'

"Mr. Allen observed, that there was a clear case against the two children, but after consulting with the other magistrates, he was of opinion that the youngest child should be given up into the charge of the parish officers of Newington, as she was too young to go into a prison; and desired that the other girl should be remanded, in order to have some of the pledged goods produced. The father was committed in default of bail, for receiving stolen goods. The child has since been found guilty. The prosecutor stated that the family consisted of five children, *not one of whom could read or write!*"

Another very cruel practice of these young delinquents is, to go into some chandler's shop, as slyly as possible, and take the first opportunity of stealing the till with its contents, there being always some older thief ready to take charge of it, as soon as the child removes it from the shop.* Many a poor woman has had to lament the loss of her till, with its contents, taken by a child, perhaps, scarcely six years of age. There is always a plan laid down for the child to act upon. Should he be unable to obtain possession of the till himself, he is instructed to pretend that he has missed his way, and to inquire for some street near the spot; or, he will address her with "Please, ma'am, can you tell me what it is o'clock?" The unsuspecting woman, with the greatest kindness possible, shows the child the street he inquires for, or

* So complete is the science of pilfering rendered by its perpetrators, that they have even a peculiar vocabulary of their own, rendering their conversation, to those who may chance to overhear them, as mysterious and incomprehensible as though they were conversing in a foreign tongue; for instance, the scutcheons they steal from the key holes are called *porcupines;* brass weights, *lueys;* while purloining the contents of a till, is called *taking the ding.* In short, they have a peculiar name for almost every thing.

leaves the shop to ascertain the hour, and for her civility, she is sure to find herself robbed, when she returns, by some of the child's companions. Should he be detected in actual possession of the property, he is instructed to act his part in the most artful manner, by pretending that some man sent him into the shop to take it, who told him that he would give him sixpence to buy cakes.

It is not uncommon for these young offenders to stop children, whom they may meet in the street un-protected, and either by artifice or violence, take from them their hats, necklaces, &c.; thus initiating them-selves, as it were, into the desperate crime of assault and highway robbery.

Young as the subjects of the foregoing narrations mostly were, I have little doubt their pupilage com-menced at a much earlier age; they could not other-wise have attained to such proficiency in the practice of crime, and hardihood on detection. However pos-sible it may be thought to reclaim children of so ten-der an age, I am convinced that thieves of more ad-vanced years become so thoroughly perverted in their wills and understandings, as to be incapable of per-ceiving the disgrace of their conduct, or the enormity of the offence. I was once told by an old thief that thieving was his profession, and he had therefore a right to follow it; and I could plainly discover from further conversation with him, that he had established in himself an opinion that thieving was no harm, provided he used no violence to the person; he seem-ed, indeed, to have no other idea of the rights of property, than that described as the maxim of a cele-brated Scottish outlaw—that,

" They should take who have the power,
  And they should keep who can."

When this most lamentable state is reached, it is to be feared all modes of punishment, as correctives, are useless; and the only thing left is to prevent further depredation by banishment.

The incorrigibility which a child may attain, who has once associated with thieves at an early age, is apparent from the following fact. " Richard Leworthy, aged fourteen, was indicted for stealing five sovereigns, the property of William Newling, his master. The prosecutor stated, that he resided in the Commercial Road, and is by business a tailor; the prisoner had been his apprentice for four months, up to the 28th of August, when he committed the robbery. On that day he gave him five pounds to take to Mr. Wells, of Bishopsgate Street, to discharge a bill; he never went, nor did he return home; he did not hear of him for three weeks, when he found him at Windsor, and apprehended him. The prisoner admitted having applied the money to his own use. He was found at a public house; and said he had spent all his money except one shilling and six-pence. A shopman in the service of Mr. Wells, stated, that in August last, the witness owed his master a sum of money; he knew the prisoner; he did not bring money to their shop, either on or since the 28th of August. The prisoner made no defence, but called his master, who said he received him from the Refuge for the Destitute, and had a good character with him. He would not take him back again. Mr. Wontner stated, that he had received two communications from the Rev. Mr. Crosby, the chaplain of the Institution, stating they would not interfere on his behalf. The jury returned a verdict of *guilty*. Mr. Justice Park observed, that the best course would be to send him out of the country."

Here we see, that notwithstanding the discipline he had undergone, and the instructions he had received during his confinement in the establishment of the Refuge for the Destitute; he had not been four months from that place before he fell into his old habits. It is moreover to be remarked, that such had been his conduct during his confinement, that the directors of the establishment thought themselves warranted in giving a good character with him. They were probably little suprised on hearing of this relapse on the part of the boy—experience had doubtless taught them it was no uncommon thing, and we plainly see they were convinced that all further attempts at reclaiming him were useless.

The facilities with which property may be disposed of should be mentioned as a powerful inducement to crime. The following case suggests it to the mind :

Thomas Jackson, a mere child, not more than nine years of age, was charged some time ago at the Town Hall, with committing a burglary on the premises of Mr. James Whitelock, a master-builder, Griffith's Rents, St. Thomas's, Southwark. Mr. Whitelock, it appears, resided in an old mansion, formerly an inn, which he had divided into two separate tenements, occupying one part himself, and letting the other to the parents of the prisoner. In his division he had deposited building materials to a considerable amount, one hundred weight of which in iron holdfasts, hinges, nails, clamps, &c., he missed one day on

entering the room, the door of which had been blocked
by a large copper, and the partition door forced.
The character of the prisoner being of the worst description, he was apprehended, when he confessed he had
taken all the property, and disposed of it to a woman
named Priscilla Fletcher, the keeper of a marine-store,
34, James Street. The receiver, who is *the last of
the family that has not been either hanged or transported*, refused to swear to the person of the prisoner, though she admitted she believed he was
the person she bought the property produced from,
at the rate of one penny for each three pounds.
It was proved to be worth three half-pence per pound.
Alderman J. J. Smith regretted that the deficiency of
evidence prevented him sending the young delinquent
for trial, and thereby rescuing him from an ignomi-
nious death, and told Mrs. Priscilla, who was all
modesty, that he was convinced she had perjured
herself,—and not to exult at her own escape from
transportation, a reward he could not help considering she richly merited, and which in due season she
would doubtless receive.

The hardened child laughed during the hearing,
and on being sentenced, by the oath of the officers, as
a reputed thief, spit at his accuser, and exclaimed, as
he was taken from the bar to be conveyed to Brixton,
—"Is this all ! I'll torment you yet!"

To add one more case, I may state that, at the
Exeter Sessions, some time since, two children were
convicted who, it is believed, were not above ten
years of age. Previously to this they had been convicted of felony, and had suffered six months imprisonment at Bodmin; and it appears that two years

before they started alone from Bristol on this circuit of youthful depredation.

Having collected the foregoing instances of juvenile delinquency and presented them to the public, I cannot refrain from adducing a few other cases which came under my own observation.

Whilst conducting the Spitalfields' Infant School, several instances of dishonesty in the children occurred. On one occasion, the mother herself came to complain of a little boy, not more than *four years old*, on the following grounds. She stated, that being obliged to be out at work all day, as well as her husband, she was under the necessity of leaving the children by themselves. She had three besides the little boy of whom she was complaining. Having to pay her rent, she put eighteen-pence for that purpose in a cup at the top of the cupboard. On stepping home to give the children their dinners, she found the boy at the cupboard, mounted on a chair, which again was placed on the top of a table. On looking for the money, she found four-pence already gone; one penny of this she found in his pocket, the rest he had divided amongst the other children, that they might not tell of him. After this relation I kept a strict watch on the child, and three or four days afterwards the children detected him opening my desk and taking half-pence out of it. They informed me of this, and while they were bringing him up to me the half-pence dropped out of his hand. I detected him in many other very bad actions, but have reason to hope, that, by suitable discipline and instruction, he was effectually cured of his sad propensities.

About the same time, I observed two little children very near the school-house in close conversation, and from their frequently looking at a fruit-stall that was near, I felt inclined to watch them ; having previously heard from some of the pupils, that they had frequently seen children in the neighbourhood steal oysters, and other things. I accordingly placed myself in a convenient situation, and had not long to wait, for the moment they saw there was no one passing, they went up to the stall, the eldest walking alongside the other, apparently to prevent his being seen, whilst the little one snatched an orange, and conveyed it under his pinafore, with all the dexterity of an experienced thief. The youngest of these children was *not four years old,* and the eldest, apparently, *not above five.* There was reason to believe this was not the first time they had been guilty of stealing, though, perhaps, unknown to their parents, as I have found to be the case in other instances.

Another little boy in the school, whose mother kept a little shop, frequently brought money with him,—as much as three-pence at a time. On questioning the child how he came by it, he always said that his mother gave it to him, and I thought there was no reason to doubt his word, for there was something so prepossessing in his appearance, that, at that time, I could not doubt the truth of his story. But finding that the child spent a great deal of money in fruit, cakes, &c. and still had some remaining, I found it advisable to see the mother, and to my astonishment found it all a fiction, for she had not given him any, and we were both at a loss to conceive how he obtained it. The child told *me,* his mother gave it

him ; and he told his *mother* that it was given to him
at school; but when he was confronted with us both,
not a word would he say. It was evident, therefore, that he had obtained it by some unfair means,
and we both determined to suspend our judgment,
and to keep a strict eye on him in future. Nothing,
however, transpired for some time ;—I followed him
home several times, but saw nothing amiss. At
length I received notice from the mother, that she had
detected him taking money out of the till in her little
shop. It then came out that there was some boy in
the neighbourhood who acted as banker to him, and
for every two-pence which he received, he was allowed one penny for taking care of it. It seems that
the child was afraid to bring any more money to
school, on account of being so closely questioned as
to where he obtained it, and this, probably, induced
him to give more to the boy than he otherwise would
have done. Suffice it, however, to say, that both
children at length were found out, and the mother
declared that the child conducted her to some old
boards in the wash-house, and underneath them there
was upwards of a shilling, which he had pilfered at
various times.

The reader may remember too that during the last
autumn, a boy of *fourteen committed suicide*, and that
another of the same age was convicted of the dreadful
crime of *murder*.

It appears he knew a boy a little younger than
himself, who was going to a distance with some
money, and having taken a pocket-knife with him,
he way-laid him and threatened to murder him. The
poor little victim kneeled down,—offered him his

money, his knife, and all he had, and said he would love him all the days of his life if he would spare him, and never tell what had happened, but the pathetic and forcible appeal, which would have melted many a ruffian-heart, was vain :—the little monster stabbed him in the throat, and then robbed him. On his trial he discovered no feeling, and he even heard his sentence with the utmost indifference, and without a tear.

It would have been easy to multiply cases of juvenile delinquency, both those which have been brought under the cognizance of the law, and those which have come to my own knowledge, but I think enough has been related to show how early children may, and do become depraved. I have purposely given most of them with as few remarks of my own as possible, that they may plead their own cause with the reader, and excite a desire in his bosom to enter with me in the next chapter on an inquiry into the causes of such early depravity.

CHAPTER II.

CAUSES OF EARLY CRIME.

"Why thus surpris'd to see the infant race
  Treading the paths of vice?   Their eyes can trace
Their *parents'* footsteps in the way they go:
  What shame, what fear, then, can their young hearts know?"

APPALLING as the *effects* of juvenile delinquency are, I think we may discover a principal *cause* of them in the present condition and habits of the adult part of the labouring classes. We shall find very frequently, that infant crime is only the natural produce of evil, by the infallible means of precept and example. I do not intend to assert, that the majority of parents amongst the poor actually encourage their children in the commission of theft; we may, indeed, fear that some do; as in the instance of the two little girls detected in shop-lifting, whose case was detailed in the preceding chapter; but still, I should hope that such facts are not frequent. If, however, they do not give them positive encouragement in pilfering, the example they set is often calculated to deprave the heart of the child, and, amongst other evil consequences to induce dishonesty; whilst in other cases we find, that from peculiar circumstances the child is deprived, during the whole day, of the controling presence of a parent, and is exposed to all the poisonous contamination which the streets of large cities afford; and hence appears another cause of evil. Here children come in contact with maturer vice, and are often drawn by it sinfluence from the paths of innocence; as we have already seen in many instances. What resistance can the infant make to the insidious serpents, which thus, as it were, steal into its cradle, and infuse their poison into its soul? The guardians of its helplessness are heedless or unconscious of its danger, and, alas! it has not the fabled strength of the infant Hercules to crush its venomous assailants. Surely such a view of the frequent origin of crime must awaken our commiseration for its miserable victims, and excite in us a desire to become the defenders of the unprotected.

It will, however, be said by some, "Where are the natural guardians of the child? Where are its parents? Are we to encourage their neglect of duty, by becoming their substitutes? It is their business to look after their children, and not ours." Frequently have I heard such sentiments put forth, and sometimes by persons in whom I knew they were rather owing to a want of reflection than of philanthropy. But a want of thought, or of feeling, it must certainly be; because, on no principle of reason or humanity can we make the unnatural conduct of fathers and mothers, a plea for withholding our protection and assistance from the helpless objects of their cruelty and neglect. If we do so, we not only

D

neglect our duty toward such children, but permit the
growth and extension of the evil.   We must recollect
that they will not merely play their own wicked parts
during their lives, but will also become models to the
next generation.

 It should be remembered here, that I am treating
of an evil which extends itself to all classes of society;
I am appealing to the prudence of men, that they
may, for their own sakes, investigate its cause; I
shall hereafter appeal to them as philanthropists, and,
still more urgently, as Christians, that they may examine the merits of the remedy I shall propose.

The culpability of many parents is beyond dispute.
They not only omit to set their children good examples, and give them good advice, but, on the contrary, instil into their minds the first rudiments of
wickedness, and lead them into the paths of vice.
Their homes present scenes which human nature
shudders at, and which it is impossible truly to describe.   There are parents who, working at home,
have every opportunity of training up their children
"in the way they should go," if they were inclined
so to do.   Instead of this, we often find, in the case
of the fathers, that they are so lost to every principle
of humanity, that as soon as they receive their wages,
they leave their homes, and hasten with eager steps
to the public house; nor do they re-pass its accursed
threshold, till the vice-fattening landlord has received
the greater part of the money which should support
their half-fed—half-clothed wives and children; and
till they have qualified themselves, by intoxication,
to act far worse than brutes on their return home.
To men of this description it matters not whether or

not their children are proving themselves skilful imitators of their evil example,—they may curse and swear, lie and steal,—so long as they can enjoy the society of their pot-companions, it is to them a matter of total indifference.

During my superintendence of the first school, I had a painful facility of examining these matters. . Frequently, when I have inquired the cause of the wretched plight in which some of the children were sent to the school,—perhaps with scarcely a shoe to their feet, sometimes altogether without,—I have heard from their mothers the most heart-rending recitals of the husband's misconduct. One family in particular I remember, consisting of seven children, two of whom were in the school; four of them were supported entirely by the exertions of the mother, who declared to me, that she did not receive a shilling from their father for a month together; all the money he got he kept to spend at the public-house; and his family, for what he cared, might go naked, or starve. He was not only a great drunkard, but a reprobate into the bargain; beating and abusing the poor woman, who thus endeavoured to support his children by her labour.

The evil does not always stop here. Driven to the extreme of wretchedness by her husband's conduct, the woman sometimes takes to drinking likewise, and the poor babes are ten thousand times more pitiable than orphans. I have witnessed the revolting sight of a child leading home both father and mother from the public-house, in a disgusting state of intoxication. With tears and entreaties I have seen the poor infant vainly endeavouring to restrain them

from increasing their drunkenness, by going into the
houses on their way home ; they have shaken off the
clinging child, who, in the greatest anxiety, waited
without to resume its painful task ; knowing all the
time, perhaps, that whilst its parents were thus throwing away their money, there was not so much as a
crust of bread to appease its hunger at home.   Let it
not be thought that this is an overcharged picture of
facts ; it is but a faint, a very faint and imperfect
sketch of a reality which defies exaggeration.   Cases
of such depravity, on the part of mothers, I with
much pleasure confess to be comparatively rare.
Maternal affection is the preventive.   But what, let
me ask, can be hoped of the children of such parents?
What are their characters likely to become under such
tuition?   With such examples before their eyes, need
they leave their homes to seek contamination, or to
learn to do evil?

And here I must say, if I were asked to point out,
in the metropolis or any large city, the greatest
nuisance, the worst bane of society, the most successful promoter of vice,—I should, without a moment's
hesitation, point to the first public-house or spirit-
dealer's that met my view.   Nor can I, in speaking
of the causes of juvenile delinquency, omit to say, I
think these houses, indirectly, a very great cause of
it.   Why I think so, my readers will readily conceive
from what I have already said.   I am sure that Satan
has no temple in which he is so devoutly worshipped,
or so highly honoured, as the ale-house,—no priest is
so devoted as its landlord,—no followers are so zealous in his behalf as its frequenters.

Let any one in the evening visit the homes of the

labouring class, in a poor neighbourhood; and he will find, in many cases, a barely-furnished room, a numerous family of small children,—perhaps forgetting the pangs of hunger in the obliviousness of sleep, —a wife, with care-worn features, sitting in solitary wretchedness, ruminating on wants which she knows not how to supply—namely, clothes and food for her children on the morrow, and on debts which she has no means of discharging. But where is *he* who should be sharing her cares, bidding her be of good cheer, and devising with her some means of alleviating their mutual distress? Where is the father of the sleeping babes,—the husband of the watchful wife? Go to the public-house; you will see him there with a host of his companions, of like character and circumstances, smoking, drinking, singing, blaspheming, gambling—ruining his health, spending his money; as jovial as though he had no wretched wife, no starving babes at home; and as lavish of money which should procure them food, as the man who is thriving on his excesses could wish him to be.

I never look on a public-house without considering it as the abode of the evil genius of a neighbourhood; the despoiler of industry, the destroyer of domestic comfort: and heartily do I wish, that some means could be devised for abolishing these resorts of wickedness; that some legislative enactment may render it unlawful for any one to keep such places. With respect to a peculiar sort of beverage, it has been declared to be illegal to afford its purchasers accommodation for drinking it on the premises. Why not extend it to other liquors? I know this would be pronounced an infringement on English liberty! The worst of men would raise this outcry against the measure.   But surely it should rather be called a preventive of English licentiousness.   All good men would consider it as such.   I would not rob the labourer of his daily allowance of a beverage which is believed by many to be of essential service, when taken in moderation ;—but I would have him drink it at home, that his wife and children may participate in his enjoyment.   Perhaps, it will be said, a man closely confined to labour all day, needs some relaxation from domestic cares—that this can only be found in change of scene, and in social company.   I will concede this. The plea of health, though often speciously advanced, cannot be denied.   But is it necessary for his health, that this change of scene should be found in a close tap-room, within a few yards of his home, where he drinks to a ruinous excess till a late hour,—breathing all the while a hot atmosphere of tobacco-smoke ? Is it not possible to obtain the change of scene, and the relaxation of social converse, by mutual visits amongst friends similarly situated, — by a ramble to the suburbs, — or, in cases where the daily occupation affords too little opportunity for exercise, are there not places established for gymnastic exercises,—and might not others be formed for the like purposes ?   Certain I am that the abolition of public-houses, in large cities, as places of daily resort for the adult labouring poor, would be attended with the most salutary consequences.   I know of nothing that must so certainly tend to their improvement both in character and circumstances.

Another measure should then be adopted, I would say—destroy the facility of spirit-drinking, by laying on a heavy duty.　It is in vain that interested sophistry would plead its benefits in particular cases—such, for instance, as the ludicrous plea of the needfulness of drams for market-women on wet and frosty mornings.*　Set these specious benefits against the dreadful results to men's health and pockets, from the present low price of spirits, and their consequent enormous consumption; and then let common sense and honesty deliver its judgment.

I have spoken thus candidly and at length upon the subject in the present chapter, though somewhat out of place, because my feelings would not allow me to be less plain or more brief, or to postpone the matter to "a more convenient season."　Perhaps in talking of legislative alterations I have been wandering upon forbidden ground; if so, in returning to my proper

* Some conception of the fearful height which drunkenness has attained, may be gathered from the fact, that in 1829, the quantity of distilled spirits on which the duty was paid in the three kingdoms, amounted to 23,000,000 of gallons.　To form a due estimate, however, of the actual consumption, an immense quantity must be added, obtained by smuggling.　Of rum imported for home consumption, allowing for that re-exported, the quantity was 5,000,000 of gallons.　Of brandy and other articles imported, 1,500,000 gallons, making a total, with the omission of all on which the duty was evaded, of 30,000,000 of gallons of ardent spirits consumed in the year.　Five millions of revenue grew out of this, but it cost the people 15,000,000l. sterling, a sum which would have paid half-a-year's interest of the national debt.

"No person," says Sir Astley Cooper, "has greater hostility to dram drinking than myself, insomuch that I never suffer any ardent spirits in my house—thinking *them evil spirits !*—and if the poor could witness the white livers, the dropsies, the shattered nervous systems which I have seen as the consequence of drinking, they would be aware that *spirits* and *poisons* were synonymous terms."

path, I will comfort myself with this thought :—the
progress of improvement, however slow, is sure, and
it is certainly making in this country ; I require no
other assurance than the establishment of Infant
Schools and Mechanics' Institutions ; it *will* advance,
and what the legislature may never be able to accomplish, the spirit of improvement eventually will.

But having considered those cases, in which wilful
neglect and bad example may be charged upon
the parents, we should not forget to tell those
who object to our interference in the duty of the
child's natural protectors, that it is not, in every
instance, from *wilful* neglect on their part, that
their children are left unprotected in the streets.
The circumstances of the labouring classes are such,
in many cases, that they are compelled to leave their
children either wholly unprotected, or in the charge
of some one who frequently becomes a betrayer instead
of a defender.   The father, perhaps, goes to his daily
labour in the morning, before the children are out of
bed, and does not return till they are in bed again at
night.   The mother goes out in like manner, the
earnings of the husband being insufficient for the
maintenance of the family, and the children are in-
trusted throughout the day to the care of some girl,
whose parents are as poor as themselves, and are glad
to let her earn something towards her support.
Numbers of little girls thus go out before they are
twelve years old, and teach the little children all they
know,—commonly to be deceitful, and not unfrequently to be dishonest.   The parents, careless or
unsuspecting, only make inquiry when they return
home if the children have been good and quiet, and

of course receive an answer in the affirmative. In the course of a few years the evil consequences begin to shew themselves, and then the good folks wonder how or when the seeds of such depravity could have been sown. Many I know will be inclined to smile at the insignificancy of the cause pointed out. I can only say, it is from such springs, however regarded, that the great stream of vice is supplied; and what we laugh at now, for its insignificant origin, will here-after, in its maturity, laugh at us for our impotence, in vainly endeavouring to stem it. What are parents to do with their children, situated as those are of whom we have just spoken? And very many are so situated. Is it possible for them to perform their duty, as protectors of their children? It requires all their time to labour for their support, and they there-fore leave them, unavoidably, either in such hands as we have described, or to take care of themselves; to range the streets, and form such associations as may there happen to fall in their way. They get into company with older delinquents, and become first their instruments, and then their associates; till at length they find their way into a gaol.

This is no delusive way of accounting for the matter;—it is a solution which experience and obser-vation have taught and established. I have traced the progress of delinquency in actual life, from its earliest stages, from the little trembling pilferer of the apple-stall, not more than four or five years old, to the confirmed thief of nine or ten years—who had been in gaol three or four times, and was as proud of his dexterity in thieving, and hardihood under punish-ment, as he could have been of the most virtuous

accomplishment, or the most becoming fortitude.
The infant thief, conscious of shame, and trembling
with fear, will tell you on detection, that "Tommy"
or "Billy," some older associate, set him to do it ;
you let him go : he joins his companions, who laugh
at the story he tells, ridicule him for his fears, praise
him for his dexterity, and rejoice in his escape.   It
will be very easy to imagine how, under a course of
such treatment, the young offender so soon dismisses
both shame and fear ; and learns to forget everything
but the gain and glory of his crimes.

It is no small matter of credit with older thieves—
(by older thieves I still mean boys of nine or ten
years old)—to have under their tuition two or three
pupils.   I have seen in my walks, as many as seven
or eight sallying forth from the alleys in the neighbourhood of Spitalfields, under the command, as it
were, of a leader, a boy perhaps not more than nine
or ten years old.   I have watched their plans ; and
have noticed that it was usual to send first the youngest boy to attempt the theft —perhaps the object to
be attained was only a bun from the open window of
a pastry-cook's shop—if he failed, another was sent,
whilst the rest were lurking at the corner of some
court, ready to flee in case their companion was detected ;—and I have sometimes seen, that after all
the rest had failed, either from the want of skill, or
the too great vigilance of the shop-keeper, the boy
who acted as leader has started out, and by a display
of superior dexterity, would have carried off the prize,
had it not happened that some one was thus purposely
watching his conduct.   When detected, if an old
offender, he will either look you in the face with the

greatest effrontery and an expression of defiance, or he will feign to cry, and tell you he was hungry, has no father nor mother, &c.; though frequently on further inquiry I have found the whole story to be false.

The two grand causes of juvenile delinquency we have seen, then, to be—the evil example of parents themselves; and the bad associations which children form at an early age, when, through neglect, they are suffered to be in the streets. In the first instance, the parents of the children are wholly without excuse; in the second, though in some cases we may blame them, in others we cannot justly do so; but must admit, as an exculpation, the unfortunate circumstances of their condition in life.

It would be easy to shew by a multitude of instances, the evil effects produced on children of a tender age by street associations. But I think enough has been said to convince every reflecting mind that it is highly necessary that we should interfere in behalf of children so situated; and I shall conclude the present chapter by some remarks on various habits and practices of the poor classes, which have at least an injurious tendency on the character of the rising generation.

As children are such imitative beings, I cannot help making a few observations on the tricks which are usually introduced into our *pantomimes*. It is well known that those of the clown form a principal part of the entertainment. It is also equally well known, that pantomimes are particularly designed to amuse children, for which reason they are generally represented during the Christmas holidays. If, however, they were merely intended to *amuse* them, they who introduced them have, perhaps, gained their object; but what kind of *instruction* they afford, I shall here attempt to shew. I do not recollect to have seen a pantomime myself without *pilfering* being introduced under every possible form, such as shop-lifting, picking pockets, &c. &c. Can it then be for a moment supposed improbable that children, after having witnessed these exhibitions, should endeavour to put the thing into practice, whenever an opportunity offers, and try whether they cannot take a handkerchief from a gentleman's pocket with the same ease and dexterity as the clown in the play did; or, if unsuccessful in this part of the business, that they should try their prowess in carrying off a shoulder of mutton from a butcher's shop,—a loaf from a baker,—or lighter articles from the pastry cook, fruiterer, or linen draper? For, having seen the dexterity of the clown, in these cases, they will not be at a loss for methods to accomplish, by sleight of hand, their several purposes. In my humble opinion, children cannot go to a better place for instruction in these matters, or to a place more calculated to teach them the art of pilfering to perfection, than to a theatre, when pantomimes are performed. To say that the persons who write and introduce these pieces are in want of *sense,* may not be true; but I must charge them with a want of sufficient thought, in not calculating on their baneful effects on the rising generation, for whose amusement it appears they are chiefly produced. Many unfortunate persons, who have heard the sentence of death passed upon them, or who are now suffering under the law, in various ways, have had to lament that the

*first seeds of vice were sown in their minds while view-
ing the pilfering tricks of clowns in pantomimes.* Alas!
too little do we calculate on the direful effects of this
species of amusement on the future character of the
young; we first permit their minds to be poisoned,
by offering them the draught, and then punish them
by law for taking it. Does not the wide world
afford a variety of materials sufficient for virtuous
imitation, without descending to that which is
vicious? It is much easier to make a pail of pure
water foul, than it is to make a pail of foul water
pure. It must not be supposed that I wish to sweep
off every kind of amusement from the juvenile part
of society, but I do wish to sweep off all that
has a pernicious tendency. The limits which
I have prescribed to myself will not allow me to enter more at large into this subject; otherwise I could
produce a number of facts which would prove, most
unquestionably, the propriety of discontinuing these
exhibitions.

A conversation which I once heard between some
boys who were playing at what is called *pitch-in-the-
hole*, will prove the truth of my assertions.—Bill,
said one of the boys to another, when did you go
to the play last? On Monday night, was the reply.
Did you see the new pantomime?—Yes. Well, did
you see any fun?—Yes, I believe I did too. I saw
the clown *bone* a whole *hank* of sausages, and put
them into his pocket, and then pour the gravy in
after them. You would have split your sides with
laughing, had you been there. A. B. and C. D.
were with me, and they laughed as much as I did.
And what do you think A. B. did the next night?—

E

How should I know.   Why, replied the other, he and
C. D. *boned* about two pounds of sausages from a pork
shop and we had them for supper.—This conversation I heard from a window, which looked into a
ruinous place where boys assembled to toss up for
money, and for other games.   This fact alone, without
recording any more, is sufficient to shew the evil of
which I have been speaking.   And I do most sincerely hope that those persons who have any influence
over the stage, will use their utmost endeavours,
speedily, to expunge every thing thus calculated to
promote evil inclinations in the minds of children,
and vicious habits in the lives of men.

As I have had much experience from being
brought up in London, I am perfectly aware of the
evil impressions and dangerous temptations that the
children of the poor are liable to fall into ; and therefore must solemnly affirm, that nothing in my view
would give so much happiness to the community at
large, as the taking care of the affections of the infant children of the poor.

There is, moreover, a practice very prevalent among
the poor, which does greater mischief than people are
generally aware of, and that is, sending their children
to the *pawnbrokers*.   It is well known that many persons send children, scarcely seven years of age, to
these people, with pledges of various sorts, a thing
that cannot be too severely condemned.   I know an
instance of a little boy finding a shawl in the street ;
and being in the habit of going to the pawnbroker's
for his mother, instead of taking the shawl home to
his parents, he actually pawned it, and spent all the
money, which might never have been known by his

parents, had not the mother found the duplicate in his pocket. It is evident, then, that many parents have no one but themselves to blame for the misconduct of their children; for had this child not been accustomed to go to such a place *for his parents*, he would never have thought of going there *for himself*; and the shawl most likely would have been carried home *to them*. Indeed, there is no knowing where such a system will end, for if children are suffered to go to such places, they may in time pledge that which does not belong to them; and so easy is the way of turning any article into money, that we find most young thieves, of both sexes, when apprehended, have some duplicates about them. Those persons, therefore, who take pledges of children (contrary to the act of parliament, whether they know it or not,) ought to be severely reprimanded; for I am persuaded, that such conduct is productive of very great mischief indeed.

Taking children to *fairs*, is another thing which is also productive of much harm. At the commencement of the first school seventy or eighty children were frequently absent whenever there was a fair near London; but the parents were afterwards cured of this, and we seldom had above twenty absentees at fair-time. Several of the children have told me that their parents wished to take them, but they requested to be permitted to come to school instead. Indeed the parents, finding that they can enjoy themselves better without their children, are very willing to leave them at school.

It is a difficult matter to persuade grown persons of the impropriety of attending fairs, who have been

accustomed to it when children ; but children are
easily persuaded from it ; for if they are properly entertained at school, they will not have the least desire
to go to such places.

I cannot quit this subject without relating one or
two more very bad habits to which children are
addicted, and which are, perhaps, fit subjects for the
consideration of the *Mendicity Society*. As it is the
object of that society to clear the streets of beggars,
it would be well if they would put a stop to those
juvenile beggars, many of whom are children of
respectable parents, who assemble together to build
what they call a GROTTO ; to the great annoyance of
all passengers in the streets. However desirous
persons may be of encouraging ingenuity in children,
I think it is doing them much harm to give them
money when they ask for it in this way. Indeed it
would appear, that some of the children have learned
the art of begging so well, that they are able to vie
with the most experienced mendicants. Ladies in
particular are very much annoyed by children getting
before them and asking for money ; nor will they take
the answer given them, but put their hats up to the
ladies' faces, saying, " Please, ma'am, remember the
grotto ;" and when told by the parties that they have
no money to give, they will still continue to follow, and
be as importunate as any common beggar. However innocent and trifling this may appear to some,
I am inclined to believe that such practices tend to
evil, for they teach children to be mean, and may
cause some of them to choose begging rather than
work. I think that the best way to stop this species
of begging is, never to give them any thing. A fact

which came under my own observation will shew that the practice may be productive of mischief. A foreign gentleman walking up Old-street-road, was surrounded by three or four boys, saying, "Please, sir, remember the grotto."—"Go away," was the reply, "I will give you none." To this followed, "Do, pray sir, remember the grotto." "No, I tell you I will give you nothing." "Do, sir, only once a-year." At length, I believe, he put something into one of their hats, and thus got rid of them; but he had scarcely gone two hundred yards, before he came to another grotto, and out sallied three more boys, with the same importunate request: he replied, "I will give you nothing; plague have you and your grotto." The boys however persevered, till the gentleman, having lost all patience, gave one of them a gentle tap to get out of the way, but the boy being on the side of the foot-path fell into the mud, which had been scraped off the road, and in this pickle followed the gentleman, bellowing out, "That man knocked me down in the mud, and I had done nothing to him." In consequence, a number of persons soon collected, who insulted the gentleman very much, and he would certainly have been roughly handled, had he not given the boy something as a recompence. He then called a coach, declaring he could not walk the streets of London in safety.

Those who know what mischief has arisen from very trifling causes, will, of course, perceive the necessity of checking this growing evil; for this man went away with very unfavourable impressions concerning our country, and would, no doubt, prejudice many against us, and make them suppose we are worse than we are.

Nearly allied to this is, " Pray remember poor Guy Faux ;" which not only teaches children the art of begging, but is frequently the means of their becoming dishonest, for I have known children break down fences, and water-spouts, and, in short, any thing that they could lay their hands upon, in order to make a bonfire, to the great danger of the inhabitants near it, without producing one good effect. Yet how easily might this practice be put down. The ill effects of it are so self-evident, that there can be no need for further enlargement.

I also disapprove of children going about begging at Christmas ; this practice is calculated to instil into the children's minds a principle of meanness not becoming the English character, and the money they get, seldom, if ever, does them any good. If persons choose to give children any thing at this time of the year, there can be no objection to it, but I dislike children going about to ask for money like common beggars ; it cannot be proper, and should be generally discountenanced. All these things, to some men, may appear trifling, but to me and others they are of consequence ; for if we mean to improve the general character of the labouring population, there is nothing like beginning in time ; and we should, amongst other things, get rid of all mean and improper customs.

Before concluding this chapter I would hint to travellers not to give children money for running after a coach. I have seen children of both sexes run until their breath failed, and, completely exhausted, drop down on the grass, merely because some injudicious persons had thrown halfpence to them. I have also seen little boys turn over and over before the horses for the purpose of getting money, to the danger of their own lives and of the passengers; and I recollect an instance of one boy being in consequence, killed on the spot. In some counties children will, in spring and summer, run after a carriage with flowers upon a long stick, thrusting it in the coach or the faces of the travellers, begging halfpence, which habit had been taught them by the same injudicious means.

CHAPTER III.

REMEDY FOR EXISTING EVILS.

———

" The most likely and hopeful reformation of the world must
begin with children. Wholesome laws and good sermons are but
slow and late ways; the timely and most compendious way is a
good education."

ARCHBISHOP TILLOTSON.

———

HAVING brought the prevalency of juvenile delinquency immediately before the eyes of my readers,
by various examples in the first chapter, and in the
second exhibited a few of the causes of it, I shall
now proceed to point out what in my humble opinion
appears to be the only efficient remedy,—namely,
the education of the infant poor. It may not be
amiss, however, to glance at the means which have
heretofore been employed, and found, though productive of some good, inefficient for the end
proposed.

As preventives, I may notice the numerous
National and Sunday Schools, Tract Societies, &c.

established throughout the kingdom. These have doubtless much good effect, and deserve the zealous support of every one who has at heart the welfare of society in general, and the improvement of the labouring classes in particular. Many have been plucked, " as brands from the burning," by these institutions; which are a blessing to the objects of their benevolence and an honour to their conductors and supporters. That Sunday Schools are not wholly efficient, in conjunction with other institutions, to accomplish the end desired, is to be attributed, on the one hand, to the small portion of time in which their salutary influence is exerted; and, on the other, to their not admitting children at a sufficiently early age. At the period usually assigned for their entrance, they have not only acquired many evil habits, but their affections have become so thoroughly perverted, as to offer great and in some cases insuperable obstacles to the corrective efforts of their teachers. Each child brings into the school some portion of acquired evil, making, when united, a formidable aggregate, and affording every facility for mutual contamination. Add to this, the counter-acting effect which the bad examples they meet with in the course of six days must have upon the good they hear on the seventh, and it will be seen how little comparatively is really practicable. I do not say this to dishearten those who are engaged in this labour of love, or to abate the zeal of its promoters. At the same time that their experience confirms the truth of my observations—and I know they would candidly confess that it does so—they must have many gratifying instances of a contrary nature, in children, who from evil habits have been won to a love of goodness and religion, shewn not merely in a punctual attendance at their school, but in that good-will toward their fellow-scholars, and grateful love to their teachers, which are the only infallible signs of a change in the affections. These things encourage them, in spite of many difficulties and mortifications, to persevere in well doing; and may the God of love bless their labours with an increase of fruitfulness! It is only my purpose here to state, that the most likely human means to produce such an increase, is the establishment of Infant Schools;— schools designed, particularly, for the cultivation of the affections,—for preparing the heart to receive that wisdom which teaches us to love God supremely, and to love our neighbour as ourselves. As to the system of instruction pursued in Sunday Schools, as well as other free schools, it is, indeed, my opinion, that some alteration for the better might be made, but as I intend to speak of this matter in a future place, I shall say no more on the subject at present, but pass on to notice prison discipline—which is, I fear, entitled to any term but that of a *remedy*.

That the end of punishment should be the prevention of future crime, rather than the gratification of vindictive feelings—whether those of states or of injured individuals—but few will venture to deny; and yet how little calculated is the punishment usually inflicted on young offenders in this country, to answer that end! They are shut up in a prison, in company with other thieves, perhaps older and more experienced than themselves, and all that was wanting to complete their education in dishonesty is here attained. Previously to their confinement within the walls of one of these places, in spite of the assertions of their hardened associates, that it was nothing to fear, it is probable, dread or apprehension hung over their minds; the last vestige of shame had not been banished by a public appearance as criminals—and this, properly taken advantage of, might have made their reformation possible! But, having encountered the object of their fears, and endured the shame of a trial—shame and fear are alike gone for ever; and when once they find their way into those sinks of iniquity, there is very little hope of amendment. From that period a prison has not the least terror for them. Being a place of idleness, it calls forth the evil inclinations of its inmates, and as they have opportunities of indulging those inclinations, it not only loses all its utility, but becomes incalculably injurious. I heard a boy who had been confined in Newgate say, that he did not care any thing about it; that his companions supplied him with plenty of victuals, that there was some good fun to be seen there, and that most likely he should soon be there again; which proved too true, for he was shortly after taken up again for stealing two pieces of printed calico, and transported. This, with a multitude of similar facts, will shew that there are few who do not become more depraved, and leave such places worse than when they entered them. A gentleman who visited Newgate informed me that he had been very much surprised at finding so many children there; some of whom were ironed; and on his inquiring the cause of such severity towards children so young, he was told by one of the turnkeys, that *he had much more trouble with them than he had with old offenders.*

To the bad habits of a prison and the association with guilt, must be added the deplorably unprovided state, in which, at the termination of their period of imprisonment, they are sent forth into society. What friends have they but their former companions? What habitations, but their former resorts of iniquity? What means of procuring a livelihood, but their former evil practices? We accordingly find, that it is not unfrequently the case, with these young offenders, that scarcely a day elapses after their liberation, before they find themselves again in custody, and within the walls of a prison. One cannot indeed view the exertions made by the " Society for the Improvement of Prison Discipline" in this respect, without feelings of gratitude to those who take an active part in it* ; neither should we forget to

---

* I will make a short extract from one of its reports, to shew that the chief end they have in view, is the prevention of crime. They state, that " in the course of their visits to the gaols in the metropolis, the Committee very frequently meet with destitute boys, who, on their discharge from confinement, literally know not where to lay their heads. To assist such friendless outcasts has been the practice of the society ; and to render this relief more efficacious, a temporary refuge has been established for such as are disposed to abandon their vicious courses. This asylum has been instrumental in affording assistance to a considerable number of distressed youths, who, but for this seasonable aid, must have resorted to criminal practices for support. On admission into this establishment, the boys are instructed in moral and religious duty, subjected to habits of order and industry, and after a time are placed in situations which afford a reasonable prospect of their becoming honest and useful members of society. To extend these objects, and to render its exertions more widely beneficial, the

return thanks to the Author of all good, that he should have encouraged the hearts of persons to venture even their lives, to improve the condition of the prisoners in Newgate and elsewhere ;—that even females are found, who, conquering the timidity and diffidence of their sex, have visited these abodes of vice and misery, for the purpose of ameliorating the condition of their inhabitants. There have been men, claiming to be considered wise men, who have ridiculed the exertions of these daughters of philanthropy, and have made them objects of ridicule, but, happily, they are impervious to the shafts of folly ; and as heedless of the unjust censures, as they are undesirous of the applause of man. Their aim is, the good of their fellow-creatures,—their reward, the pleasure of doing good, and the approbation of Him who is goodness itself. That their well-meant and praise-worthy exertions are not more successful can only be accounted for by the awfully depraved affections which habitual vice produces ; when every principle of action, which should be subservient to virtue becomes actively employed in the cause of wickedness ; for, whatever may be the impulse which first induces offenders to do wrong, they become, in course of time, so totally lost to all sense of what is good as to " glory in their shame." Whether it may

society solicits the aid of public benevolence. Its expenses are unavoidably serious, and its funds are at present very low ; but it is trusted that pecuniary support will not be withheld, when it is considered, that on the liberality with which this appeal is answered, depends, in a great measure, the success of the society's objects—the reformation of the vicious, and the prevention of crime."

be possible to devise any plan of prison discipline sufficient to remedy the evil, I cannot pretend to say; and I shall only repeat the burthen of my song— *educate and protect the infant poor;* and it will be found that *to prevent* is not only better, but easier, than *to cure.*

That this remedy is effectual, experience has taught me and many others; and experience is a guide on whom we may safely rely. It has shewn me that by taking children at an early age out of the reach of contamination in the streets, and removing them in a great measure from the no less baneful influence of evil example at home, we may lay such a foundation of virtue, as is not likely to be shaken. Nor do I think it difficult to shew the reason of this. It is confessed on all hands that our first impressions are the most powerful, both as to their immediate effects and future influence; that they not only form the character of our childhood but that of our maturer years. As the mind of a child expands, it searches for new objects of employment or gratification; and this is the time when the young fall an easy prey to those who make a business of entrapping them into the paths of dishonesty, and then of urging them to crimes of deeper dye. What, then, but a most salutary result can ensue from placing a child in a situation, where its first impressions will be those of the beauty of goodness,—where its first feelings of happiness will consist in the receiving and cherishing kindness towards its little neighbours? In after years, and in schools for older children, it is reckoned an unavoidable evil, that they should be congregated together in numbers; not so in the infant school; it

is there made use of as a means of developing and
exercising those kindly feelings, which must conduce
to individual and general comfort, not only there,
but in society generally. It is not merely by instructing them in *maxims* of honesty that we seek to provide against the evil ; but by the surer way of exciting
that feeling of love towards each other—towards
every one—which, when found in activity, must not
only prevent dishonesty, but every other species of
selfishness.

Consider the difference of the cases. In the one
case we behold a child associated, in happy commu-
nion, with a society—a little world—of its own age
and feelings,—continually proving the possibility of
giving and imparting happiness by receiving and
exercising kindness to its companions—secured from
every danger—supplied with a constant variety of
amusement, which is at the same time instruction ;
and all this under the care of a master or mistress,
acting the part, not of a petulant school-dame, or a
stern pedagogue, but of a kind and judicious parent.

In the case of the child not thus befriended, we see
it, either exposed to the dangerous associations of
the street, or to the bad examples of its parents ; to
their unkindness and severity, or misguided indulgence ; and presented, moreover, with every facility,
as well as every temptation, to do wrong. Now, is
it to be wondered at, that, in the former case, kind,
obedient, honest characters should be the result ; and
in the latter, such as we have, in our preceding examples, exhibited ?—Reason tells us such a consequence
is likely, and experience has shewn us that it really
happens. I could enumerate a thousand cases of

honest principle in the infants who have been under
my own care ; but I can only mention one or two circumstances illustrative of the matter.

I once had, for example, two little boys to travel
with me ; their assistance was exceedingly valuable
in organizing schools.   They were often invited
to accompany me at dinner ; the guests generally
gave them presents.   I have watched them under
many tempting circumstances, and never found them
steal.   It is my firm conviction, that dishonesty is
only the effect of neglect.   No child can be *born a
thief*, in the strict sense of the term.   In many schools,
too, there are fruit-trees planted in the play-ground,
to which the children will not do the least injury, nor
will they touch the fruit.   Flowers in pots, such as
geraniums, auriculas, and other plants, are placed in
the middle of the play-ground, without the least
danger of being injured.   Such is their respect to
private property.

Another instance particularly excited my notice
amongst the children in the first establishment in
London.   They were permitted to bring their dinners with them, and there were boxes in the
school to put them in.   Every child in the school had
access to these boxes, for they were never locked,
and yet I never knew a child to lose his dinner, or
any part of it, notwithstanding many of the children,
to my knowledge, had been kept extremely short of
food.   I have known an instance of a slice of bread
and butter being left in the box for several weeks, by
some child that could not eat it, but none of the other
children would dare to touch it.   I have found in the
boxes two or three pieces of bread, as hard as possi-

ble, and as a proof that many were hungry, and that it did not remain there because they could not eat it, but out of pure honesty, I have offered it to some of the children, and they have eaten it in that state. Cold potatoes, pieces of fat, &c. were not unacceptable to them when given; but sooner than take any thing without leave, they have actually left it to spoil. These are facts which shew, that notwithstanding all the disadvantages to which poor children are exposed, their character may be so far formed as to produce the effects above described. " Would you take a piece of bread out of this box that did not belong to you?" said I to the children one day. "No, sir," replied a little girl of four years old.— " Why not?" " Because," said the child, " it would be thieving." " Well, but suppose no one saw you?" Before I could speak another word, a number of the children answered, " God can see every thing that we do." " Yes," added another little boy, " if you steal a cherry, or a piece of pencil, it is wicked." " To be sure," added another, " it is wicked to steal any thing."

I cannot do better than introduce in this place the opinion of the present Judge Bosanquet, on the subject of the education of the infant poor; and some valuable hints will likewise be found in his remarks on prison discipline. It is an extract from a charge to the jury delivered at the Gloucester assizes for April, 1823. " Gentlemen, I have reason to believe, that the offences for trial on this occasion, are rather less than usual at this season, and, to whatever the diminution of crime may be ascribed, I cannot forbear earnestly to press upon your attention, a constant perseverance in two things, *which, above all others, are calculated to diminish crime*—the first, is an unremitted attention to the education of the children of the poor, and of all classes of society, in the principles of true morality and sound religion—the next is the constant and regular employment of such persons as may be sentenced to imprisonment, in such labour as may be adapted to their respective ages and conditions. I believe that these observations may be considered as quite superfluous in this county, and therefore I have taken the liberty of using the word perseverance, because I believe your attention is already strongly drawn to that subject, and it requires no exhortation of mine to induce your attention to it. I am not quite sure whether in the gaol for this city, the same means are provided for the employment of those persons sentenced to terms of imprisonment which are provided in the gaol for the county. The magistrates for the city are equally desirous of promoting the education of all the poor under their care, I have no doubt; and I do hope and trust, if the means of labour have not been provided in their gaol, that no time will be lost in providing those means by which imprisonment may be made a real punishment, by which offenders may be reformed during their imprisonment, and by which the idle and dissolute may be prevented from any inclination to return there."

I have hitherto only been considering the *prudential* motives which should induce us to promote the education of the poor. I have shewn, that it will be for the benefit of society, inasmuch as it is likely to decrease the number of those who transgress its laws—that it will prove a greater security to our persons

and property than laws or prisons afford.   But, there
are other motives, which, if these selfish ones were
wholly wanting, might be sufficient to advocate, in
every humane heart, the same course of conduct.   If
the duty of promoting honesty amongst the labouring
classes did not exist, that of increasing happiness and
piety amongst them would not be the less imperative.
That there is much room for an augmentation of both,
few, I think, will be inclined to deny ; the less so in
proportion as they have had the greater opportunity of
ascertaining their actual condition.

Let us now for a few moments consider how great
a blessing an Infant School is, even when regarded
as a mere asylum, to take charge of the child's bodily
welfare. I have mentioned before, that the poor are unable to take that care of their children which their tender age requires, on account of their occupations, and
have shewn, that it is almost certain, that the children
of such persons will learn every species of vice.   But
there are other kinds of dangers which more immediately affect the body, and are the cause of more
accidents than people in general imagine.   I shall
here notice some of the most prominent, and hope to
be able to convince the unprejudiced mind, that it
would be a charity to take charge of the infant poor,
even leaving the idea of their learning any thing good
at school entirely out of the question ; and surely
those persons, who disapprove of educating the poor
at all, will see the propriety of keeping, if possible,
their children safe from accidents, and preserving the
lives of many little ones, who would otherwise be
lost to their country, from their falling a prey to
surrounding dangers.

It is well known that many poor people are obliged to live in garrets, three or four stories high, with a family of six or seven children; and it will not appear improbable that when the children are left by themselves, they should frequently meet with accidents by tumbling down stairs; some breaking their backs, others their legs or arms; and to this cause alone, perhaps, may be traced a vast number of the cripples that daily appear as mendicants in our streets. When the poor parents return from their daily labour, they sometimes have the mortification of finding that one, or probably two of their children, are gone to an hospital; which of course makes them unhappy, and unfits them for going through their daily labour. This dead weight, which is continually on the minds of parents, is frequently the cause of their being unable to please their employers, and the consequence sometimes is, they are thrown out of work altogether; whereas, if they were certain that their children were taken care of, they would proceed with their daily labour cheerfully, and be enabled to give more satisfaction to their employers than they otherwise can do.

Other parents I have known, who, when obliged to go out, have locked their children in a room to prevent them from getting into the street, or falling down stairs, and who have taken every precaution, as they imagined, to protect their children; but the little creatures, perhaps after fretting and crying for hours at being thus confined, have ventured to get up to the window, in order to see what was passing in the street, when one, overreaching itself, has fallen into it and been killed on the spot. A gentleman said, at a public meeting at Exeter, when referring to this subject, " I have myself, twice in my life, nearly occasioned the death of children. In one instance, a child left to itself, ran out of the hedge by the roadside; I was fortunately able to stop, and found the child, unconscious of its escape, raising its hands to the reins of the horse. And on another occasion, my horse threw a child down, and I had but just time to pull up, and prevent the wheels from passing over the infant's head." And it was stated in a Bristol paper, that in the short space of *one fortnight, seven* children were taken to the infirmary of that city so dreadfully burnt that four of them died. Numerous cases of this kind are to be found in the public prints, and hundreds of such accidents occur which are not noticed in the papers at all. Many children, again, strolling into the fields, fall into ponds and ditches and are drowned. So numerous, indeed, are the dangers which surround the infant poor, as to make a forcible appeal to the hearts of the pious and humane, and to call loudly on them to unite in rescuing this hitherto neglected part of the rising generation from the evils to which they are exposed.

It is much to be regretted that those persons who most need employment, should be the last to procure it, but such is the fact, for there are so many obstacles thrown in the way of married persons, and especially those with a family, that many are tempted to deny that they have any children, for fear they should lose their situations, though it is certainly an additional stimulus to a servant to behave orderly, when he knows that he has others to look to him for support.

Shall I close this appeal for the necessity of educating the infant poor by another and weightier argument? They are *responsible* and *immortal* beings. It may be thought that I should have given this plea the precedence of every other. I did not, because, I felt more anxious to make good my ground with the prudent and the philanthropic—to shew them that self-interest and humanity demand our exertions in this cause. I knew that when I came to urge such efforts upon the attention of the Christian, I could not possibly fail. No one who is a sincere follower of Him who said " Suffer little children to come unto me, and forbid them not, for of such is the kingdom ;" no one who professes to abide by the maxims of Him whose commandment was, " Love thy neighbour as thyself," can turn a deaf ear to the entreaties of those who are necessitous and suffering. Thousands there are among those of whom we have been speaking, who are brought up in as great ignorance of God and religion, as though they had been born in a country where the light of Revelation has never shone—where the glad tidings of salvation have never been proclaimed. With examples of evil continually before their eyes, both at home and abroad, we see and hear its consequences daily, in the wickedness with which our streets abound, and in the lisped blasphemy and profanity of those who learn to curse and swear before they can well walk.

Whilst I was at Lincoln, I was shocked beyond measure by the horrid language of the boys; to such a pitch had the evil come, that the magistrates were determined to fine all the men who were brought before them for profane swearing; and I had the satisfaction of hearing that four men had been fined whilst I was there.   What a blessing it would be, if other magistrates throughout the kingdom would follow their example !

Any person who has been accustomed to walk the streets of London, must have heard how frequently children take the name of the Almighty in vain ; seldom or ever mentioning it but to confirm some oath. I have seen boys playing at marbles, tops, and other games, and who, on a dispute arising about some frivolous thing, would call upon the Supreme Being to strike them deaf, dumb, or blind ; nay, even dead, if what they said were not true ; when, nevertheless, I have been satisfied from having observed the origin of the dispute, that the party using the expressions has been telling a falsehood. Indeed so common is this kind of language in the streets, that it often passes without notice.   I am inclined to think, that children accustomed to use such expressions on every trifling occasion, will, when they grow to riper years, pay very little respect to the sanctity of an oath.   It is, perhaps, one of the reasons why we hear of so much perjury in the present day.   At all events, little children cannot avoid hearing such expressions, not only from those who are rather older than themselves, but, I am sorry to say, even from their parents.   I have known repeated instances of this kind.   Many little ones, when they first come to our schools, make use of dreadful expressions, and when told that it is wrong, will say that they did not know it was so ; others, with the greatest simplicity, have declared, that they had heard their fathers or mothers say the same words.   Hence I have had much difficulty in persuading them that it was wrong, for they very naturally thought, that if their parents made use of such language, they might do the same. How great is the necessity of good example; and did parents generally consider how apt children are to receive impressions, and to become imitators, both in their words and actions, they would be more cautious than they are. There are many parents who make use of very bad expressions themselves, that would correct their children for using the same;—as a proof of this, I will mention one circumstance, out of many others, that took place in the school I super-intended many years since. We had a little girl there, five years old, who was so fond of the school, that she frequently stopped after the usual hours to play with my children and some others who chose to stay in the play-ground. Many of them would stop till eight or nine o'clock at night, to which I had no objection, provided their parents approved of it, and they did not get into mischief; it being desirable to keep them out of the streets as much as possible. It happened, however, one day, that some of the children offended this child, and she called them by dreadful names, such as I cannot repeat; and, of course, the others were terrified, and told me of them immediately. I was soon satisfied that the child was igno-rant of the meaning of what she said, for, as an excuse for her conduct, she declared that she heard her father and mother use the same words. I told the child, that notwithstanding her parents might have done so, it was very wicked, and that I could not let her stay another time to play, if she ever did so again. Hav-ing sent for the mother, I informed her of the expres-sions the child had used, but did not tell her what she had mentioned relative to her parents, for if I had, she would have beaten her most unmercifully. The mother, after having heard me relate the circumstance, immediately flew into a violent passion with the child, and declared, that she would "skin her alive," (this was her expression,) and I had much difficulty to restrain her from correcting the child in the school. Having pacified her a little, I inquired where the child could have heard such wicked expressions. She said she could not tell. I then told her, I hoped the child did not learn them of her, or her father. To this she made no answer, but I could perceive that she stood self-convicted, and having said what I conceived necessary upon the occasion, I dismissed her, observing that it was useless for ladies and gentlemen to establish schools for the education of the infant poor, if the parents did not assist by setting them a good example.

I am happy to state, that the advice I gave her was not thrown away, as I never knew the child guilty of saying a bad word afterwards; and the mother soon brought me another child, of two years and a half old, and said she should be very glad if I would take it into the school, and that she wished a blessing might always attend the gentlemen who supported the institution. She also requested me to take an opportunity of speaking a few words to her husband, for she was thankful for what had been said to her. And here I would observe, that although it is most undoubtedly true, that the good taught to children in our Infant Schools is greatly counteracted by the conduct they witness on their return home, yet we occasionally see, that these little children, by the

G

blessing of God, are made the means of reforming their own parents. What a gratifying fact it is, that the adult and hardened sinner, may be turned from his evil ways—from death unto life—by an infant's precept or example !

Nor is it only in profane expressions that we see the influence of evil. Some children I have known, in the same neighbourhood, who even beat their parents. There was a poor widow, very near the school, who was frequently to be seen with her face dreadfully bruised by blows from her own son. He had been taken before a magistrate, and imprisoned for three months, but it did him no good, for he afterwards beat his mother as much as ever, and the poor woman had it in contemplation to get the miscreant sent out of the country. One Sunday, I remember to have seen a boy, under twelve years of age, take up a large stone to throw at his mother: he had done something wrong in the house, and the mother followed him into the street with a small cane, to correct him for it ; but he told his mother, that if she dared to approach him, he would knock her down. The mother retired, and the boy went where he pleased. These and many similar scenes I have witnessed ; and I am afraid that many such characters have been so completely formed as to be past reformation. So essential is it, to embrace the first opportunity of impressing on the infant mind the principles of duty and virtue.

I am aware that many excellent institutions are in existence for the spread of the gospel amongst the ignorant and depraved at home as well as abroad ; but I must here again advert to the readier reception of religious truths in infancy, than by the adult and confirmed sinner. I would not say to those who are engaged in the painful task—painful because so often unsuccessful—forego your labours; but I would call upon all who have at heart the everlasting welfare of the souls of men, to exert themselves, that the rising generation may not likewise grow up into that state of perverseness—that they may not in future years prove themselves to be a generation, which "like the adder, turneth a deaf ear to the charmer, charm he ever so wisely." I am satisfied, from the experience I have had, that an amount of good is attainable from early and judicious culture, which far, very far surpasses all that has heretofore been accomplished; and on which not a few are even unprepared to calculate.

It was a Christian-like wish expressed by King George III., that every child in his dominions should be able to read the bible; and from the increased facility of doing so from gratuitous education, the number of those who cannot is much less than formerly; but in many cases the necessitous circumstances of the parents prevent them from allowing their children, except during their infant years, the advantage of instruction, even though it cost nothing. The time for the children of the poor to receive instruction, is between the ages of two and eight; after that period many are sent out to work, or detained at home, for they then become useful to their parents, and cannot be sent to school. There are many little girls who, having left the infant school, go out to work for a shilling a week, and the mothers have declared to me, when I have endeavoured to persuade them to send them to the National School, for at least one year, that they could not do it, for, they were so poor, that every shilling was a great help; they have, however, promised me that they would send them to a Sunday School. This may account, in some measure, for there being so many more boys than girls, in almost every school in London, and shews the great good that has been done, and is doing, by those valuable institutions.*

Many of my readers, who have been in the habit of noticing and pitying the poor, may think the detail into which I have entered superfluous, but I can assure them the want of information on the subject is but too general, and is sufficient to account for the indifference which has so long been exhibited.

The objection, that education is altogether improper for poor people is not quite obsolete. There are not wanting persons who still entertain the most dreadful apprehensions of the *" march of intellect,"* as it has been termed; who see no alternative but that it must overturn everything that is established, and subvert the whole order of society. I would willingly impart comfort to the minds of those who

---

* It is to be observed here, that the children do not come to our schools on Sundays, but many of them between five and six years old, who have brothers or sisters in the National School, go with them to church, and others of the same age go to a Sunday School in the neighbourhood. In short, I may venture to say, that almost all the children that are able go either to a Sunday School, or to church; but to take them all in a body, at the early age that they are admitted into an Infant School, to any place of worship, and to keep them there for two or three hours, with a hope to profit them, and not to disturb the congregation, is, according to my view, injurious if not impracticable.

are afflicted with such nervous tremors, but I fear, if the demonstration of experience has not quieted them, the voice of reason never will. It cannot fail to remind us of the apprehensions of the popish clergy in former times, who decried the art of printing, then recently introduced, as a branch of the *black art*, which, if encouraged, must eventually demolish the social fabric, and introduce civil wars and discord into every country. Time, that test of truth, has shewn us how groundless their apprehensions were. Instead of injuring that fabric, it has strengthened its foundation, so that it cannot be shaken, and has surrounded it with defences, which bid defiance to assault.

The first idea of an Infant School was suggested by the asylums provided by Mr. Owen of New Lanark, for the infant children of the adult part of the population. That they might not be an hindrance to the daily labours of their parents, they were put under the charge of several women, and the whole was placed under the superintendence of one man, Mr. Buchanan. Instead of wandering about the streets unprotected, liable to accidents, or to form bad associations, these children were observed to be taken care of, and made happy; amusement and exercise for them were not forgotten, and they were frequently seen dancing and capering about to the sound of a flute. The introduction of these institutions into England is to be traced to the active philanthropy of the present Lord Chancellor.

Mr. Buchanan was engaged, and came over from New Lanark, and a school was opened under his management in Brewer's Green, Westminster.

A school was afterwards established, of which I was requested to become the superintendent. This was, indeed, the only Infant School then existing; for the former institution was merely an asylum to contain children from two to ten or twelve years of age ; with none of the apparatus yet to be described in this volume. *I regret, however, to state that on a recent visit I found it in a very unfavourable condition.* No blame attaches to the master, but the zeal of its founder appears to have declined, and thus it has become a wreck. Great was the interest I once took in it, and most gratifying was the inspection of it to multitudes, but now it presents but little resemblance to what it once was, or what I desire it to be. *With great pain I make this statement, but it is due to myself and to the system, since were strangers to go thither from what has been said and published respecting it, their disappointment would be great, and serious obstacles might arise to the education of the Infant poor.* I was afterwards invited to re-organize a school in Vincent's Square on my own plan. Others soon arose, and since that time the system has been adopted in most of the principal towns of England, in many parts of Scotland, and in several instances in Ireland and Wales. For full particulars on this subject the reader is referred to a volume entitled, "Early Discipline illustrated, or the Infant System Progressing and Successful;" dedicated, by permission, to the Right Honourable the Lord Chancellor, and published by Messrs. Westley and Davis.

To the furtherance of this object I have devoted for many years my utmost energies and resources, and to it I purpose to give them so long as I am permitted by the gracious Providence of God. I shall be happy to render it any aid either by supplying information to those who need it, or by personal exertions, the expenses of so doing being defrayed; on application to my depot, Alpha House, Cheltenham.

In order to urge the necessity, and explain the design of Infant Schools, I have for some years been accustomed to deliver a course of lectures, of which the following is an outline :—

FIRST LECTURE.—Affecting state of the children of the poor—Lamentable condition of the offspring of the higher classes—Dreadful increase of young delinquents—What are the causes ?—The question answered—Bodily and mental injuries now sustained by children of all ranks described and prevented—What is the best remedy for existing evils ?—Answer given—Origin and history of the Infant System—Its progress in Scotland, where it might least have been expected—What are the objections to the system ?—A practical refutation of them—Modes of instruction :—The alphabet, spelling, reading, arithmetic—Moral cultivation enforced, and the means explained.

SECOND LECTURE.—A play-ground made not only delightful, but *mentally and morally* improving—The class-room adapted to produce and confirm religious impressions—Music, its application to improve the feelings and the memory—Representations of natural objects and scriptural subjects—Variety and extent of information attainable—Lying, dishonesty, injustice, and cruelty corrected.

THIRD LECTURE.—New plans of reward and

punishment—Influence of fear and love—Great difference in the result—Infant system more fully explained—Appeals to conscience—Emulation unnecessary—Elliptical plan of teaching described—Trials by jury—Effect of sympathy—Infants the instruments of improving one another.

FOURTH LECTURE.—Methods of teaching the elements of grammar, geography, and geometry—Gallery described, and its application to many useful purposes—Qualifications of instructors—Injury sustained from their deficiencies and errors—The system contrasted with former methods—Ultimate effects of its diffusion—Servants prepared to become blessings to families—Hints to parents, and the application of the whole system to children of every grade.

These lectures I am ready to deliver wherever it may be deemed desirable, and to follow up the effect by the organization of schools. The necessary apparatus may be obtained at my depot, and as it has been pirated, it is due to myself and the public to request that all orders may be addressed to *me*.

CHAPTER IV.

PRINCIPLES OF INFANT EDUCATION.

" The business of education, in respect of knowledge, is not, as I think, to perfect a learner in all or any one of the sciences; but to give his mind that disposition, and those habits, that may enable him to attain any part of knowledge he shall stand in need of in the future course of his life."

LOCKE.

" When the obligations of morality are taught, let the sanctions of Christianity never be forgotten; by which it will be shewn that they give lustre and strength to each other: religion will appear to be the voice of reason, and morality the will of God."

JOHNSON.

WHEN Agesilaus, king of Sparta, was asked, " What should boys be taught?" he answered, " What they ought to do when they become men." Such a declaration was worthy of later times, since the most intelligent now admit that the great end of all education is the formation of solid, useful, and virtuous character. This work should be, doubtless, commenced at the earliest possible period, to it the sys-

tem explained in this volume is considered to be
adapted, and the principles on which it proceeds are
now to be illustrated. And here it ought to be particularly observed that nothing is admissible, except
what is appropriate to the state of infancy, calculated
to exercise the physical energies, and likely, by their
invigoration, to lay the basis of a sound and powerful intellect. And yet all this is too often forgotten.
Look at the infant, the very embodying of vivacity
and activity, and its confinement to a particular pos-
ture, or the requirement of a peculiar expression of
countenance, is manifestly unnatural. An inactive
and healthy child under six years of age is never
seen. Whatever compels it to be otherwise consequently produces what is artificial in character. A
parent or a teacher may keep his children quiet, and
in what he terms order; but it does not follow that
this is a good preparation for after years. On the
contrary, bondage may issue in excess. The feelings
and propensities which, instead of being corrected,
are unduly restrained, will be manifested in some
other ways, and under less favourable circumstances,
and frequently the reaction will be violent in maturity.
Hence the system now recommended is expressly one
for *infants*, adapted to them just as they are, and
wholly designed to repress what is evil, and to cherish
what is good.

Accordingly, the utmost attention is given to the
cheerfulness and happiness of those on whom it acts.
Instruction in reading, arithmetic, geometry, and
various other things is made exceedingly amusing;
smiling countenances and sparkling eyes are observ-
able all around when it is communicated; and what

was dull and soporific, according to the old plan, is now insinuated so agreeably, that the child, while literally at play, is acquiring a large amount of valuable knowledge. Music has proved a most important auxiliary for this purpose, and a stranger would be astonished at the hilarity and delight with which much is rehearsed, with a full perception of its meaning, when in any other way it would be irksome and unintelligible.

These attainments, moreover, are accompanied by various movements and evolutions which exercise the limbs, the joints, the muscles ; in addition to which, set times are appointed every morning and afternoon for its exclusive enjoyment.

The conduct of inferior animals, when young, shews the propriety of giving exercise to children. Every other creature makes use of its organs of motion as soon as possible, and many of them, when under no necessity of moving in quest of food, cannot be restrained without force. Such is the case with the calf, the lamb, and many more. If these creatures were not permitted to frisk about at pleasure, they would soon die, or become diseased. The same inclination appears very early in the human species ; but as they are not able to take exercise themselves, it is the business of their parents and nurses to give it them. This may be done in various ways, and the methods included in the system are shewn in other parts of this work. It is to be regretted that men should be so inattentive to this matter ; their negligence is one reason why females know so little of it. Women will always be desirous to excel in such accomplishments as recommend them to the other sex; but men generally avoid even the slightest acquaintance with the affairs of the nursery, and many would reckon it an affront were they supposed to know any thing of them. Not so, however, with the kennel or the stables; a gentleman of the first rank who is not ashamed to give directions concerning the management of his dogs or horses, would blush were he surprised in performing the same office for that being who is to be the heir of his fortunes, and, perhaps, the future hope of his country.

Arguments to show the importance of exercise might be drawn from every part of the animal economy. Without it, the circulation of the blood cannot be properly carried on, nor the different secretions duly performed; neither can the fluids be properly prepared, nor the solids rendered firm or strong. The action of the heart, the motion of the lungs, and all the vital functions, are greatly assisted by exercise. But to point out the manner in which these effects are produced, would lead us beyond the present subject. We shall therefore only add, that when exercise is neglected, none of the animal functions can be duly performed; and when this is the case, the whole constitution must go to wreck. Healthy parents, wholesome food, and suitable clothing will avail little where it is disregarded. Sufficient exercise will supply many defects in nursing, but nothing can compensate for its want. A good constitution ought certainly to be our first object in the management of children. It lays a foundation for their being useful and happy in life; and whoever neglects it, not only fails in his duty to his offspring, but to society.

While this is forgotten, let us not complain of weak and thoughtless children, or of weak and thoughtless servants; for the former are so from the neglect of their parents and the public; and the latter from not having been taught to think at all—and yet the very persons that object to the education of the poor are the first to complain of their servants.

A notion that habits of industry must be established, has, however, been the means, I regret to state, of a sad perversion of the system in these respects. The time allowed for amusement and exercise has been, in some cases, very much abridged that the children might learn and practise sewing, knitting, plaiting, &c. Now, no one can be more disposed to the encouragement of industrious habits than myself, but I would say not at the expense of health; which I am certain in these cases it must be. Deprive the children of their amusement, and they will soon cease to be the lively, happy beings, we have hitherto seen them, and will become the sickly, inanimate creatures, we have been accustomed to behold and pity, under the confinement and restraint of the Dames' Schools. I do not scruple to affirm, that if the *play-grounds* of Infant Schools are cut off from the system,—they will from that moment cease to be a blessing to the country.

The first faculties which develop themselves in childhood, are those of observation. The infant, who is two months old, will notice a lighted candle; immediately that sense is gratified, it seeks to please another, that of *touch*, and every mother knows, if not prevented, it will put its hand in the flame. The next effort is to examine other objects : these it will

H

seize if it can, and after having examined one, it will put it aside to observe another.   On its being able to move about, it seeks objects within its reach, and, wishing to gratify the sense of taste, applies every thing to the mouth; by this it distinguishes the bitter from the sweet, and on seeing what is sweet a second time, will point to it and wish to obtain it, whilst what is bitter will not be desired.

The *mental* part of the system should now be adverted to.   Hence it has been well remarked, "From the time that children begin to use their hands, nature directs them to handle every thing over and over, to look at it while they handle it, and to put it into various positions, and at various distances from the eye.   We are apt to excuse this as a childish diversion, because they must be doing something, and have not reason to entertain themselves in a more manly way.   But if we think more justly, we shall find that they are engaged in the most serious and important study; and if they had all the reason of a philosopher, they could not be more properly employed.   For it is this childish employment that enables them to make the proper use of their eyes. They are thereby every day acquiring habits of perception, which are of greater importance than any thing we can teach them.   The original perceptions which nature gave them are few, and insufficient for the purposes of life; and therefore she made them capable of many more perceptions by habit.   And to complete her work, she has given them an unwearied assiduity in applying to the exercise by which those perceptions are acquired."

Such is the education which nature gives her children, and we may add that another part of her dis-cipline is, that by the course of things, children must exert all their muscular force, and employ all their ingenuity, in order to gratify their curiosity and sa-tisfy their little appetites. What they desire is only to be obtained at the cost of labour, patience, and many disappointments. By the exercise of the body and mind necessary for satisfying their desires, they acquire agility, strength, and dexterity in their mo-tions, as well as constitutional health and vigour; they learn to bear pain without dejection, and disappoint-ment without despondency. The education of nature is most perfect in savages, who have no other tutor; and we see that in the quickness of all their senses, in the agility of their motions, in the hardiness of their constitutions, and in their ability to bear hun-ger, thirst, pain, and disappointment, they commonly far exceed civilized nations. On this account, a most ingenious writer seems to prefer savage to social life. But it is the intention of nature, that human education should assist to form the man, and she has fitted us for it, by the natural principles of imita-tion and belief, which discover themselves almost in infancy, as well as by others which are of later growth.

When the education which we receive from men does not give scope to that of nature, it is erroneous in its means and its tendency, and enervates both the body and the mind. Nature has her way of rearing men, as she has of healing their maladies. The art of education is to follow her dictates, and the art of education is equally to obey her laws. The ancient inhabitants of the Baleares followed nature in their manner of teaching their children to be good archers, when they hung their dinner aloft by a thread, and left them to bring it down by their skill in the use of the bow.

The education of nature, without any more human care than is necessary to preserve life, makes a savage. Human education joined to that of nature, may make a good citizen, a skilful artizan, or a well-bred man ; but a higher power is wanting in order to produce a Bacon or a Newton.

The error of the *past* system (for such I hope I may venture to call it) as to *mental development* was, that the inferior powers of the mind were called into activity, in preference to its higher faculties. The effort was to exercise the memory, and store it with information, which, owing to the inactivity of the understanding and the judgment, was seldom or never of use. To adopt the opinions of others was thought quite enough, without the child being troubled to think for itself, and to form an opinion of its own. But this is not as it should be. Such a system is neither likely to produce great nor wise men; and is much better adapted to parrots than children. Hence, the first thing attempted in an Infant School is, to set the children thinking,—to induce them to examine, compare, and judge, in reference to all those matters which their dawning intellects are capable of mastering. It is of no use to tell a child, in the first place, *what it should think,*— this is at once inducing mental indolence, which is but too generally prevalent among adults ; owing to this erroneous method having been adopted by those who had the charge of their early years. Were a

child left to its own resources, to discover and judge
of things exclusively by itself, though the opposite
evil would be the consequence, namely, a state of
comparative ignorance, yet I am doubtful whether it
would be greater or more lamentable than that issuing
from the injudicious system of giving children dog-
mas instead of problems, the opinions of others
instead of eliciting their own. In the one case we
should find a mind, uninformed and uncultivated, but
of a vigorous and masculine character, grasping the
little knowledge it possessed, with the power and
right of a conqueror; in the other, a memory occupied by a useless heap of notions,—without a single
opinion or idea it could call its own,—and an understanding indolent and narrow, and, from long-in-
dulged inactivity, almost incapable of exertion. As
the fundamental principle of the system, I would
therefore say, let the *children think for themselves*.
If they arrive at erroneous conclusions, assist them
in attaining the truth; but let them with such assistance arrive at it by their own exertions. Little
good will be done, if you say to a child,—*That* is
wrong, *this* is right, unless you enable it to perceive
the error of the one and the truth of the other. It is
not only due to the child as a rational being that you
should act so, but it is essentially necessary to the
development of its intellectual faculties. It were not
more ridiculous for a master in teaching arithmetic,
to give his pupil the problem and answer, without
instructing him in the method of working the question, than it is for a person to give a child results of
reasoning, without shewing how the truth is arrived
at. But some, perhaps, will be ready to exclaim,

" Surely the teacher should not withhold the benefit of his knowledge and experience,—the child will have time enough to examine the merits of his information when he grows older and be more competent to do so!" To this I answer: in the first place, nothing should be submitted to the child which it is not fully competent to understand. To give the child tasks or subjects too difficult for its mental powers, is a violation of nature; and as foolish and detrimental as though you were to place a hundred pounds weight on its shoulders, when it is incapable of supporting ten. The teacher's experience can only be of service to the child so far as it is applicable to its own state; and as to postponing the period when it is to think for itself, there is certainly no occasion for it. Nature has provided food adapted to the powers of the infant's stomach, and those who would rightly conduct the work of education, should imitate her in providing its intellectual food. That this may be done, I am attempting to shew in theory in the pages of this work; and, that it answers equally well in practice, any one who has a doubt, may assure himself by visiting any school conducted upon the plan here laid down.

The charge has been brought against the system, that we are not sufficiently anxious to teach the children to read. Now, though I may venture to say, that under no other plan, do the children acquire a knowledge of alphabetical characters, and the formation of words, so soon as under the present, yet I am quite ready to concede that I consider their learning to read a secondary object, to that of teaching them to examine and find out the nature and properties of things, of which words are but the *signs*. It is with *things*, and not *words* merely, we wish to make our children acquainted. If they first learn the nature and properties of an object, there is no fear of their afterwards inquiring its name; but we too frequently find, that having acquired *names*, they are indifferent to, and forgetful of, the objects represented.

Our first endeavour is, therefore, to excite a spirit of inquiry,—to foster that curiosity which is so natural to young children;—till this is properly done, your information will not be well received, and it is most likely soon to be forgotten; but having once made them inquisitive, you are more likely to tire of communicating than they are of receiving. The skilful teacher will, indeed, rather leave them with an appetite still craving, than satiate them by repletion. I have frequently found the most beneficial results arise from the sudden cessation of a lesson or lecture on an interesting topic. The children have looked for its renewal with the utmost impatience, pondering over what they had already heard, and anticipating what was yet to come with the greatest interest. Give a child a *task*, and you impose a burthen on him,—permit him to learn something and you confer a favour.

Having excited a spirit of inquiry, the next endeavour is to direct it to proper objects. These, of course, will be things which relate to the senses of the child; the nature and properties of bodies, which may be ascertained by the application of those senses, &c. Having induced it to examine for itself, you are now to elicit its ideas of each object respectively; and having taught it to use its reason and judgment freely, and to express its own notions fearlessly and candidly,—you are to attempt the correction of what is erroneous, by putting forth your own views in as simple a way as possible. Not so as to induce the child to give up its own opinions and adopt yours, but in such a way as to direct it to the attainment of truth; to induce a comparison between his thoughts and yours, and thus to discover its own error.

The powers of observation will speedily be improved under such a course of instruction, and in all the subsequent stages of existence, will not fail to constitute an independent and shrewd observer. But some may think we are straining the child's faculties by the plan recommended — overstepping nature's laws,—and that the result must be detrimental to the child, both in mind and body. So far, however, is this from being true, that we have taken nature for our guide. We deprecate that unnatural system, which gives children tasks beyond their powers, and for which their infantine faculties are not qualified; —we would lead them on in the path which nature has marked out—step by step—taking care that one thing should be thoroughly mastered before another is attempted.

As soon as a child enters the school he is under command. He is required to occupy certain places, to go through various motions, and to attend to diversified instruction, at the sound of a foot, or the raising of a hand. From this course no departure is allowed. At first it is the work of sympathy and imitation, but afterwards it becomes a matter of principle. Thus, then, the native reluctance of the infant mind to obey is overcome, and a solid basis laid for future efforts. So far, however, the discipline is general; to be particular, the individual character must be minutely observed. The movements of the child, when unrestrained, must be diligently watched, its predominant qualities ascertained, and such a mode of treatment adopted as sound judgment of character may dictate. Wherever this is forgotten, some evils will arise. The orders which are given to any other power than those of sympathy and imitation are not likely to be obeyed by the untrained babe; the fact is, that as yet it has no other means of obedience, and for this, on higher principles we must wait till nature furnishes instruments and opportunities for their exercise. When, however, success is gained thus far, the way is prepared for further development and culture, and the powers of observation and discrimination, then gradually tasked, will accomplish all that is desired. Thus the infant sits or rises, repeats or is silent, at first, because those about him do so, afterwards he perceives a reason for doing so; for example, that when in the gallery, he can see what he could not any where else, and, *therefore*, that he must march thither, and then he judges that one thing is wrong because the doing it was forbidden, and that another is right because it was commanded, or because the one makes him happy and the other the contrary.

Under the old system of education, I must candidly say, *moral* treatment has been often altogether omitted, and still more frequently has it been erroneous, and consequently inefficient. Let me ask,—would it

promote a child's health, to teach it to repeat certain
maxims on the benefits resulting from exercise? The
answer is obvious.   Neither can it be of any service
to the moral health of the child, to teach it to repeat
the best maxims of virtue, unless we have taken care
to urge the practical observance of those precepts.
And yet this has rarely been the case.   How frequently do we hear persons remark on the ill conduct
of children, " It is surprising they should do so ;—
they have been taught better things !"   Very likely ;
and they may have all the golden rules of virtue
alluded to, carefully stored up in their memories ;—
but they are like the hoarded treasures of the miser :
the disposition to use them is wanted. It is this which
we must strive to produce and promote in the child.
Indeed, if we can but be the instruments of exciting
a love of goodness, it will not err, nor lack the knowledge how to do good, even though we were to forget to give it any rules or maxims.   It is to the heart
we must turn our attention in the moral treatment of
children.   Another grand object of the master or
mistress of an Infant School, is, therefore, to win their
love, by banishing all slavish fear.   They are to be
invited to regard their teacher, as one who is desirous
of promoting their happiness, by the most affectionate
means—not only by kind words, but by kind actions;
one of which influences a child more than a volume
of words.   Words appeal only to the understanding,
and frequently pass away as empty sounds ; but kind
actions operate on the heart, and, like the genial
light and warmth of spring, that dispels the gloom
which has covered the face of nature during the chilly
season of winter, they disperse the mists which cold

and severe treatment has engendered in the moral atmosphere. The fundamental principle of the Infant School system is *love;* nor should any other be substituted for it, except when absolutely necessary. Let the children see that you love them, and *love* will beget *love,* both toward their teacher and each other. Without the aid of example nothing can be done; it is by this magnetic power alone that sympathetic feelings can be awakened. It acts as a talisman on the inmost feelings of the soul, and excites them to activity; which should be the constant aim of all persons engaged in the important work of education. As we find that vicious principles are strengthened by habit, and good principles proportionally weakened, so, on the contrary, immoral dispositions are weakened by the better feelings being brought into action.

The great defect in the human character is *selfishness,* and to remove or lessen this is the great desideratum of moral culture. How happy were mankind, if, instead of each one living for himself, they lived really for one another ! The perfection of moral excellence cannot be better described than as the attainment of that state in which we should ''love our neighbour as ourselves.'' The prevalence of self-love will be very obvious to the observant master or mistress, in the conduct of the children under their care,—and it is this feeling that they must be ever striving to check or eradicate. Nor need they despair of meeting with some degree of success. The children may be brought to feel, that to impart happiness is to receive it,—that, being kind to their little schoolfellows, they not only secure a return of kindness, but actually receive a personal gratification from so doing; and that there is more pleasure in forgiving an injury than in resenting it. Some I know will be apt to say,—that after all, this is nothing but *selfishness* or *self-love*. It is an old matter of dispute, and I leave those to quarrel over it who please. Every one knows and feels the difference between that which we call *selfishness*, and that which is comprehensively termed by the lips of divine truth, the " *love of our neighbour*." If it must be called self-love, I can only say that it is the proper direction of the feeling which is to be sought.

In the work of moral culture, it will be necessary not only to observe the child's conduct under the restraint of school observation and discipline ; but at those times when it thinks itself at liberty to indulge its feelings unnoticed. The evil propensities of our nature have all the wiliness of the serpent, and lurk in their secret places, watching for a desirable opportunity of exercise and display. For the purpose of observation the *play-ground* will afford every facility, and is on this account, as well as because it affords exercise and amusement to the children, an indispensable appendage to an Infant School. Here the child will shew its character in its true light. Here may be seen what effects the education of children have produced; for if they are fond of fighting and quarrelling, here it will be apparent; if they are artful, here they will seek to practise their cunning ; and this will give the master an opportunity of applying the proper remedy; whereas, if they are kept in school (which they must be, if there be no play-ground), these evil inclinations will not manifest themselves until they go into the street, and consequently, the antidote will

not be applied. I have seen many children behave
very orderly in the school, but the moment they entered the play-ground they manifested their selfishness
to such a degree, that they would wish all the rest of
the children to be subservient to them ; and, on their
refusing to let them bear rule, they would begin to
use force, in order to compel their compliance. This
is conduct that ought to be checked—and what time
so proper as the first stages of infancy ?

To take another case, a quarrel like this may arise :
a boy has six gooseberries ; another boy comes and
asks one ; by a little solicitation he obtains it :—he
wishes another ;—but the boy who has them says he
cannot spare any more ; he has only five, and cannot
part with another. The second boy, however, duns
him. He even acts the hypocrite, and puts into play
many of the worst artifices of human nature, which
we so often see in daily practice, and he gains his
end. But he is not yet satisfied ; he wishes another.
The first boy, however, will on no account give him
more. He again tries all his arts, but in vain. Seeing
he cannot by art or entreaty gain another, he has recourse to violence. He snatches one out of his companion's hand and runs off with it. The first boy is
irritated at such conduct, he pursues the fugitive, over-
takes him, and gives him a blow on the face. The
second boy is as great a coward as he is a thief. He
comes up and makes his complaint to the master.
The master then has a trial by jury. He does not
knock one head against the other, according to the
old custom, but he hears both plaintiff and defendant,
and having got the facts, he submits to the children
themselves whether it was right in the one boy to

I

take with violence what was not his own, and shews
them which is the more to blame. Then they decide
on the sentence; perhaps some one suggests that it
should be the utmost infliction allowable, a slight pat
on the hand; while a tender-hearted girl says, "Please,
sir, give it him very softly;" but the issue is, a marked
distinction between right and wrong;—appropriate
expressions of pleasure and disapprobation:—and on
the spot, "a kissing and being friends." I am, indeed,
so firmly convinced, from the experience I have had,
of the utility of a play-ground, from the above reasons, and others, elsewhere mentioned, that I scruple
not to say, an Infant School is of little if any service
without one.

Where the play-ground is ornamented with flowers,
fruit-trees, &c. (and I would recommend this plan to
be invariably adopted) it not only affords the teacher
an opportunity of communicating much knowledge to
the children, and of tracing every thing up to the
Great First Cause, but it becomes the means of establishing principles of honesty. They should not on
any account be allowed to pluck the fruit or flowers;
every thing should be considered as sacred; and being
thus early accustomed to honesty, temptations in
after-life will be deprived of their power. It is dis-
tressing to all lovers of children, to see what havoc
is made by them in plantations near London; and
even grown persons are not entirely free from this
fault, for, not content with a proper foot-path, they
must walk on a man's plantations, pull up that which
can be of no use, and thereby injure the property of
their neighbour. These things ought not to be, nor
do I think they would be so common, if they were

noticed a little more in the education of children. It has been too much the practice with many, to consider that the business of a school consists merely in teaching children their letters; but I am of opinion, that the formation of character while there is of the greatest importance, not only to the children, but to society at large. How can we account for the strict honesty of the Laplanders, who can leave their property in the woods, and in their huts, without the least fear of its being stolen or injured, while we, with ten times the advantages, cannot consider our property safe, with the aid of locks and bolts, brick walls, and even watchmen and police-officers besides? There must be some cause for all this, and perhaps the principal one is defective education, and the total neglect of the morals of the infant poor, at a time when their first impressions should be taken especial care of; *for conscience, if not lulled to sleep, but called into vigorous action, will prove stronger than brick walls, bolts, or locks: and I am satisfied, that I could have taken the whole of the children under my care in the first Infants' School, into any gentleman's plantation, without their doing the least injury whatever; and this I could now do in any similar circumstances.* I will mention, however, one fact.

One day, while I was walking in the play-ground, I saw at one end of it about twenty children, apparently arguing a subject, pro and con.; from the attitude of several of the orators, I judged it was about something that appeared to them of considerable importance. I wished to know the subject of debate, but was satisfied that if I approached the children it might put an end to the matter altogether. Some of the bystanders saw me looking very attentively at the principal actor, and, as I suppose, suggested to the party the propriety of retiring to some other spot, for immediately afterwards they all went behind a partition, which afforded me an opportunity of distinctly hearing all that passed, without being observed by them. I soon found that the subject of debate was a *song*. It seems that one of the children had brought a song to the school, which some of the monitors had read, and having decided that it was an improper thing for the child to have in his possession, one of them had taken it from the owner, and destroyed it. The aggrieved party had complained to some of the other children, who said that it was *thieving* for one child to take any thing from another child, without his consent. The boy, nettled at being called a thief, defended himself by saying that he, as a monitor, had a right to take away from any of his class any thing that was calculated to do them harm; and was, it seems, backed in this opinion by many others. On the other hand, it was contended that no such right existed; and it was doubtful to me for a considerable time, on which side the strength of the argument lay. At last one of the children observed to the following effect:—" You should have taken it to *master*, because he would know if it was bad better than you." This was a convincing argument, and to my great delight, the boy replied—" How much did the song cost?" The reply was, " A halfpenny." " Here, then, take it," says the child, " I had one given me to-day; so now remember I have paid you for it, but if you bring any more songs to school I will tell master." This seemed to give general satisfaction to the whole party, who immediately dispersed to their several amusements. A struggle like this, between the principles of *duty and honesty*, among children so very young, must prove highly interesting to all who love them, and exemplifies, beyond a doubt, the immense advantage of early instruction.

Another thing to be noticed is a regard for *truth*. Nothing is so delightful as this. There is no conversation so agreeable as that of the man of integrity, who hears without any design to betray, and speaks without any intention to deceive; and this admitted, we should strive to the utmost to induce children to remember it. But our success, in a great measure, will depend on the means we employ. Many children are frightened into falsehood by the injudicious methods of those who have the care of them. I have known a mother promise a child forgiveness if it would speak the truth, and, after having obtained confession, she has broken her engagement. A child, once treated in this manner, will naturally be guarded against a similar deception. I have known others who would pretend not to punish the child for confession, but for first denying it, and afterwards confessing. I think that children should not be punished, on any account, after having been promised forgiveness, truth being of too great importance to be thus trifled with; and we cannot wonder if it is lightly esteemed by children, after the example is set by their parents. Having had several thousand children under my care, I have had favourable opportunities of observing the bias of the infant mind, and I must say, that I have not found them so inclined to evil and falsehood as I had previously imagined.

When morality is adverted to in this chápter, let it not be forgotten that by it is meant the morality of the Scriptures. From thence the great means are derived of regulating the conscience and improving the heart. The Infant System, however, steers clear of the various theological opinions entertained by Christians of different denominations, conceiving, as I do, that such institutions should receive the support of all. What kind of religious doctrine and faith infants ought to be taught I do not venture to declare, as I think it must be the wish and desire of *all* the dis-ciples of Christ that they should be instructed in the fundamental truths of the everlasting gospel.

CHAPTER V.

REQUISITES FOR AN INFANT-SCHOOL.

" Wisdom seeks the most desirable ends in the use of the most appropriate means."

I SHALL now lay before my readers an account of the things necessary for the establishment of an Infant School; previously to presenting them with the detail of the plan to be pursued in it.

In the first place, it is necessary to provide an airy and spacious apartment, with a dry, and, if possible, a large play-ground attached to it. The plot of ground, I conceive, should not be less than fifty feet wide, and one hundred feet long; but if the ground were one hundred and fifty, or two hundred feet long, it would be so much the better, as this would allow one hundred or one hundred and fifty feet for a play-ground; which is of such importance, that I consider the system would be very defective without it, for reasons which will be spoken of hereafter.

There should likewise be a room about fifteen feet square, for the purpose of teaching the children in classes, which may be formed at one end of the large room; this is absolutely necessary. As the master and mistress should live on the premises, a small house, containing three or four rooms, should be provided for them. The reason for their living on the premises is, that the children should be allowed to bring their dinners with them, as this will keep them out of the streets; and, indeed, of those who do go home to dinner, many will return in a very short time, and if there be no persons on the premises to take care of them, they will be lost; and not only so, but strange boys will come in from the streets, and do a great deal of mischief, if no one be there to prevent it.

The portion of sitting-room that I have allowed for each child is twelve inches. The scholars should sit all round the school room, with their backs against the wall; double seats should be round the sides of the school, like the two first seats in the gallery. A school according to the engraved plan, will be found large enough for all the purposes of an Infant School; but if it is wished to be more commodious, it may be of the same length as the plan, and instead of twenty-two feet wide, may be made thirty feet wide; this will hold as many children as ought to be collected together in one place, and as many as any man and woman can possibly do justice to. If it be any longer, it will be difficult for all the children to hear the master. An oblong building is the cheapest, on account of the roof. Economy has been studied in the plan given, without any thing being added that is unnecessary. This, of course, is a matter of opinion, and may be acted upon or not, just as it suits those who may choose to build. The mas-

ter's house in the plan, it will be seen, projects a
little into the play ground, to afford him an opportunity of seeing the children at play while he is at
dinner, that he may notice any improper conduct on
the part of the children, and mention it when the accounts of the day are made up.

As children are very apt to get into danger, even
when at school, it becomes expedient to exercise the
utmost vigilance, in order to prevent the possibility of
an accident; for where two hundred children are assembled together, the eldest not seven years of age, it
is most certain that if there be danger, some will get
into it.   For this reason, all the doors on the premises should be so secured, that the children cannot
swing them backwards and forwards; if they are not,
they will get their fingers pinched, or greater accidents
may occur.   The forms also should be so placed that
the children may not be likely to fall over them.
Every thing, in short, should be put out of the way,
that will be likely to occasion any danger.

The master's desk should be placed at the end of
the school, where the class-room is.   By this means
he will be able to see the faces of all the children, and
they can see him, which is absolutely necessary.   They
may then be governed by a motion of his hand.

The *furniture* necessary for the school consists of
a desk for the master; a small rostrum; seats for the
children; lesson-stands; stools for the monitors;
slates and pencils; pictures and lessons on scriptural
subjects; pictures and lessons on natural history;
alphabets and spelling lessons; brass letters and
figures, with board for them; geometrical figures, &c.;
and the transposition-frame, or arithmeticon, as it has

been called.   To these may be added little books, &c.
The particular use of these articles will be particularly
shewn in the succeeding pages.

The following is a representation of a lesson-
post.

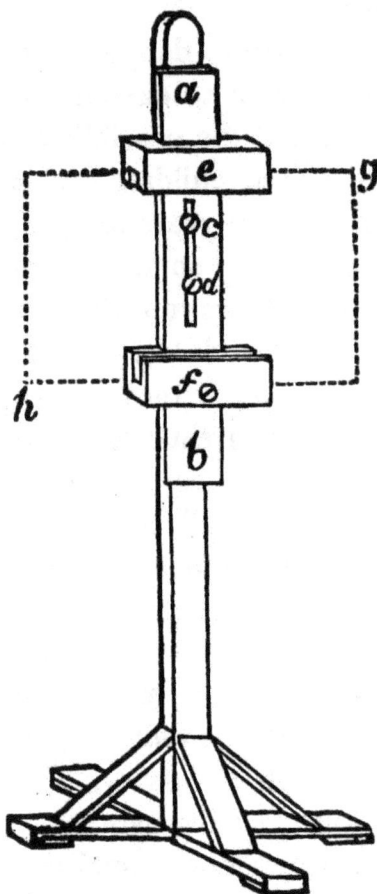

a b is a slip of wood with a groove in it, fixed to the post by means of the screws *c* and *d*, on which slip are two blocks *e* and *f*; the bottom one, *f*, is fixed with a groove in the upper side, for the lower edge of the board *g h* to rest in; the upper block, *e*, has a groove in the lower side, for the upper edge of the board *g h* to rest in, and rises and falls according to the width of the board on the slip *a b*. — Instead of being made with feet, the lesson-post is generally, and perhaps better, fixed into the floor of the school-room, and should be very slight, and 4 feet 4 inches in height.

The *lessons*, pasted on wood, to render them sufficiently stiff, are put into the grooves of the lesson-post; and can then be placed in any position which is most convenient, and adjusted to any height, as the master may see proper.

The arithmeticon, of which a description will be

given in a subsequent chapter, is simple in its construction, but, as will be seen hereafter, may be variously and beneficially applied.   It is indeed indispensable in an Infant School, as it is useful for teaching the first principles of grammar, arithmetic, and geometry.   The expense of furnishing a large School is about 16*l.* ; that of a smaller one about 10*l.*

I must here protest against a violation of the freedom of the infant mind.   A fold, as it is called, is erected in some schools for the youngest of the children ; and thus they are cut off from the society of the rest, from whom they would learn much more than they could from any teacher.   The monitors having charge of this class, are also cooped up in the same cage, and therefore suffer the same privation. The result of my own experience, as well as that of others, is, that a child is decidedly incompetent to the duties of a monitor, if he cannot keep the youngest class in order without any such means.   I would therefore deprecate, in the strongest terms, the separation referred to, as not only altogether unnecessary, but exceedingly injurious.

To have one hundred children, or upwards, in a room, however convenient in other respects, and not to allow the children proper relaxation and exercise, which they could not have without a play-ground, would materially injure their health, which is a thing, in my humble opinion, of the first importance.   I would rather see a school where they charged two-pence or three-pence per week for each child, having a play-ground, than one where the children had free admission without one ; for I think the former institution would do the most good. The play-ground, likewise, is one of the most useful parts of the system. It is there the child shews itself in its true character, and thereby gives the master an opportunity of nipping in the bud its evil propensities. I am, therefore, most anxious humbly to recommend that this necessary appendage to an Infant School should not be dispensed with. I moreover observe, that where there is a play-ground attached to the school, instead of playing in the streets, where scarcely anything but evil is before their eyes, the children will hasten to the school, with their bread and butter in their hands, in less than a quarter of an hour after they have left it, knowing that they have an opportunity of playing there the remainder of their dinner-time, so that they love the school, and but rarely wish to be anywhere else.

The play-grounds of some schools are paved with bricks, which I have found to answer very well, as they absorb the rain so quickly, that ten minutes after a shower, the place is dry enough for the children to play in; which, perhaps, would not be the case with any other kind of paving. They are commonly placed flat on the ground, but I should prefer them being put edgways, as they would last many years longer, yet it would take nearly double the number of bricks were they so placed. If it be not paved, the ground will be soft, and the children will make themselves dirty. It should be so managed that the water may be carried off, for, if there are any puddles, the children will get into them. Some persons have recommended a few cart-loads of good iron mould gravel, there being a sort which will bind almost like a rock, if well rolled; but the children are liable to dig holes if it is only gravel. If this is noticed in time it may be prevented; but if they are suffered to proceed, and no notice be taken of it, it will be very difficult to prevent them from continuing the practice. If money can be saved by any plan, perhaps it is as well to notice it; but after having weighed the advantages and disadvantages of gravelling, I am of opinion, that bricks are preferable. I should also recommend that fruit trees be planted in the centre of the play-ground, and likewise round the walls; which will delight the children, and teach them to respect private property. If any person doubts the propriety of this plan, I can only say we have many play-grounds thus ornamented: and instead of proving a temptation to the children, it has so far become the means of confirming principles of honesty in them, that they never touch a single flower or even a leaf in the garden. There should also be a border of flowers round the play-ground, of such sorts as will yield the most fragrance, which will tend to counteract any disagreeable smell that may proceed from the children, and thereby be conducive to their health, as well as to that of those who have the charge of them. They will, besides, afford the teacher an opportunity of giving the children many useful lessons; for the more he teaches by things, and the less he teaches by signs, the better. These things need be no expense to the establishment, except the purchase in the first instance, for they will afford an agreeable occupation for the master before and after school hours, prepare him in some measure for the duties of the day, and afford him an ample opportu-

K

nity of instilling a variety of ideas into the minds of
the children, and of tracing every thing up to the
Great First Cause. I have witnessed the good effects
of these things, which makes me desirous of humbly
but earnestly recommending them to others.

With regard to the expense; if two hundred children pay two pence each per week*, which is now the
usual charge, the annual receipts will be, deducting
four weeks for holidays, about 80*l*., and if the deficiency be made up by subscriptions and donations from
the friends of the system, it may be easily adopted,
and all its advantages secured. A village school
might be furnished for half the money, and supported
at less than half the expense. I QUESTION
WHETHER IT DOES NOT COST THE COUNTRY AS
MUCH FOR EVERY INDIVIDUAL THAT IS TRANS-
PORTED OUT OF IT. Perhaps I shall be excused
in this place for indulging in a few thoughts on the
practicability of establishing Infant Schools throughout the United Kingdom by means of a legislative
provision. It appears to me as much a duty of government to erect schools for children to prevent ignorance and crime in them, as it is to employ means
to prevent ignorance and crime in men; and notwithstanding the outcry that has been made against the
new System for educating the poor of Ireland, I am
certain it will do much good, and would they only
add the Infant System, which I know suits the Irish

---

* In some parts of St. Giles's, Wapping, &c. &c., many of the
parents are not able to pay, and many that are, would sooner let
their children run the streets than pay a penny; yet the children
of the latter persons are the greater objects of charity; and it is
the children of such persons that chiefly fill our prisons.

children, much more would be done, and much
crime prevented in that country; but I see no reason why the English, thousands of whom are deplorably ignorant and desperately profane, should not
have the same advantages. None can be aware of
the extent of such evils, unless they have visited the
poor in the different countries, counties, and towns
that I have. Could they but see what I have seen,
they would at once be convinced.

Every year increases my conviction of the great
importance of the play-ground, and of the folly of
some of my early views respecting it. Finding a
great variety of lessons and objects necessary to arrest
the attention of children, diversified as they are in
disposition and taste, it was supposed that an equal
variety of toys was required for the play-ground. A good
supply of balls, battledores, shuttlecocks, tops, whips,
skipping-ropes, hoops, sticks, and wheelbarrows, was
therefore obtained, and we flattered ourselves that
this must produce universal happiness. In this,
however, we were most grievously disappointed; for
the balls frequently bounced over the wall,— the
players not being able to throw them with the preci-
sion of Spartan children, sometimes struck their
comrades, perhaps in the eye,—if we could succeed
in quieting the sufferer by a kiss and a sugar-plum,
the ear was immediately afterwards saluted with the
cry of "O my chin, my chin," from some hapless
wight having been star-gazing, and another, anxious
for as many strokes as possible, mistaking that part
for the bottom of his shuttlecock,—while this would
be followed by "O my leg," from the untoward
movement of a stick or a barrow. In short, such

scenes were insupportable; and what with the accidents that arose, and the tops without strings, and the
strings without tops, the hoops without sticks, and
the sticks without hoops, the seizure of the favourite
toy by one, and the inability of another to get any
thing, it was evident that we were wrong, but not so
clear how we could do otherwise.

It then occurred that we might provide some wood
bricks, about four inches long, an inch and a half
thick, and two inches and a half wide, and of these a
thousand were obtained. With these children are exceedingly amused, from the variety of forms in which
they may be placed, and of buildings which may be
erected with them.

In addition to these, all that is required is a rota-
tory swing, of which the above is a representation.
To make one, a pole eighteen or twenty feet long
should be firmly fixed in the ground, three feet of
the but-end should be sunk secured by sleepers to
keep it steady, it should be at least three quarters of
a yard in girth at bottom, and taper gradually to the
top to half that size.   An iron rim is to be driven on

the head of the pole to keep it from splitting, and then a spindle at least an inch in diameter, with a shoulder, is to be fixed in it; an iron wheel with four spokes turned up at the end like a hook, to which four ropes are to be fastened, must then be made to revolve on the spindle. As the ropes reach the ground, four children may take hold of them and run round until they can bear the whole weight of the body on the arms, and this exercise will be found to strengthen the muscles, and give vigour to the whole frame. In a large school there should be two swings of this kind, one for the girls and the other for the boys. The teachers must however be careful the first few weeks, to train the children to look about them; this they are but little disposed to do, hence the most impressive manner should be adopted, and I will venture to say, should any injury be sustained by the children, the fault *will not be theirs*. The effect of the instruction thus urged will be valuable in other cases; for a child thus taught to watch against accident will be careful in passing crossings, and going through crowded streets, and thus be likely to escape many dangers into which others fall. This exercise may also be accompanied by instruction, as the children may repeat the cow or the sheep, or any other lesson, as the measure of the time during which four may have the swing. It will, moreover, afford an opportunity for detecting the selfishness of some children by their wishing to keep the ropes too long, and the passion of others from the vehemence with which they will insiston their rights; but, as on such occasions, both are to be forbidden to swing any more that day, they will soon learn to bear and forbear.

In the event of a child being thrown down from standing in the way, all the children should be placed in the gallery, and this one shewn them. If it appear hurt, all will pity it; let then the question be put, How did this happen? and the answer will be, perhaps, "Please sir, because he did not make use of his eyes." Here, then, is full opportunity to inculcate caution, and to inform and benefit the whole. For example, the master may say, How many senses have we? The children will answer, five. *Master*—Name them. *Children*—Hearing, seeing, smelling, tasting, and feeling. *M*. Where are the organs of sight? *C*. Here (pointing to the eyes). *M*. Look at this child, and see if he has them (here an inspection will take place, the sufferer will look sheepish, and begin to perceive he has not made the best use of the sense of seeing, whilst the singular observations of the children will sharpen his faculties, and make such an impression as to cause him to be more cautious in future; and many a scholar who is sitting in judgment will profit by the circumstance). I have known the lives of several children saved by such simple lessons, and they are of as much importance as any that are taught, though I am not quite sure that all the teachers will think so. Too many, to save trouble, will find fault with the swing; and I have known several instances where the swing had been taken down in consequence.

CHAPTER VI.

QUALIFICATIONS OF TEACHERS.

——————————

———————————— " Such authority in shew,
" When most severe and minist'ring all its force,
" Is but the graver countenance of love,
" Whose favour, like the clouds of spring may lower,
" And utter now and then an awful voice,
" But has a blessing in its darkest frown,
" Threat'ning at once and nourishing the plant."

Thomson.

——————————

I ENTER on this chapter with a full recollection of
the painful sense of incompetency I endured on becoming " a teacher of babes," and this I trust will
enable me to offer any remarks on the present subject
with the humility that is desirable, blended with the
confidence of experience. It is a very common idea,
that almost any person can educate little children,
and that it requires little or no ability; but it will be
found, on an enlightened and correct estimate of the
work, that this is a great mistake, and I regret that
this mistake has been made by those who professed
to understand the system, and who have written upon

it; but there is just this slight difference between theory and practice : theory supposes such and such things to be correct, which was my own case, but twelve months only of practical effort very soon convinced me I was wrong. How frequently, for instance, may we find children, ten or twelve years of age, who cannot answer the most simple question, and who nevertheless have been to school for several years. To give the children ideas, is a part of education seldom thought of : but if we really wish to form the character of the rising generation, and to improve the condition of society generally, the utmost attention must be given to this object. Little, I should think, need be said to prove, that few ideas are given in Dame Schools. There may be a few as to which an exception should be made ; but generally speaking, where the children of mechanics are usually sent before the age of seven years, no such thing is thought of. The mind of a child is compared by Mr. Locke to a sheet of blank paper, and if it be the business of a tutor to inscribe valuable lessons on the mind, it will require much patience, gentleness, perseverance, self-possession, energy, knowledge of human nature, and above all, piety,—to accomplish so great a work with propriety and success.

Whoever is in possession of these requisites, with the addition of a lively temper, pleasing countenance, and some knowledge of music, may be considered as a proper person to manage an infant school, and whoever has charge of such an institution will find numerous opportunities of displaying each and all of these qualifications. It would be almost useless to attempt to cure the bad tempers of children, if the master should encourage and manifest such evil tempers in his own conduct; for children are not indifferent to what they see in others : they certainly take notice of all our movements, and consequently the greatest caution is necessary. It will be of little purpose to endeavour to inculcate suitable precepts in the minds of the children, unless they see them shine forth in the conduct of the teacher.

How strangely it would sound, if, when a teacher was explaining to his pupils the sin of swearing, a child should say, " Please, sir, I heard you swear;" and it is just the same as to those faults which some may consider of minor importance,—such as the indulgence of angry passions,—in the presence of children.

Persons, in such circumstances, cannot be too circumspect, as every trifling fault will be magnified both by parents and children. Indeed, character is of so much importance, that the designs of benevolent individuals are very often frustrated by appointing improper persons to fill such situations. I have seen more than once the interests of two hundred babes sacrificed to serve one individual, and persons have been chosen merely because they had been unfortunate, and to serve them they have been placed in a situation disagreeable to themselves, and unprofitable to the children. It is one thing to possess certain information, but it is another to be able to communicate that information to infants. Patience is a virtue absolutely indispensable, as it will frequently take the master or mistress a whole hour to investigate a subject that may appear of little or no importance; such as one child accusing another of stealing a trifle, as a plum, a cherry, a button, or any other thing of like value. The complainant and defendant will expect justice done to them by the master or mistress, and in order to do this, much time and trouble will, in some cases, be necessary. Should a hasty conclusion be formed, and the accused be punished for what he has not been guilty of, the child will be sensible that an injury has been done him, feel dissatisfied with his tutors, and consequently will not pay them the respect they ought to have. Besides, it will frequently be found, on examination, that the accuser is really the most in fault, and I think I have convinced many children that this has been the case, and they have retired satisfied with my decision. For when a child is convinced that justice will be done him, he will open his case freely and boldly ; but if he has any idea that it will be otherwise, he will keep one half of the facts in hisown mind, and will not reveal them. I once formed a hasty conclusion in the case of two children, and happened to decide directly contrary to what I ought to have done ; the consequence was, that the injured child endeavoured to do that for himself which he found I had not done for him, and pleaded his own cause with the opposite party in the playground, but finding that he could not prevail on him, and being sensible that he had been wronged, he was so much hurt, that he brought his father the next day, and we re-considered the case ; when it was found that the child was correct, and that I was wrong. Here I found how necessary it was to exercise the utmost patience, in order to enable me to judge rightly, and to convince my little pupils, that I had the greatest desire to do them justice. I compare an Infant School to a little commonwealth, the head or governor of which is naturally the master. An Infant-school master or mistress is not to consider anything relating to the rights of his little community as trifling or unimportant. However justly it might be considered such in itself, yet comparatively, it is a matter of moment to the parties concerned, and such therefore it should be esteemed by him, who is the arbitrator of their rights, and the legislator and judge of the infant state. He will have, indeed, to act the part of counsel, judge, and jury, and although the children cannot find words to plead their own cause, yet by their looks and gestures, they will convince you that they know when you have rightly decided; and it appears to me, that the future conduct of the children in the world, will depend, in a great measure, upon the correctness of the master's decisions.

One would suppose, to hear the observations of some persons, that mere automatons would do for masters and mistresses. By them the system is considered as every thing, while the persons who are to teach it, have been considered as secondary objects; but a system, however perfect in itself, will be productive of little good, unless it be committed to persons possessed of some degree of skill; as the best watch will go wrong, if not properly attended to. We cannot, therefore, be too circumspect in the choice of the persons to whom we commit the care and education of the rising generation. There is something so powerful in correctness of deportment, that even infants respect it; and this will operate more on their minds than many imagine. It does not appear necessary to me, that children should be kept under excessive restraint by their tutors; they should rather be encouraged to make their teacher their confidant, for by this means he will become acquainted with many things, the knowledge of which it is essential he should possess, both as it regards himself, and the welfare of his pupils. If the child be enthralled, he will seek some other persons to whom he may open his little mind, and should that person be ill-disposed, the most serious consequences will not unfrequently follow. I know the source from whence all assistance is derived, and I am taught to believe, that such assistance will not be withheld from those who diligently seek it. I am well aware that I shall have to render an account of my stewardship to the Almighty, for every child that may have been placed under my care, and I feel that to do so unblameably requires much assistance from above.

Let not those, then, who are similarly circumstanced with myself, think that I address them in the spirit of arrogance, with a pre-conceived opinion of my own sufficiency. I wish that all who teach may be more fit for the situation than I am. I know many who are an honour to their profession, as well as the situation they fill; but, I am sorrow to say, I think they do not all meet with the encouragement they merit. It is not always those who do their duty the best that are most valued; but if a man's conscience do not upbraid him, he has in its approval a high reward.

And now, as to a matter on which there is some difference of opinion, *viz.* whether women are or are not as fit for conductors of Infant Schools as men; my decided opinion is, that *alone* they are not. There should be in every school a master and a mistress. In the first place, in an Infant School, the presence of the man, as of a father in a family, will insure a far greater degree of respect and attention on the part of the children. This does not arise from the exercise of any greater degree of harshness or severity than a mother would be capable of using; nor is it to be attributed, as some suppose, to the less frequent presence of the father in the case of many families, but is rather to be accounted for by an intuitive perception of the greater firmness and determination of the character of the man. To those who deny this, I would give as a problem for solution, a case by no means unfrequent, and which most of my readers will have witnessed,—a family in which the mother—by no means incurring the charge of spoiling the child, by sparing the rod—is less heeded, less promptly obeyed in her commands, than a father who seldom or never makes use of any such means. The mother scolds, threatens, scourges, and is at last reluctantly and imperfectly obeyed—the father, either with reference to his own commands, or seconding those of the mother, *speaks*, and is instantly regarded. The idea of disputing his authority, or neglecting or disobeying his laws, never once enters the minds of his children. Exactly the same is it in an Infant School,—the presence of a man insures attention and gains respect from the children, not only at first, whilst the novelty of such control might be supposed to operate, but permanently; as I am sure all who have candidly examined the schools where two women preside, and those conducted by a man and a woman, must have seen.

Another objection to the sole government of females (I mean the class of females who are likely to accept such situations) in these schools, is—they have not the physical strength, nor, at present, intellectual powers sufficient for the task. In saying this, I trust I shall not be suspected of wishing to offend my fair country-women. That they have not sufficient physical strength is the intention of nature; that they are deficient in mental energy is the defect of education. I trust, therefore, that no offence will be assumed where no blame is attached. It has been a point much disputed, whether there be really an original and intrinsic difference in the mental powers of the two sexes, and it has been of course differently decided by the respective disputants. With this I shall have nothing to do; but these things are certain; that the minds of *both* are capable of much greater activity and more important results than have been generally supposed; and that whilst education has not done what it ought for man, it has done far less for woman. This it is, then, which affords an additional argument in my mind for a master and a mistress. For let it not be imagined, that I would dismiss women altogether from the System—that I think them useless or even dispensable in an Infant School. If, indeed, one or the other *must* be done without, and I had my choice, I should certainly give my voice for a woman; but to carry the system into full effect requires *both*. There is ample opportunity for the offices of maternal love, of which man is at best but a poor imitator; neither can it be denied, that an active intelligent woman is a useful auxiliary to the labours of the man in the duties of the school. The authoritative

presence of the man is the more necessary in the Infant System, because one grand object is, to rule
without harshness, and by that principle of love
which is in no degree incompatible with the respect
felt for a kind but judicious schoolmaster.   Some
children, indeed, so far as regards authority, might
be very well managed by a mistress only, but then it
must be recollected that an Infant School exhibits
every variety of temper and disposition; and even
were it otherwise, the objection as to intellectual in-
competence, before adverted to, would still hold good.

Such, indeed, is the opinion of the unfitness of
females for the occupation of teaching, in Scotland,
that in many places the very idea of it is scouted.
The people of that country have scarcely heard of a
school-mistress, even for the youngest children; and
certain it is, that education is much better conducted
in Scotland than in most other places.   If the minds
of children are to be cultivated, and a firm and decided
tone given to their characters, say they, what can be
the use of sending them to a school conducted by a
woman only ?   And I must candidly admit, that I perfectly agree with them on this head, and have therefore
deemed it my duty to be thus explicit on the matter.

One thing I must add, by way of conclusion— to
render any man or woman competent to discharge
the duties of the situation efficiently, the *heart* of the
teacher must be in the school.   If there be not the
zeal of the amateur, the skill of the professor will be
of little avail.   The maxim will apply to every species
of occupation, but it is peculiarly true as to that of an
infant-school teacher.   To those who can feel no
other interest than that which the profit gives to the

employment, it will soon become not only irksome, but exceedingly distasteful. But certain I am that it is possible to feel it to be what it is—an employment not only most important, but likewise most interesting. It is one which a philosopher might choose for the study of the human character, and a philanthropist for its improvement.

One word more, and I have done. I have seen what I could have wished had been otherwise, viz. not sufficient discrimination used in giving *religious instruction;* improper times have been chosen, too much *shew* has been made of it, too much freedom has been used with *the divine names;* and I have sometimes been so shocked at the levity displayed, as to have considered it little less than *profanation.*

I wish to lay the utmost stress on what has been stated, as a failure on the part of a master and mistress is most grievous and lamentable. I have seen schools, where little or nothing has been done, because of the inefficiency of the teachers. Moral and religious qualifications are confessedly of the first importance, but those which are mental are to be highly estimated. I differ with a gentleman who has written on this subject when he says, that any clever boy who has been educated in a national school, will accomplish the end; because the system through which he has passed neither gives a sufficient knowledge of *things* nor of *words,* nor does it sufficiently develop the faculties to prepare him for such a service.

One cause of failure in these respects has been undoubtedly the paltry remuneration which some receive, and I would earnestly recommend the supporters and conductors of Infant Schools to try the effect of liberality by all the means they can command. Persons of talent ought to be found for this work, and then they should be appropriately paid; but if *any* are to be deemed suitable, and if the having them at a low rate be a special reason for their engagement, it would be better at once to revert to the old system, than to destroy by such means the public confidence in the plans now suggested.

I entertain a full conviction that the Infant System will flourish most where I once least expected its adoption—I mean in Scotland, because of the high importance attached to the essential qualifications of teachers, and because of the attention and kindness which they continually receive.

CHAPTER VII.

HINTS FOR CONDUCTING AN INFANT SCHOOL.

———

" Whate'er is best administer'd is best."—*Pope.*

———

As I have had considerable practice in teaching children in various parts of England, Scotland, Ireland, and Wales, I hope I may be allowed to give a few hints on the subject of organizing an Infant School. I have generally found on opening one, that the children had no idea of acting together. In order, therefore, to gain this object, it will be found necessary to have recourse to what we call *manual lessons,* which consist in the children holding up their hands all at one time, and putting them down in the same manner; throwing the right or the left foot out; putting their hands together, or behind them, or rising from their seats all at one time; and many things of a similar kind.

This we do in the first instance, because it is calculated to please the infants, and is one grand step towards order. After the first day or two, the children will begin to act together, and to know each other, but until this is the case, they will be frequently peevish, and want to go home; any method, therefore, that can be taken at first to gratify them, should be adopted : for unless this can be done, you may be sure they will cry. Having proceeded thus far, we have then to class them according to their capacity and age, and according as they shew an aptitude in obeying your several commands. Those who obey them with the greatest readiness may be classed together.

I have found it difficult, at all times, to keep up the attention of infants, without giving them something to do ; so that when they are saying the tables in arithmetic, we always cause them to move either their hands or feet, and sometimes to march round the school. The best way we have yet discovered is the putting their hands one on the other every time they speak a sentence. If they are marching they may count one, two, three, four, five, six, &c.

Having classed them, and found that each child knows its own place in the school, you may select one of the cleverest of each class for a monitor. Some of the children will learn many of the tables sooner than the others ; in this case, the teacher may avail himself of their assistance, by causing each child to repeat what he knows in an audible manner, the other children repeating after him, and performing the same evolutions that he does ; and by this means the rest will soon learn. Then the master may go on with something else, taking care to obtain as much assistance from the children as he can, for he will find that unless he does so, he will injure his lungs, and render himself unfit to keep up their attention, and to carry on the business of the school.

When the children have learned to repeat several of the tables, and the monitors to excite their several classes, and keep them in tolerable order, they may go on with the other parts of the plan, such as the spelling and reading picture lessons, &c. which will presently be described. But care must be taken that in the beginning too much be not attempted. The first week may be spent in getting them in order, without thinking of anything else; and I should advise that not more than sixty children be then admitted, that they may be reduced to order, in some measure, before any more are received, as all that come after will quickly imitate them. I should, moreover, advise visitors not to come for some time after a school is opened, for several reasons; first, because the children must be allowed time to learn, and there will be nothing worth seeing; secondly, they take off the children's attention, and interfere with the master; and, lastly, they may go away dissatisfied, and thereby injure the cause which they intend to promote.

In teaching infants to sing, I have found it the best way to sing the psalm or hymn several times in the hearing of the children, without their attempting to do so until they have some idea of the tune: because, if all the children are allowed to attempt, and none of them know it, it prevents those who really wish to learn from catching the sounds. Nothing, however, can be more ridiculous or absurd than the attempts at singing I have heard in some schools.

You must not expect order until your little officers

are well drilled, which may be done by collecting them together after the other children are gone, and instructing them in what they are to do. Every monitor should know his work, and when you have taught him this, you must require it to be done. To get good order, you must make every monitor answerable for the conduct of his class. It is astonishing how some of the little fellows will strut about, big with the importance of office; and here I must remark, it will require some caution to prevent them from taking too much upon themselves; so prone are we, even in our earliest years, to abuse the possession of power.

The way by which we teach the children hymns, is to let one child stand in the rostrum with the book in his hand; he then reads one line, and stops until all the children in the school have repeated it, which they do simultaneously; he then repeats another, and so on successively, until the hymn is finished. This method is adopted with everything that is to be committed to memory, so that every child in the school has an equal chance of learning.

I have mentioned that the children should be classed: in order to facilitate this, there should be a board fastened to the wall perpendicularly, the same width as the seats, every fifteen feet, all round the school; this will separate one class from another, and be the cause of the children knowing their class the sooner. Make every child hang his hat over where he sits, in his own class, as this will save much trouble. "Have a place for everything, and everything in its place." This will bring the children into habits of order. Never do anything for a child that he is able to do for himself, but teach him to put his own hat and coat on, and hang them up again when he comes to school. Teach every child to help himself as soon as possible. If one falls down, and you know that he is able to get up himself, never lift him up; if you do, he will always lie till you can give him your aid. Have a slate, or a piece of paper, properly ruled, hanging over every class; let every child's name that is in the class be written on it, with the name of the monitor; teach the monitor the names as soon as you can, and then he will tell you who is absent. Have a semicircle before every lesson, and make the children keep their toes to the mark; brass nails driven in the floor are the best. When a monitor is asking the children questions, let him place his stool in the centre of the semicircle, and the children stand around him. Let the monitors ask what questions they please, they will soon get fond of the process, and their pupils will soon be equally fond of answering them. Suppose the monitor ask, What do I sit on? Where are your toes? What do you stand on? What is before you? What behind you? At first, children will have no idea of this mode of exercising the thinking powers. But the teacher must encourage them in it, and they will very speedily get fond of it, and be able to give an answer immediately. It is very pleasing to witness this. I have been much delighted at the questions put, and still more so at the answers given. Assemble all the very small children together as soon as you can: the first day or two they will want to sit with their brothers or sisters, who are a little older than themselves. But the sooner you can separate them the better, as the elder children frequently plague the younger ones; and I have always found, that the youngest are the happiest by themselves.

Supposing the little flock brought by this time into something like order; we are next to consider the means of securing other objects. Although the following rules for this purpose are given, it must not be supposed, that they are presented as a model not to be departed from. If they can be improved so much the better, but some such will be found indispensable.

RULES

To be observed by the Parents of Children admitted into the —————— Infant School.

1.

Parents are to send their children clean washed, with their hair cut short and combed, and their clothes well mended, by half past eight o'clock in the morning, to remain till twelve.

2.

☞ If any child be later in attendance than nine o'clock in the morning, that child must be sent back until the afternoon; and in case of being later than two in the afternoon, it will be sent back for the day.

3.

Parents may send their children's dinners with them in the morning, so that the children may be taken care of the whole day, to enable the mother to go out to work. This can only be done where the teachers reside on the premises.

4.

If a child be absent, without a notice being sent to the master or mistress, assigning a satisfactory reason for the absence, such child will not be permitted to return again to the school.

Saturday afternoon is half-holiday.

*** It is earnestly hoped, that parents will see their own interest, as well as that of their children, in strictly observing these rules; and they are exhorted to submit to their children being governed by the master and mistress; to give them good instruction and advice; to accustom them to family prayer; but particularly to see that they repeat the Lord's Prayer, when they rise in the morning, and when they retire to rest, and to set before them a good example; for in so doing, they may humbly hope that the blessing of Almighty God will rest upon them and their families; for we are assured in the holy Scriptures, that if we train up a child in the way he should go, when he is old he will not depart from it, Prov. xxii. 6. Therefore parents may be instrumental in the promotion of the welfare of their children in this life, and of their eternal happiness in the world to come.

On each of these rules I will make a few remarks. *First rule.* Some parents are so habitually dirty,

M

that they would not wash their children from one week's end to another, unless required so to do; and if it be done for them, they will not be so thankful as when compelled to do it themselves. This I have found from experience.

Second rule. This has its advantages; for it would not be right to punish the children when the fault rests with their parents; consequently, by sending them home, the real authors of the evil are punished. Many parents have told me, that when their children were at home, they employed themselves in singing the alphabet, counting, patting their hands, &c. &c. ; that it was impossible to keep an infant asleep, that they were glad to get them out of the way, and that they would take care that they should not be late again.

But there is no rule without an exception. I have found that this has its disadvantages; for some of the elder children, when they wanted a half-holiday, would take care to be late, in order to find the door shut, although they were sent in proper time by their parents; this, when detected, subjects them to a pat on the hand, which is the only corporeal punishment we have. If this rule were not strictly enforced, the children would be coming at all hours of the day, which would put the school into such disorder, that we should never know when all the children had said their lessons.

Third rule. This is of great service to those parents who go out to work; for by sending their children's dinners with them, they are enabled to attend to their employment in comfort, and the children, when properly disciplined, will be no additional trouble to the teacher, for they will play about the play-ground, while he takes his dinner, without doing any mischief.

Fourth rule. Many persons will keep their children away for a month or two when nothing is the matter with them, consequently the children will lose almost all they have learned at school. Besides this, children are kept out, who perhaps would attend regularly, and we should never know how many children were in the establishment. If, therefore, a parent does not attend to this rule, the child's name is struck off the book.

On the admission of every child, the parents should be supplied with a copy of the preceding rules, as this will prevent them from pleading any excuse; it should be fastened on pasteboard, otherwise they will double it up and put it into their pockets, and forget all about it; but being on pasteboard, they may hang it up in their dwellings. The short exhortation that follows, it is hoped, may have its use, by reminding the parents of their duty to co-operate with those persons who have the welfare both of themselves and their children at heart.

I shall next speak of the *daily routine* of instruction.

If we would be successful in our labours, we must ask for help,—we must solicit aid from that Being who never yet denied it when sincerely and fervently implored. A minister who desires to instruct his flock with effect, never fails to commence his work with supplication; and certainly every teacher must ask for help, and instruct his pupils to do so too, if he really wish to be successful. If the wisest and best of men ask assistance from God to teach their fellow-men, and feel and know it to be necessary so to do, who would not ask assistance to instruct infants?

"To lead them into virtue's path,
And up to truth divine."

If we had only to educate the *head*, prayer might be less necessary. But the promoters of *Infant Schools* want to affect the *heart;* to operate upon the will and the conscience, as well as on the understanding; to make good men rather than learned men—men of *wisdom*, rather than men of *knowledge;* and he who has this work to accomplish, should remember the Saviour's declaration, " Without me ye can do nothing."

But to proceed. The children being assembled, should be desired to stand up, and immediately afterwards to kneel down, all close to their seats, and as silently as possible : those who are not strong enough to kneel, may be allowed to sit down. This being done, a child is to be placed in the centre of the school, and to repeat the following prayer :—

"O God, our heavenly Father, thou art good to us: we would serve thee; we have sinned and done wrong many times. Jesus Christ died on the cross for us. Forgive our sins for Jesus' sake ; may the Holy Spirit change our hearts, and make us to love God; help us to-day to be good children and to do what is right. Keep us from wicked thoughts and bad tempers; make us try to learn all that we are taught ; keep us in health all the day. We would always think of God, and when we die may we go to heaven. God bless our fathers and mothers, and sisters and brothers, and our teachers, and make us obedient and kind, for Jesus Christ's sake. Amen."

The children afterwards repeat the Lord's prayer, and then sing a hymn; for instance, the following :

> When first the morning light we see,
>   And from our beds arise;
> We to our God should thankful be,
>   Who every want supplies.
>
> 'Twas God who made the pretty sun,
>   That gives all day its light;
> And it was God who made the moon
>   And stars, which shine at night.
>
> The fish that in the water swim,
>   The beasts upon the land,
> Were all created first by him,
>   And shew his mighty hand.
>
> The food we eat, the clothes we wear,
>   'Tis God alone can give;
> And only by his love and care,
>   Can little children live.
>
> Then let us ever caution take,
>   His holy laws to keep;
> And praise him from the time we wake
>   Until again we sleep.

Immediately after this they proceed to their lessons; which are fixed to what are called lesson-posts. To each of these posts there is a monitor, who is provided with a piece of cane for a pointer. This post is placed opposite to his class; and every class has one, up to which the monitor brings the children three or four at a time, according to the number he has in his class. We have fourteen classes, and

M 3

sometimes more, which are regularly numbered, so that we have one hundred children moving and saying their lessons at one time. When these are gone through, the children are supplied with pictures, which they put on the post, the same as the spelling and reading lessons, but say them in a different manner. We find that if a class always go through their lesson at one post, it soon loses its attraction; and consequently, although we cannot change them about from post to post in the spelling and reading lessons, because it would be useless to put a child to a reading post that did not know its letters, yet we can do so in the picture lessons, as the children are all alike in learning the objects. One child can learn an object as quick as another, so that we may have many children that can tell the name of different subjects, and even the names of all the geometrical figures, who do not know all the letters in the alphabet; and I have had children, whom one might think were complete blockheads, on account of their not being able to learn the alphabet so quickly as some of the other children, and yet those very children would learn things which appeared to me ten times more difficult. This proves the necessity of variety, and how difficult it is to legislate for children. Instead, therefore, of the children standing opposite their own post, they go round from one to another, repeating whatever they find at each post, until they have been all round the school. For instance, at No. I. post there may be the following objects; the horse, the ass, the zebra, the cow, the sheep, the goat, the springing antelope, the cameleopard, the camel, the wild boar, the rhinoceros, the elephant, the hippopotamus, the lion, the tiger, the leopard, the civet, the weazel, the great white bear, the hyena, the fox, the greenland dog, the hare, the mole, the squirrel, the kangaroo, the porcupine, and the racoon. Before commencing these lessons, two boys are selected by the master, who perhaps are not monitors. These two boys bring the children up to a chalk line that is made near No. 1 post, eight at a time; one of the boys gets eight children standing up ready, always beginning at one end of the school, and takes them to this chalk line, whilst the other boy takes them to No. 1 post, and delivers them up to the charge of No. 1 monitor. No. 1 monitor then points to the different animals with a pointer, until the name of every one that is on his plate has been repeated; this done, he delivers them to No. 2 monitor, who has a different picture at his post; perhaps the following: the fishmonger, mason, hatter, cooper, butcher, blacksmith, fruiterer, distiller, grocer, turner, carpenter, tallow-chandler, milliner, dyer, druggist, wheelwright, shoe-maker, printer, coach-maker, book-seller, bricklayer, linen-draper, cabinet-maker, brewer, painter, book-binder. This done, No. 2 monitor delivers them over to No. 3 monitor, and No. 3 monitor to No. 4, and so on successively, until there are about one hundred children on the move at one time, all saying different objects. Every child says the whole of the objects at each post. This great variety keeps up the attention, and their moving from post to post promotes their health.

As a further guide to the master or mistress of Infant Schools, I subjoin a synopsis of a week's course of instruction, which I drew up for my own use.

TIME.—*Mornings*. School to assemble at 9 o'clock, and to leave at 12.

Afternoons. School to assemble at 2 o'clock, and to leave at 5.

MONDAY.

Morning. When assembled, to offer the appointed prayer, after which a hymn is to be sung; then slates and pencils are to be delivered to the children; after which they are to proceed with their letters and spelling. At half past 10 o'clock to play, and at 11 o'clock to assemble in the gallery, and repeat the picture lessons on natural history after the monitor in the rostrum.

Afternoon. Begin with prayer and hymn as in the morning; picture lessons on Scripture history to be repeated from the lesson-post, and to be questioned on them afterwards in the gallery.

TUESDAY.

Morning. Usual prayer and hymn. Letters and spelling from the lesson-posts. Play. Gallery; repeat the addition and subtraction tables.

Afternoon. Prayer and hymn. Multiplication table; the monitor asking the question, and the children answering. Reading lessons. Play. Gallery; numeration and spelling with brass figures and letters.

WEDNESDAY.

Morning. Prayer and hymn. Letters and spelling. Play. Gallery; master to teach geometrical figures and musical characters.

Afternoon. Prayer and hymn. Practice, pence, and shilling tables. Play. Gallery; master to give lessons on arithmetic. Extempore teaching on men and things, &c. &c.

THURSDAY.

Morning. Prayer and hymn. Letters and spelling. Division, weights, measures, and time, from the rostrum. Play. Gallery; same lessons as Monday morning.

Afternoon. Prayer and hymn. From the lesson posts, epitome of geometry and natural history. Gallery; brass letters and figures. Extempore teaching on men and things, taking care that all such teaching shall be illustrated by substances.

FRIDAY.

Morning. Prayer and hymn. Letters and spelling. Tables in arithmetic, at the master's discretion. Play. Gallery; lessons on geography, maps, globes, &c.

Afternoon. Prayer and hymn. Scripture pictures on the lesson-posts, and questions on them in the gallery.

SATURDAY.

Morning. Prayer and hymn. Letters and Spelling. Tables of arithmetic from the rostrum. Play. Gallery. Lessons on the transposition frame, and on geometry from the brass instrument. Religious instruction should have a prominent part in the business of every day, and especially so every Saturday morning.

N.B. If visitors wish any particular lessons to be gone through, and the children appear disposed, the master is not bound to adhere to the above rules, neither at any other time if the children appear particularly disinclined.

———————

There are a few other matters, on which, before concluding this chapter, I must speak, as claiming the attention of Infant-School conductors. First, attend to

CLEANLINESS.

Although we have referred to this before, yet, as it is of considerable importance not only to the children but

to those around them, it may not be amiss to take
up a little more of the reader's time, and to state the
different plans that have been devised, in order to
make the children as clean as possible. In one case,
a trough was erected, and a pipe provided to convey
the water into it; but before it had been up a month,
it was found, that instead of answering the end intended, it had quite a contrary effect; for the children
dabbled in the trough, and made themselves ten times
worse than they were, by wetting themselves from
head to foot; besides which, it frequently caused them
to take cold, of which the parents complained. Some
took their children away without notice; others
came and gave the master what they called " *a good
set down*." It was, therefore, thought necessary to
forbid the children washing themselves, and to wash
all that came dirty. But it was soon found that the
dirty children increased so fast, that it required one
person's time to attend to them; besides which, it
had another bad effect, it encouraged the parents in
laziness; and they told me, when I complained of their
sending the children to school dirty, " That indeed
they had no time to wash their children; there was
a trough in the school for that purpose, and the persons who had charge of the school, were paid for it,
and ought to do it." In consequence of this, the
trough was taken away, and it was represented to the
parents, that it was their duty to keep their children
clean; that unless they did so, they would be sent
home to be washed; and if they persisted in sending
them without being washed, there would be no alternative left but to dismiss them from the school altogether. This offended some of the parents, and they

took their children out of the school, but many afterwards petitioned to have them re-admitted. I mention this, merely to prevent others, who may be concerned in the establishment of Infant Schools, from incurring an unnecessary expense, and to shew that the parents will value the school equally as well if you make them wash their children, as if you did it for them.

The plan that we have acted upon to enforce cleanliness, is as follows. As soon as the children are assembled in the school, the monitors cause them to hold out their hands, with their heads up; they then inspect their hands and their faces, and all those who are dirty are desired to stand out, to be examined by the master, who will easily perceive whether they have been washed that morning; if not, they are sent home to be washed, and if the mother has any sense of propriety, she will take care that it shall not often occur. But it may be found, that some have been washed, and have been playing with the dirt, when coming to school, which some children are very apt to do; in this case they have a pat on the hand, which generally cures them. There is much trouble, at first, to keep the children quite clean; some of their parents are habitually dirty, and in such cases the children will be like them; these will therefore require more trouble than others, but they will soon acquire cleanly habits, and, with proper management, become as cleanly as any of the other children. As soon as a child is taken into the school the monitor shews him a certain place, and explains to him, that when he wants to go into the yard, he is to ask him, and he will accompany him there. Of course there are separate accommodations for each sex, and such prudential arrangements made as the case requires, but which it is unnecessary further to particularize.

2. NEVER FRIGHTEN CHILDREN.

It is common for many persons to threaten to put children into the black hole, or to call the sweep to take them away in his bag, when they do not behave as they ought; but the ill effects of this mode of proceeding may be perceived from the following fact. I knew a child, who had been to one of those schools, where the children of mechanics are usually sent, called dames' schools, which was kept by an elderly woman, who, it seems, had put this child into the coal-hole, and told him, that unless he was a good boy, the black man would come and take him away; this so frightened the child, that he fell into a violent fit, and never afterwards could bear the sight of this woman. On the mother getting the child admitted into our school, she desired me to be very gentle with him, relating to me all the above story, except that the child had had a fit. About a fortnight after the admission of the child, he came running one day into the school, exclaiming, "I'll be a good boy, master! master! I'll be a good boy." As soon as he caught sight of me, he clung round, and grasped me with such violence, that I really thought the child was mad; in a few minutes after this he went into strong convulsions, and was such a dreadful spectacle, that I thought the child would die in my arms. In this state he remained for about twenty minutes, and I fully expected he would be carried out of the school a corpse. I sent for the mother, but on her arrival I perceived she was less alarmed than myself; she immediately said, the child was in a fit, and that I had frightened him into it. I told her she was mistaken; that the child had only just entered the school, and I was ignorant of the cause of his fright; but several of my little scholars soon set the matter at rest, by stating the particulars of the fright, which they observed when coming to school. It seems that a man was in the street, who sweeps chimnies with a machine, and just as the little fellow passed him, he called out "Sweep;" this so alarmed the child, that he thought the man was going to take him, and was affected by his fears in the way I have stated. The child, however, getting better, and the mother hearing what the children said, begged my pardon for having accused me wrongfully, and then told me the whole particulars of his first fright with the woman and the coal-hole. I had the greatest difficulty imaginable to persuade him, that a sweep was a human being, and that he loved little children as much as other persons. After some time, the child got somewhat the better of his fears, but not wholly so. He never had but one fit afterwards. This shows how improper it is to confine children by themselves, or to threaten them in the manner described. Many persons continue nervous all their lives through such treatment, and are so materially injured, that they are frightened at their own shadow.

It is also productive of much mischief to talk of mysteries, ghosts, and hobgoblins, before children, which many persons are too apt to do. Some deal so much in the marvellous, that I really believe they frighten many children out of their senses. I recollect, when I was a child, hearing such stories, till I have actually been afraid to look behind me. How many persons are frightened at such a little creature as a mouse, because the nature of that little creature has not been explained to them in their infancy. Indeed children should have all things shown them, if possible, that they are likely to meet with; and above all, it should be impressed upon their minds, that if they meet with no injury from the living, it is most certain the dead will never hurt them, and that he who fears God, need have no other fear. It is also common with many persons, to put a disobedient child into a room by himself. I cannot approve of this method, as the child is frequently frightened into quietness without improving his temper in the least; if it be day time it is not so bad, but if it be dark the consequences are often serious, and materially injure the constitution of the child.

3. GUARD AGAINST FORGETFULNESS.

The circumstance I am about to mention, shews how necessary it is to teach by example as well as precept. Many of the children were in the habit of bringing marbles, tops, whistles, and other toys, to the school, which often caused much disturbance; for they would play with them instead of attending to their lessons, and I found it necessary to forbid the children from bringing any thing of the kind. After giving notice therefore two or three times in the school, I told them that if any of them brought such things, they would be taken away from them. In consequence of this, several things fell into my hands which I did not always think of returning, and among other things a whistle belonging to a little boy. The child asked me for it as he was going home, but having several visitors at the time, I put him off, telling him not to plague me, and he went home. I had forgotten the circumstance altogether, but it appears the child had not; for some time after, while I was lecturing the children upon the necessity of telling truth, and on the wickedness of stealing, the little fellow approached me, and said, "*Please, sir, you stole my whistle.*" "Stole your whistle!" said I "did I not give it you again?" "No, teacher, I asked you for it, and you would not give it to me." I stood self-convicted, being accused in the middle of my lecture, before all the children, and really at a loss to know what excuse to make, for I had mislaid the whistle, and could not return it to the child. I immediately gave the child a halfpenny, and said all I could to persuade the children that it was not my intention to keep it.

However, I am satisfied that this trifling mistake of mine did more harm than I was able to repair during some time, for if we wish to teach children to be honest, we should never take any thing from them without returning it again. Indeed, persons having charge of children can never be too cautious, and should not on any account whatever break a promise; for experience has taught me that most children have good memories, and if you once promise a thing and do not perform it, they will pay very little attention to what you say afterwards.

4. OBSERVE PUNCTUALITY.

A little girl, whose mother was dead, was often

absent from school. She was never at a loss for excuses, but from their frequency I was at last induced
to suspect their truth. None of the children knew
where she resided; so I was obliged to send the
eldest boy in the school home with her, to ascertain
whether or not her stories were true. I gave the boy
positive directions to make haste back ; but, much to
my surprise, I saw no more of him for six hours.
When he returned he told me that the little girl refused to shew him where she lived ; and had taken
him so far, that he at last determined to leave her,
but could not find his way back sooner. In the evening I went myself according to the direction I had
entered in the admission-book, but found that the
family were removed, and the persons in the house
could not tell me where they had gone to reside. I
saw nothing of the child for the five following days,
when a woman who had the care of her and her
little brother in arms, came to inquire the reason why
the girl came home at such irregular hours, stating,
that sometimes she came home at half-past eleven, at
other times not till two, and sometimes at three in
the afternoon : in short, often an hour after school
was over. I told her that the child was frequently
absent, and that it was five days since I had seen her.
The woman appeared quite surprised, and told me,
that she had always sent the child to school at the
regular time ; that when she came home before the
usual hour, she said her governess had sent all the
children home a little sooner ; and if she came home
after the time, then she said that there had been some
ladies visiting the school, and that the children had
been kept for their inspection.

Here I must acknowledge, that I have frequently detained children a little while after school hours, when we have had visitors, but since it furnishes the children with an excuse for going home late, I think it would be better to discontinue the practice; and would hint to those ladies and gentlemen who feel inclined to visit such schools, that they should come between the hours of nine and twelve in the forenoon, or two and four in the afternoon. I have only to observe, that the child I have been speaking of came to school very regularly afterwards.

5. BE STRICTLY ACCURATE IN YOUR EXPRESSIONS.

One day, when the children were assembled in the gallery, having none of their usual lessons at hand, I took from my pocket a piece of paper, and promised them that if they would answer me every question I put concerning the paper, I would at last make a paper boat. I proceeded in the following manner : " What is this ?" " What colour ?" " What is its use?" "How made?" "What made of ?" &c. These questions being answered according to their different views ; and having folded the paper into a variety of forms, and obtained their ideas upon such forms, I proceeded to fulfil my promise of forming it into the shape of a boat; but the children, seeing me at a loss, exclaimed, " Please, sir, you can't do it ;" which proved the fact, as I had forgotten the plan, and was obliged to make the confession. " Then, sir," rejoined one of the boys, " you should not have promised."

In the course of my observations I had frequently enjoined the children to make every possible use of their thinking powers, but it appears I had at the same time forgotten to make use of my own, and consequently had been betrayed into a promise which I was not able to perform.

I remember some other instances :

One of the children happened to kick another. The injured party complained to the person who then had the charge of the school, saying, "Please, sir, this boy kicked me." It being time for the children to leave school, the master waved his hand towards the gate through which the children pass, thoughtlessly saying, at the same time, " Kick away ;" meaning that the complainant was to take no more notice of the affair, but go home. The complainant, however, returning to the other child, began kicking him, and received some kicks himself. A friend was present, and seeing two children kicking each other, he very naturally inquired the reason. " Please, sir," replied the children, " Master told us!" " Master told you," says the gentleman, " that cannot be ; I'll ask him." He accordingly inquired into the truth of the affair, and received for answer, " Certainly not." " Yes," said the child, " you did, sir, did not I tell you just now that a boy kicked me?" " Yes," says the master, "you did." " Then, please, sir," says the child, "you told me to go and kick away !" The master immediately recollected that he had said so.

This fact shews how improper it is to say one thing to a child and mean another. These children were under the influence of obedience, *and in the light of truth*, and being in that light, they could see from no other, and very naturally concluded the master meant what he had said.

One day some visitors requested I would call out a class of the children to be examined. Having done so, I asked the visitors in what they would wish the children to be examined; at the same time stating that they might hear the children examined in natural history, scriptural history, arithmetic, spelling, geography, or geometry. They chose the latter, and I proceeded to examine the children accordingly; beginning with straight lines. Having continued this examination for about half an hour, we proceeded to enter into particulars respecting triangles; and having discoursed on the difference between isosceles triangles and scalene triangles, I observed that an acute isosceles triangle had all its angles acute, and proceeded to observed that a right-angled scalene triangle had all its angles acute. The children immediately began to laugh, for which I was at a loss to account, and told them of the impropriety of laughing at me. One of the children immediately replied, "Please, sir, do you know what we were laughing at?" I replied in the negative. "Then, sir," says the boy, "I will tell you. Please, sir, you have made a blunder." I, thinking I had not, proceeded to defend myself, when the children replied, "Please, sir, you convict yourself." I replied, "How so?" "Why," says the children, "you said a right-angled triangle had one right angle, and that all its angles are acute. If it has one right angle, how can all its angles be acute?" I soon perceived the children were right, and that I was wrong. Here, then, the reader may perceive the fruits of teaching the children to think, inasmuch as it is shewn that children of six years of age and under were able

to refute their tutor.   If children had been taught to
think many years ago, error would have been much more
easily detected, and its baneful influence would not
have had that effect upon society which at this day
unfortunately we are obliged to witness.

At another time I was lecturing the children in the
gallery on the subject of cruelty to animals; when
one of the little children observed, " Please, sir, my
big brother catches the poor flies, and then sticks a
pin through them, and makes them draw the pin
along the table."   This afforded me an excellent opportunity of appealing to their feelings on the enormity of this offence, and among other things I observed, that if the poor fly had been gifted with the
powers of speech like their own, it probably would
have exclaimed, *while dead*, as follows :— " You
naughty child, how can you think of torturing me so?
Is there not room in the world for you and me? Did
I ever do you any harm ? Does it do you any good
to put me in such pain ?   Why do you do it, you are
big enough to know better ?   How would you like a
man to run a piece of wire through your body, and
make you draw things about ?   Would you not cry
at the pain?   Go, then, you wicked boy, and learn to
leave off such cruel actions."   Having finished, one
of the children replied, " How can any thing speak if
it is dead ?"   " Why," said I, " supposing it could
speak." " You meant to say, sir," was the rejoinder,
" *dying*, instead of *dead*."

It will of course be understood that in this case I
purposely misused a word, and the children being
taught to think, easily detected it.

6. WATCH AGAINST THE ENTRANCE OF DISEASE.

It may, probably, be considered presumption in me, to speak of the diseases of children, as this more properly belongs to the faculty; but let it be observed, that my pretension is not to cure the diseases that children are subject to, but only to prevent those which are infectious from spreading. I have found that children between the ages of two and seven years, are subject to the measles, hooping cough, fever, ophthalmia, and the small pox. This last is very rare, owing to the great encouragement given to vaccination; and were it not for the obstinacy of many of the poor, I believe it would be totally extirpated. During the whole of the time I superintended a school, I heard of only three children dying of it, and those had never been vaccinated. I always made a point of inquiring, on the admission of a child, whether this operation had been performed, and, if not, I strongly recommended that it should be. If the parents spoke the truth, I had but few children in the school who had not been vaccinated: this accounts, therefore, for having lost but three children through the small pox.

The measles, however, I consider as a very dangerous disorder, and we lost a great many children by it, besides two of my own. It is preceded by a violent cough, the child's eyes appear watery, and it will also be sick. As soon as these symptoms are perceived, I would immediately send the child home, and desire the parents to keep it there for a few days, in order to ascertain if it have the measles, and if so, it must be prohibited from return ing to school until well. This caution is absolutely necessary; as some parents are so careless, that they will send their children when the measles are thick out upon them.

The same may be said with respect to other diseases, for unless the persons who have charge of the school attend to these things, the parents will be glad to get their children out of the way, and will send them, though much afflicted, without considering the ill-effects that may be produced in the school. Whether such conduct in the parents proceeds from ignorance or not, I am not able to say, but this I know, that I have had many parents offer children for admission, with all the diseases I have mentioned, and who manifested no disposition to inform me of it. The number of children who may be sick, from time to time, may be averaged at from twenty to thirty-five. Out of two hundred and twenty, we have never had less than twenty absent on account of illness, and once or twice we had as many as fifty.

Soon after I first took charge of the establishment, I found that there were five or six children in the school who had the measles; the consequence was, that it contaminated the whole school, and about eight children died, one of my own being of that number. This induced me to be very cautious in future, and I made a point of walking round the school twice every day, in order to inspect the children; and after the adoption of this plan, we did not have the measles in the school.

The hooping-cough is known, of course, by the the child hooping; but I consider it the safest plan to send all children home that have any kind of cough; this will cause the mother to come and inquire the reason why the child is sent home; and it can be ascertained from her whether the child has had the hooping-cough or not.

With respect to fever, I generally find the children appear chilly and cold, and not unfrequently they are sick. I do not however feel myself competent to describe the early symptoms of this disorder, but the best way to prevent its gaining ground in the school is to send all the children home who appear the least indisposed.

As to the ophthalmia, I can describe the symptoms of that disease, having had it myself, together with the whole of my family. It generally comes in the left eye first, and causes a sensation as if something was in the eye, which pricks and shoots, and produces great pain : the white of the eye will appear red, or what is usually called bloodshot; this, if not speedily attended to, will cause blindness ; I have had several children that have been blind with it for several days. In the morning the patients are not able to unclose their eyes for some time after they are awake. As soon as I observe these appearances, I immediately send the child home ; for I have ascertained, beyond a doubt, that the disease is contagious, and if a child be suffered to remain with it in the school, the infection will speedily spread among the children.

As children are frequently apt to burn or scald themselves, I will here insert a method for adoption in such cases. It is very simple, and yet infallible ; at least, I have never known it to fail. It is no other than the application of common writing ink. One of my own children burnt its hand dreadfully, and was cured by immediately washing it all over with that liquid. Several children burnt their hands against the pipe that was connected with the stove in the school-room, and were cured by the same means. One boy, in particular, took hold of a hot cinder that fell from the fire, and it quite singed his hand; I applied ink to it, and it was cured in a very short time. Let any one, therefore, who may happen to receive a burn, apply ink to it immediately, and he will soon witness the good effects of the application.

7. NEVER CORRECT A CHILD IN ANGER.

8. NEVER OVERLOOK A FAULT.

9. IN ALL THINGS SET BEFORE THE CHILDREN AN EXAMPLE WORTHY OF IMITATION.

————

I should recommend the adoption of the following resolutions of an intelligent and zealous committee, and that a copy of them be sent to each master and mistress.

"That as this Infant School is established for the express purpose of carrying into the fullest effect the System of Mr. Wilderspin, which the committee are convinced is practicable and excellent, the master be desired to make himself perfectly acquainted with it, in its physical, mental, and moral bearings, by a study of Mr. Wilderspin's work on the subject, and particularly of the last and most complete edition.

" That the Rules as printed be strictly adhered to by the master. That children who are ill, having hooping-cough, ringworm, or other contagious disease, be refused admission until perfectly restored. That the business of the school begin precisely at the time appointed, and that during the shortest days the signals for leaving school be not given till 4 o'clock precisely.

" That except during the time given according to the System to play, the whole be occupied by the mistress as well as the master in the instruction of the children, and that the plan laid down in Mr. Wilderspin's book, be followed as nearly as possible, so that the apparatus already provided may be gradually brought into action, and the children have all the advantages of the System; the master and mistress so dividing their labour that all the children may be occupied.

" That the master and mistress pay the utmost attention to the children learning to read.

" That when a child is absent a week, the master state the cause to the treasurer to prevent mistakes as to the payments, and that when a child declines attending or is excluded, immediate notice be given to the secretary of the ladies' committee.

" That the master be desired to go on with the business of the school when visitors who are members of the committee are present, and only to pay particular attention to those who may be strangers, and who require information.

" That all applications from the master be made to the Committee."

o

CHAPTER VIII.

ON REWARDS AND PUNISHMENTS.

———

" A very frequent recourse to rewards does but lessen their effect and weaken the mind, by accustoming it to an unnecessary stimulus, whilst punishment, too freely administered, will fret the temper, or, which is worse, break the spirit."—*Hoare.*

———

As man comes into the world with a propensity to do that which is forbidden, it has been found necessary at all times, to enact laws to govern and even to punish him, when he acts contrary to them; and who will deny the man a just reward who has done any act whereby his fellow-men have been benefited? " The hope of reward sweetens labour." If, then, rewards and punishments are necessary to make *men* active, and to keep them in order, how can it be expected that children can be governed without some kind of punishment? I am aware that I am taking the unpopular side of the question, by becoming an advocate for punishment, but notwithstanding this, I must say, that I think no school in England has ever been governed without it; and that the many theories ushered into the world, on this sub-

ject, have not been exactly acted upon. Indeed, it
appears to me, that while men continue to be imperfect beings, it is not possible that either they or their
offspring, can be governed without some degree of
punishment. I admit that it should be administered
with great prudence, and never employed but as a
last resource; and I am sorry to say, that it has descended to brutality in some schools, which, perhaps,
is one reason why so many persons set their faces
against it altogether.

The first thing that appears to me necessary, is
to find out, if possible, the real disposition and
temper of a child, in order to be able to manage it
with good effect. I will allow that it is possible to
govern some children without corporal punishment,
for I have had some under my charge whom I never
had occasion to punish, to whom a word was quite
sufficient, and who, if I only looked displeased, would
burst into tears. But I have had others quite the reverse; you might talk to them till you were tired,
and it would produce no more effect half an hour afterwards, than if they had not been spoken to at all.
Indeed, children's dispositions are as various as their
faces; no two are alike; consequently, what will do
for one child will not do for another; and hence the
impropriety of having an invariable mode of punishment. What should we think of a medical man,
who was to prescribe for every constitution in the
same manner? The first thing a skilful physician
does, is to ascertain the constitution of the patient,
and then he prescribes accordingly; and nothing is
more necessary for those who have charge of little
children, than to ascertain their real character. Hav-

ing done this, they will be able, should a child offend, to apply some appropriate antidote.

To begin with rewards: the monitors I have generally allowed one penny a week each, as I found much difficulty in procuring monitors; for, whatever *honours* were attached to the office, children of five years old could not exactly comprehend them. They could much more easily perceive the use of a penny; and as a proof how much they valued the penny a week above all the honours that could be bestowed, I always had a good supply of monitors after this remuneration was adopted. Before this time, they used to say, "Please, sir, may I sit down? I do not like to be a monitor." Perhaps I might prevail on some to hold the office a little longer, by explaining to them what an honourable office it was: but, after all, I found that the penny a week spoke more powerfully than I did, and the children would say to each other, "I like to be a monitor now, for I had a penny last Saturday; and master says, we are to have a penny every week; don't you wish you were a monitor?" "Yes, I do; and master says, if I be a good boy, I shall be a monitor by and bye, and then I shall have a penny." I think they richly deserve it. Some kind of reward I consider necessary, but what kind of reward, must, of course, rest entirely with the promoters of the different schools.

A most important means of discipline appears in what we term "trial by jury," which is composed of all the children in the school. It has been already stated that the playground is the scene for the full development of character, and, consequently, the spot where circumstances occur which demand this peculiar treatment. It should be also particularly observed, that it is next to prayer in solemnity, and should only be adopted on extraordinary occasions. Any levity manifested either by the teacher or the pupils will be fatal to the effect. But to illustrate it, I will state a fact. In the play-ground of an Infant School there was an early dwarf cherry tree, and which, from its situation, had fruit, while other trees had only flowers. It became, therefore, an object of general attraction, and ordinarily called forth a variety of important observations. Now it happened that two children, one five years of age, and the other not quite three, entered the school in the autumn, and on the return of spring, they, having had only a winter's training, were charmed by this object, and in consequence fell into temptation. Accustomed to watch new scholars narrowly, I particularly observed them; when I marked the elder one anxiously, intently, and wishfully gazing on the fruit, and especially on one amazingly large cherry pendent from a single shoot. While thus absorbed, the younger child was attracted to the spot, and imitated his example. The former then asked if he did not think it a large one, and the reply was of course, in the affirmative. Having thus addressed the powers of observation, the next appeal was to the taste, by the inquiry, "Is not it a nice one?" The answer to which was "Yes." Then followed the observation, "It is quite soft," when the young one, being thus excited by the touch of the other, touched it also. This act, he subsequently repeated, by desire of the elder, who, having charged him to hold it tight, struck his hand, and thus detached the cherry. I now withdrew to some distance, and it was evident that the little one was distressed by what he had done, as he did not eat it, but began to cry faintly, on which the elder took the cherry out of his hand, and ate it. This increased the crying, when, on approaching, he ran up to me, saying that the other took my cherry. The little one continuing to cry, the other stated that he saw him take it; to which I replied, "We will try him by and bye." As soon, therefore, as the proper time arrived, the bell was rung; prior to which, however, I was apprized of the loss by several children, and when all were seated in the gallery, I proceeded as follows: "Now little children, I want you to use all your faculties, to look at me attentively, and to think of what I am about to say, for I am going to tell you a tale of two little boys. Once on a time they were amusing themselves with a great many other children in a play-ground, where there were a great many flowers and some fruit trees. But before I go on, let me ask you is it right to take the flowers or fruit which belong to others?" to which the general reply was "No," with the exception of the culprits. I then described their age, stated that one boy was five years old, and the other three; that the former was looking at one of his master's fine cherries, which was growing against the wall, and that the latter approached, and looked at it too; on which several exclaimed, "Please, sir, your big cherry is gone;" which caused an inspection of each others' countenances. To this, I replied, I am sorry for it, but let me finish my tale. "Now, children, while they were both looking at the cherry, the elder one asked the younger if it were not large, to which he replied, Yes; he then inquired, whether it were not nice, when he again answered, Yes ; afterwards, he told him, having touched it himself first, to touch it because it was soft, and the little boy unfortunately did so, on which the big one pulled his arm, and the cherry came off in his hand." While this was proceeding, the two delinquents sat very demurely, conscious that they were pourtrayed, though all the rest were ignorant of the fact. I then said, "Which do you think the worst of these boys ?" when several answered " The biggest was the worst." On inquiring, " Why," the reply was " Because he told the little one to take it ;" while others said, " Because he pulled his arm." I added, "I have not told you the whole tale yet, but I am glad to see that you know right from wrong, and presently you will be still better prepared to judge. When the big boy had told the little one to take the cherry, he then robbed him of it, and immediately betrayed him by telling the master. Now which do you think was the worst ?" When a great number of voices vociferated "The big one." I then inquired, if they thought we had such children in our school ? the general reply was "No," but the scrutiny among themselves was redoubled. To this I rejoined, " I am sorry to say such children are now sitting among you in the gallery." At this crisis the little one burst into tears, on which the children said, " Please, sir, that's one of them, for his face is so red, and he cries." I answered, " I am sorry it is so," and called the culprit down with " Come here, my dear, and sit by the side of me until we examine into it." This was followed by the outcry, "Please, sir, we have found the other, he hangs his head down, and his face looks so white."

This child was then called down in the same mild

manner to sit on the other side of me.   I then told
them, that they would find, when they became men
and women, that in our courts of law, wintesses of
what was done were called, and as the elder boy had
seen the young one take the cherry, it was necessary
and desirable to hear what he had to say.   On being
desired to stand up, I therefore said, " Did you see
him take the cherry ?"   To which he promptly answered " Yes."   The next inquiry was, What did he
do with it ?   To this he was silent, on which the little
one, not being able to contain himself, called out,
" He took it from me, and ate it."   All eyes were
now turned to the big one, and all felt convinced that
he was the most guilty, whilst the confidence of the
little one increased by the prospect of having justice
done him, as he previously feared that being accused
by the elder one, he should be condemned without
ceremony.

Finding that the elder one had no more to say, it
only remained to hear the defence of the young one,
who, sensible of having done what was wrong, said, in
broken accents, " He told me to take it,—he hit my
hand,—and he ate the cherry."   To which it was necessary to give the admonition, That he never ought
to do wrong, though required to do so by others; and
that such a defence would avail him nothing were he
a man.   Both the children were now exceedingly distressed, and hence this was the time to appeal to the
rest, as to the measure of the punishment that was
due.   The general opinion was, that the eldest should
be punished, but no one mentioned that the young one
should have even a pat on the hand ; the next thing
was to appeal to the higher faculties of the little culprit,

who, seeing that he had thus far got off, required to be softened down in reference to the other, though he had betrayed him, while the best way of operating on the elder was by a display of love on the part of the younger; he was therefore asked if he would forgive the other, and shake hands with him, which he immediately did to the evident delight and satisfaction of all the children, while the countenance of the elder shewed that he felt himself unworthy of the treatment he received. I then inflicted the sentence which had been pronounced,—two pats of the hand, which the girls asked might be soft ones, and sent him to his seat, while I concluded the whole with some appropriate exhortations. It is pleasing to add that the elder proved one of the most useful monitors I ever had.

Should any persons be disposed to object to such a process, they may be reminded that the Infant System deals with children as rational creatures, and is designed to prepare them for future life. I have seen numerous instances of its beneficial effects; these have induced me to pursue the plan, and in the strongest terms to recommend it to others. In all cases, the matter should be stated to the children simply, calmly, and slowly, and they will seldom, if ever, come to a wrong conclusion.

With regard to punishments, they are various, and must be adapted to the disposition of the child. The only corporal punishment that we inflict, is a pat on the hand, which is very great service in flagrant cases of misconduct. For instance, I have seen one child bite another's arm, until it has almost made its teeth meet. I should suppose few persons are prepared to say, such a child should not be punished for it. I have seen others who, when they first came to school, would begin to scream as if they were being punished, as soon as their mother brought them to the door, while the mother continued to threaten the child without ever putting one threat into execution. The origin of all this noise, has been, perhaps, because the child has demanded a half-penny, as the condition of coming to school, and the mother probably has not had one to give him, but has actually been obliged to borrow one in order to induce him to come in at the school door. Thus the child has come off conqueror, and set it down as a maxim, that, for the future, he may do just as he pleases with his mother. I have sometimes made my appearance at this time, to know what all the noise was about, when the mother has entered into a lamentable tale, telling me what trouble she has had with the child, and that he would not come to school without having a half-penny each time. But the moment the child has seen me, all has been as quiet as possible. I have desired him to give me the half-penny, which he has done directly, I have returned it to the mother, and the child has gone into school, as quietly as any child could do. I have had others who would throw their victuals into the dirt, and then lie down in it themselves, and refuse to rise up, crying, "I will go home ; I want to go into the fields; I will have a half-penny." The mother has answered, "Well, my dear, you shall have a half-penny, if you will stay at school." "No, I want to go and play with Billy or Tommy;" and the mother at length has taken the churl home again, and thus fed his vanity and nursed his pride, till he has completely mastered her, so that she has been glad to apply to the school again, and beg that I would take him in hand.

At another time a girl came with a pillow; she had insisted on having it for a doll; but, so far from contributing to her happiness, it had a contrary effect. Nevertheless, the parent, for want of that firmness so necessary with children, had allowed her to bring it to school, and on her journey she cried all the way, to the amusement of the lookers on. When I remonstrated with the mother, she replied, "What could I do? she would not come without it." The child, however, gave it up to me without any trouble, and the over *indulgent mother* took it back with her. Numerous have been the instances of a similar kind, and all for the want of firmness.

I have found it necessary, under such circumstances, to enter into a kind of agreement with the mother, that she should not interfere in any respect whatever: that on such conditions, and such only, could the child be admitted; observing, that I should act towards it as if it were my own, but that it must and should be obedient to me; to which the mother has consented, and the child has been taken in again; and, strange to say, in less than a fortnight, has been as good, and has behaved as orderly as any child in the school. But I should deem myself guilty of duplicity and deceit, were I to say that such children, in all cases, could be managed without corporal punishment, for it appears to me, that this, in moderation, has been the mode of correcting refractory children, from the earliest ages; for it is expressly said in the Scriptures, "*He that spareth his rod, hateth his son, but he that loveth him chasteneth him betimes;"* and again, *"He that knoweth his Lord's will, and doeth it not, shall be beaten with many stripes."* There is certainly something very pleasing in the sound, that several hundred infant children may be well managed, kept in good order, and corrected of their bad habits, without *any sort* of punishment. But as I have not been able to attain to that state of perfection in the art of teaching, I shall lay before the reader what modes of punishment I have adopted, and the success that attended them.

The first offence deserving punishment, which I shall notice, is playing the truant; and I trust I may be permitted to state, that, notwithstanding the children are so very young, they frequently, at first, stay away from the school, unknown to their parents; nor is this to be wondered at, when we consider how they have been permitted to range the streets and get acquainted with other children in similar circumstances. When this is the case, they cannot be brought into order in a moment; it is a work of time, and requires much patience and perseverance to accomplish it effectually. It is well known that when we accustom ourselves to particular company, and form acquaintances, it is no easy matter to give them up; and it is a maxim, that a man is either better or worse for the company he keeps. Just so it is with children; they form very early attachments, and frequently with children whose parents will not send them to school, and care not where they are, so long as they keep out of their way. Hence such children will persuade others to accompany them, and of course they will be absent from school; but as night approaches, the child will begin to think of the consequences, and mention it to his companions, who will instruct him how to deceive both his teacher and his parents, and perhaps bring him through his trouble; this will give him fresh confidence, and finding himself successful, there will be little difficulty in persuading him to accompany them a second time. I have had children absent from school, two or three half days in a week, and sometimes whole days, who have brought me such rational and plausible excuses, as completely to put me off my guard; but who have been found out by their parents, from having stayed out till seven or even eight o'clock at night. The parents have applied at the school, to know why I kept the children so late, and have then informed me that they had been absent all day. Thus the whole plot has been developed; it has been found that the children were sent to school at eight o'clock in the morning, and had their dinners given them to eat at school; but instead of coming, they have got into company with their older companions, who, in many cases, I have found, were training them for every species of vice. Some have been cured of truant-playing by corporal punishment, when all other means I could devise have failed. Others, by means the most simple, such as causing the child to hold a broom for a given time.

The most powerful punishment I have yet discovered, is to insist on the child sitting still without moving hand or foot, for a given time, say *half an hour at most*. Long punishment always has the tendency to harden the child; he soon gets contented in his situation, and you defeat your own object.

P

By keeping a strict eye upon them, it will be re-marked, they soon begin to form an attachment with some of their own school-fellows, and ultimately become as fond of their new companions, their books, and their school, as they were before of their old companions and the streets. I need scarcely observe, how strong our attachments formed in early years at school are; and I doubt not but many who read this, have found a valuable and real friend in a school-fellow, for whom they would do anything within their power.

There were several children in the school who had contracted some very bad habits, entirely by their being accustomed to run about the streets; and one boy in particular, only five years of age, was so frequently absent, and brought such reasonable excuses for his being so, that it was some time before I detected him. I thought it best to see his mother, and therefore sent the boy to tell her that I wished her to come; the boy soon returned, saying, his mother was not at home: the following morning he was absent again, and I sent another boy to know the reason, when the mother waited on me immediately, and assured me that she had sent the child to school. I then produced the slate, which I kept for that purpose, and informed her how many days and half-days her child had been absent for the last month; when she again assured me, that she had never kept the child at home a single half-day, nor had he ever told her that I wanted to see her; at the same time observing, that he must have been decoyed away by some of the children in the neighbourhood. She regretted that she could not afford to send him to school before; adding, *that the Infant School was " a blessed institution,"* and one, *she thought, much wanted in the neighbourhood.* I need scarcely observe, that both the father and mother lost no time in searching for their child, and, after several hours, they found him in the nearest fruit market, in company with several other children, pretty well stored with apples, &c., which they had, no doubt, stolen from the fruit baskets that are continually placed there. They brought him to school, and informed me that they had given him a good flogging, which I found to be correct, from the marks that were on the child; this, they said, they had no doubt would cure him. But he was not so soon conquered, for the very next day he was absent again; and after the parents had tried every expedient they could think of, in vain, they delivered him over to me, telling me to do what I thought proper. I tried every means that I could devise with as little success, except keeping him at school after school hours; for I had a great disinclination to convert the school into a prison, as my object was, if possible, to cause the children to love the school; and I knew I could not take a more effectual method of causing them to dislike it, than by keeping them there against their will. At last, I tried this experiment, but to as little purpose as the others, and I was about to exclude the child altogether as incorrigible; but unwilling that it should be said, a child of only five years of age had mastered us, I at last hit upon an expedient which had the desired effect. The plan I adopted, was to put him on an elevated situation, within sight of all the children, so secured that he could not hurt himself. I believe it was the force of *ridicule* which effected the cure ; this I had never tried before, and I must say I was extremely glad to witness it. I never knew him absent without leave afterward, and what is more surprising, he appeared to be very fond of the school, and became a very good child. Was not this, then, a brand plucked from the fire ?

I have been advised to dismiss twenty such children rather than retain them by the above means, but if there be more joy in heaven over one sinner that repenteth than over ninety and nine just persons who need no repentance, ought not such a feeling to be encouraged on earth—particularly when it can be done by means that are not injurious to the orderly, but, on the contrary, productive of the best effects? The child just mentioned afterwards went into the national school, with several others who had been nearly as bad as himself, but they scarcely ever failed to come and see me when they had a half-holiday ; and the master of the school told me, that not one of them had ever been absent without leave, and that he had no fault to find with them. I have further to observe, that the moment I perceived a bad effect produced by any method of punishment, it was relinquished.

I believe that there was not a child in the school who would not have been delighted to *carry the broom*, if I had called it play. The other children might have laughed as long as they pleased, for he would have laughed as heartily as any of them ; and as soon as he had done, I should have had a dozen applicants, with " Please sir, may I ? please sir, may I ?" But it was called a *punishment*, and hence I had no applications whatever. They all dreaded it as much as they could a flogging. I am aware, that this plan of punishment may appear ridiculous; and, perhaps, it would be so to use it for older children, but with such young children I have found it answer well, and therefore have no wish to dispense with it. I would, however, have care taken not to encourage the children to ridicule each other while undergoing this or any other punishment, except in extraordinary cases like this. On the contrary, we should encourage them to sympathize with and comfort a child as soon as his punishment is over; and I can truly add, that I do not recollect a single instance, when any child has been undergoing the broom punishment, but what some of the others have come and attempted to beg him off, with "Please, sir, may he sit down now?" and when asked the reason why they have wished the little delinquent to be forgiven, they have answered, "May be, sir, he will be a good boy." Their request has been complied with, and the culprit forgiven; and what have I seen follow? Why, that which has taught me an important lesson, and convinced me that *children can operate on each other's minds, and be the means of producing, very often, better effects than adult persons can.* I have seen them clasp the child round the neck, take him by the hand, lead him about the play-ground, comfort him in every possible way, wipe his eyes with their pinafores, and ask him if he was not sorry for what he had done. The answer has been, " Yes ;" and they have flown to me with— "Master, he says he is sorry for it, and that he will not do so again." In short, they have done that which I could not do ; they have so won the child over by kindness, that it has caused the offender not only to be fond of them, but equally as fond of his master and the school. To these things I attribute the reclaiming of the children I have mentioned; and so far from punishment being productive of the "*worst effects,*" I have found it productive of the best.

The ill effects of expelling children as incorrigible, may be seen in the case of Hartley, who was executed some years back. He confessed before his execution that he had been concerned in several murders, and upwards of two hundred burglaries; and by the newspaper account, we learn, that he was dismissed from school at nine years of age, there being no school-master who would be troubled with him, when, finding himself at full liberty, he immediately became a robber. "Hartley's father (the account proceeds) formerly kept the Sir John Falstaff inn, at Hull, in Yorkshire. He was put to school in that neighbourhood, but his conduct at school was so marked with depravity, and so continually did he play the truant, that he was dismissed as unmanageable. He then, although only nine years of age, began with pilfering and robbing gardens and orchards, till at length his friends were obliged to send him to sea. He soon contrived to run away from the vessel in which he had been placed, and having regained the land, pursued his old habits, and got connected with many of the principal thieves in London, with whom he commenced business regularly as a housebreaker, which was almost always his line of robbery."

Should not every means have been resorted to

with this child, before proceeding to the dangerous mode of expulsion? For it is not the whole who need a physician, but those that are sick; and I strongly suspect, that if judicious punishment had been resorted to, it would have had the desired effect. I can only say, that there never was a child expelled from the Infant School under my care, as incorrigible. In conclusion, I have to observe that the broom punishment is only for extraordinary occasions, and I think we are justified in having recourse to any means that are consistent with duty and humanity, in preference to turning a child out into the wide world.

Of all the difficulties I ever had to encounter, to legislate for rewards and punishment gave me the most trouble. How often have I seen one child laugh at that which would make another child cry. If any one department in teaching requires knowledge of character more than another it is this, many a fine child's spirits are broken through the ignorance of parents and teachers in this particular, but for me to lay down *invariable rules* to manage *every child,* would be like undertaking to describe a voyage to the moon: every person's own good sense must decide for them according to character and circumstances; and as to rewards, the same discrimination must be used. One child will set much value on a little book whilst another will destroy it in a day; and although the book might be worth sixpence, a half-penny worth of what *they* call good stuff, would be valued at double the amount. I have had more business done sometimes for a plum, than for a sixpenny book. It is never necessary to give the child *badges of distinction,* and to allow it as many orders and degrees as an Austrian field marshal; crosses at the button holes, and bits of ribbon on the shoulders are unnecessary, they throw an apple of discord between the young creatures, who have sense enough to see that these things are frequently given with a wondrous lack of discrimination, and sometimes to please parents more than to reward merit. A carraway comfit put into the mouth of an infant will do more good than all the badges of distinction I have mentioned.

CHAPTER X.

LANGUAGE.

" Without things, words, accumulated by misery in the memory, had far better die than drag out a useless existence in the dark; without words, their stay and support, things unaccountably disappear out of the store-house, and may be for ever lost. But bind *a thing with a word*, a strong link, stronger than any steel, and softer than any silk, and the captive remains for ever happy in its bright prison-house."— *Wilson.*

THE senses of children having revealed each object in its true light, they next desire to know its name, and then express their perceptions in words. This you have to gratify; and from the time you tell them the name of an object, it is the representative of the thing in the mind of the child. If the object be not present, but you mention the name, this suggests it to the infant mind. Had this been more frequently thought of by instructors, we should have found them less eager to make the child acquainted with names of things of which it has no knowledge or conception. Sounds and signs, which give rise to no idea in the mind, because the child has

never seen or known the things represented, are of
no use and can only burden the memory. It is
therefore the object of our system to give the children
a knowledge of things— and then a knowledge of
the *words* which represent those things.   These remarks not only apply to the names of visible things;
but more particularly to those which are abstract.
If I would say, show a child a *horse*, before you tell
it the name of the animal;   still more would I urge it
upon the teacher to let the child see what *love, kindness, religion,* &c. &c. are, before it is told what name
to designate these principles by.   If our ignorance
as to material things be the result of instructing
children in names, instead of enabling them to become acquainted with things; so, on the other hand,
I believe, we may account in the same way to some
extent for *virtue* being so frequently a mere word, an
empty sound amongst men, instead of an active
principle.

Our next endeavour is to teach the children to express their thoughts upon things;—and if they are
not checked by injudicious treatment, they will have
some on every subject.   We first teach them to express their *own notions*—we then tell them ours—
and truth will prevail, even in the minds of children.
On this plan it will operate by its own strength, not
by the power of coercion, which renders even truth
disagreeable and repulsive.   The children will adopt
it from choice in preference to error, and it will be
firmly established in their minds.

It will no doubt be perceived, that for the promotion of the course here recommended, it will be advisable to connect with our *alphabetical* and *reading*

lessons, as much information as we possibly can. By so doing the tedium of the task to the child will be considerably lessened, as well as much knowledge attained. The means of doing this in a variety of ways will, no doubt, suggest themselves to the intelligent teacher; but, as an illustration of what we mean, the following conversational plan may not be useless.

We have 26 cards, and each card has on it one letter of the alphabet, and some object in nature. The first, for instance, has the letter A on the top and an apple painted on the bottom. The children are desired to go into the gallery, which is formed of seats elevated one above another, at one end of the school, like stairs; the master places himself before the children, so that they can see him, and he them, and being thus situated, proceeds in the following manner :—

Q. Where am I ? *A.* Opposite to us. *Q.* What is on the right side of me ? *A.* A lady. *Q.* What is on the left side of me ? *A.* A chair. *Q.* What is behind me ? *A.* A desk. *Q.* Who are before me ? *A.* We children. *Q.* What do I hold up in my hand ? *A.* Letter A for apple. *Q.* Which hand do I hold it up with ? *A.* The right hand. *Q.* Spell apple.* *A.* A-p-p-l-e. *Q.* How is an apple pro-

---

* It is not supposed that all or many of the children will be able to spell this, or the subsequent words, or to give such answers as we have put down, but *some* amongst the older or more acute of them will soon be able to do so, and thus become instructors of the rest. It may be proper to mention, also, that the information on natural history, &c. &c., displayed in some of the answers, is the result of the instructions in natural history, which the children

duced? *A.* It grows on a tree. *Q.* What part of the tree is in the ground? *A.* The root. *Q.* What is that which comes out of the ground? *A.* The stem. *Q.* When the stem grows up straight, what would you call its position? *A.* Perpendicular. *Q.* What are on the stem? *A.* Branches. *Q.* What are on the branches? *A.* Leaves. *Q.* Of what colour are they? *A.* Green.

Q. Is there any thing besides leaves on the branches? *A.* Yes; apples. *Q.* What was it before it became an apple? *A.* Blossom. *Q.* What part of the blossom becomes fruit? *A.* The inside. *Q.* What becomes of the leaves of the blossom? *A.* They fall off the tree. *Q.* What was it before it became blossom? *A.* A bud. *Q.* What caused the buds to become larger and produce leaves and blossom? *A.* The sap. *Q.* What is sap? *A.* A juice. *Q.* How can the sap make the buds larger? *A.* It comes out of the root and goes up the stem. *Q.* Where next? *A.* Through the branches into the buds. *Q.* What do the buds produce? *A.* Some buds produce leaves, some blossoms, and some a shoot. *Q.* What do you mean by a shoot? *A.* A shoot is a young branch, which is green at first, but becomes hard by age. *Q.* What part becomes hard first? *A.* The bottom.

B.

Q. What is this? *A.* B, for baker, for butter,

simultaneously receive, and which is spoken of in a subsequent chapter.

Mr. Galt's simple arrangement of the alphabet I much approve of, and no doubt it will come into general use.

for bacon, for brewer, for button, for bell, &c. &c.
[The teacher can take any of these names he pleases,
for instance, the first:] Children, let me hear you
spell baker. *A.* B-a-k-e·r. *Q.* What is a baker?
A. A man who makes bread. *Q.* What is bread
made of? *A.* It is made of flour, water, yeast, and
a little salt. *Q.* What is flour made of? *A.* Wheat.
Q. How is it made? *A.* Ground to powder in a
mill. *Q.* What makes the mill go round? *A.* The
wind, if it is a windmill. *Q.* Are there any other
kinds of mills? *A.* Yes; mills that go by water,
mills that are drawn round by horses, and mills that
go by steam. *Q.* When the flour and water and
yeast are mixed together, what does the baker do?
A. Bake them in an oven. *Q.* What is the use of
bread? *A.* For children to eat. *Q.* Who causes
the corn to grow? *A.* Almighty God.

C.

Q. What is this? *A.* It is letter C for cow,
c-o-w, and for cat, &c. *Q.* What is the use of the
cow? *A.* The cow gives us milk to put into the
tea. *Q.* Is milk used for any other purpose besides
putting it into tea? *A.* Yes; it is used to put into
puddings, and for many other things. *Q.* Name
some of the other things? *A.* It is used to make
butter and cheese. *Q.* What part of it is made into
butter? *A.* The cream which swims at the top of
the milk. *Q.* How is it made into butter? *A.* It
is put into a thing called a churn, in the shape of a
barrel. *Q.* What is done next? *A.* The churn is
turned round by means of a handle, and the motion
turns the cream into butter. *Q.* What is the use of

Q

butter? *A.* To put on bread, and to put into pie-crust, and many other nice things. *Q.* Of what colour is butter? *A.* It is generally yellow. *Q.* Are there any other things made of milk? *A.* Yes, many things; but the principal one is cheese. *Q.* How is cheese made? *A.* The milk is turned into curds and whey, which is done by putting a liquid into it called rennet. *Q.* What part of the curd and whey is made into cheese? *A.* The curd, which is put into a press; and when it has been in the press a few days it becomes cheese. *Q.* Is the flesh of the cow useful? *A.* Yes; it is eaten, and is called beef; and the flesh of the young calf is called veal. *Q.* Is the skin of the cow or calf of any use? *A.* Yes; the skin of the cow is manufactured into leather for the soles of shoes. *Q.* What is made with the calf skin? *A.* The top of the shoe, which is called the upper-leather. *Q.* Are there any other parts of the cow that are useful? *A.* Yes; the horns, which are made into combs, handles of knives, forks, and other things. *Q.* What is made of the hoofs that come off the cow's feet? *A.* Glue, to join boards together. *Q.* Who made the cow? *A.* Almighty God.

D.

Q. What is this? *A.* Letter D, for dog, for dove, for draper, &c. *Q.* What is the use of the dog? *A.* To guard the house and keep thieves away. *Q.* How can a dog guard the house and keep thieves away? *A.* By barking to wake the persons who live in the house. *Q.* Is the dog of any other use? *A.* Yes; to draw under a truck. *Q.* Does he do as his master bids him? *A.* Yes; and knows his master from any other person. *Q.* Is the dog a faithful animal? *A.* Yes, very faithful; he has been known to die of grief for the loss of his master. *Q.* Can you mention an instance of the dog's faithfulness? *A.* Yes; a dog waited at the gates of the Fleet prison for hours every day for nearly two years, because his master was confined in the prison. *Q.* Can you mention another instance of the dog's faithfulness? *A.* Yes; a dog lay down on his master's grave in a churchyard in London for many weeks. *Q.* How did the dog get food? *A.* The people who lived near noticed him, and brought him victuals. *Q.* Did the people do any thing besides giving him victuals? *A.* Yes; they made a house for him for fear he should die with wet and cold. *Q.* How long did he stay there? *A.* Until the people took him away, because he howled dreadfully when the organ played on Sundays. *Q.* Is it right to beat a dog? *A.* No; it is very wrong to use any animal ill, because we do not like to be beaten ourselves. *Q.* Did Almighty God make the dog? *A.* Yes; and every thing else that has life.

E.

Q. What letter is this? *A.* E, for egg. *Q.* What is the use of an egg? *A.* It is useful for many purposes; to put into puddings, and to eat by itself. *Q.* Should country children keep an egg if they find it in the hedge? *A.* No, it is thieving; they should find out the owner and take it home. *Q.* Do children ever throw stones at the fowls? *A.* Yes; but they are mischievous children, and perhaps do not go to school. *Q.* What ought children to learn by going to school? *A.* To be kind and good to every body, and every thing that has life.

F.

Q. What letter is this? *A.* Letter F, for frying-pan, for father, &c. *Q.* Let me hear you spell frying-pan. *A.* F-r-y-i-n-g p-a-n. *Q.* What is the use of the frying-pan? *A.* To fry meat and pan-cakes. *Q.* Spell me the names of the different kinds of meat. *A.* B-e-e-f, p-o-r-k, v-e-a-l, m-u-t-t-o-n, l-a-m-b, h-a-m, &c. *Q.* Of what shape are frying-pans? *A.* Some circular, and some are like an ellipsis.* *Q.* Are there any other utensils into which meat is put that are circular? *A.* Yes, please sir, my mother has some circular plates; and please sir, my mother has some elliptical dishes. *Q.* Any thing besides? *A.* Yes, please sir, my mother has a circular table; and, please sir, my mother has a rectangular one, and it is made of deal.

G.

Q. What letter is this? *A.* Letter G, for goat, for good girl, &c. *Q.* Spell goat. *A.* G-o-a-t. *Q.* What is the use of the goat? *A.* In some countries people drink the goat's milk; and the skin is useful

* It may possibly strike some of my readers as strange that a geometrical question should be put in a conversation on the alphabet, but it should be remembered that, according to the Infant School system, *language* is not taught exclusively, but in connection with *number* and *form*;—questions like the above, therefore, are calculated to excite their memories, and induce an application of their geometrical knowledge.

to make the upper-leather of shoes. *Q.* Are goats fond of going into the valleys and low places? *A.* No; they are fond of going up hills and high places. *Q.* If a goat is coming down a high hill which has only one narrow path merely wide enough for one goat to walk on without falling down, and another goat is coming up the same path, what do they do? *A.* The goat that is coming up lies down and lets the other goat walk over him. *Q.* Why does not one of the goats turn round and go back again? *A.* Because there would not be room, and the one which should try to turn round would fall down and be killed.

H.

Q. What letter is this? *A.* Letter H, for horse, for house, &c. *Q.* What is the use of the horse? *A.* To draw carts, coaches, stages, waggons, fire-engines, &c. *Q.* Spell horse and cart and coach. *A.* H-o-r-s-e, c-a-r-t, c-o-a-c-h. *Q.* What is the difference between a cart and coach? *A.* A cart has two wheels, and a coach has four. *Q.* Tell me some other difference. *A.* The horses in a cart go before each other, but the horses in a coach go side by side. *Q.* What is the use of a fire-engine? *A.* To put the fire out when the house is on fire. *Q.* Is it right for children to play with the fire. *A.* No, very wrong; as many children are burnt to death, and many houses burnt down from it. *Q.* Should the horse be cruelly used? *A.* No; he should be kindly treated, as he is the most useful animal we have. *Q.* Who created him? *A.* Almighty God.

I.

Q. What letter is this? *A.* Letter I, for iron, for idleness, &c. *Q.* Spell iron. I-r-o-n. *Q.* What is the use of an iron? *A.* To iron the clothes after they are washed, and to make them smooth. *Q.* How do they iron the clothes? *A.* Make the iron hot, and then work it backwards and forwards on the clothe *Q.* Should little chil dren come with clean clothes to school? *A.* Yes; and clean hands and faces too. *Q.* Is not iron used for other purposes? *A.* Oh, yes; for a great many things, as knives, forks, &c.

J.

Q. What letter is this? *A.* J, for jug, John, &c. *Q.* What is the use of the jug? *A.* To hold water, or beer, or any other liquid. *Q.* What is a jug made of? *A.* Of clay, which is worked round into the shape of a jug, and then burnt, and that hardens it. *Q.* Should children be careful when they are carrying a jug? *A.* Yes; or else they will let it fall and break it. *Q.* Then it is necessary for children to be careful? *A.* Yes, every body should be careful.

K.

Q. What letter is this? *A.* Letter K, for kite, &c. *Q.* What is the use of the kite? *A.* For little children to fly. Please sir, my big brother has got a kite. *Q.* What does your brother do with his kite? *A.* Please sir, he goes into the fields when he has got time, and flies it. *Q.* How does he fly it? *A.* Please sir, he has got a long string, which he fixes to another called a loop, and then he unwinds the string, and gets some boy to hold it up. *Q.* What then ? *A.* Please sir, then he runs against the wind, and the kite goes up. *Q.* What is the use of the tail of the kite? *A.* Please sir, it will not fly without a tail. *Q.* Why not ? *A.* Please sir, it goes round and round without a tail, and comes down. *Q.* Then what do you suppose is the use of the tail ? *A.* Please sir, I don't know. Another child will probably supply the answer. Please sir, to balance it.

L.

Q. What letter is this ? *A.* Letter L, for lion, &c. *Q.* Spell lion. *A.* L-i-o-n. *Q.* What is the size of a full grown lion ? *A.* A full grown lion stands four feet and a half high, and is eight feet long. *Q.* How high do you stand ? *A.* Please sir, some of us stand two feet, and none of us above three. *Q.* Has the lion any particular character among beasts ? *A.* Yes, he is called the king of beasts on account of his great strength. *Q.* When he seizes his prey, how far can he leap ? *A.* To the distance of twenty feet. *Q.* Describe some other particulars concerning the lion. *A.* The lion has a shaggy mane, which the lioness has not. *Q.* What other particulars ? *A.* The lion's roar is so loud that other animals run away when they hear it. *Q.* Where are lions found? *A.* In most hot countries : the largest are found in Asia and Africa.

M.

Q. What letter is this ? *A.* Letter M, for Monday, for mouse, &c. *Q.* What is the use of the mouse ? *A.*

To make the servants diligent and put the things out of the way. *Q.* How can mice make servants diligent? *A.* If people don't put the candles in a proper place the mice will gnaw them. *Q.* Are mice of any other service? *A.* Please sir, if the mice did not make a smell, some people would never clean their cupboards out.*

N.

Q. What letter is this? *A.* Letter N, for nut, &c. *Q.* What is a nut? *A.* A thing that is hard, and it grows on a tree. *Q.* What shape is it? *A.* Something in the shape of a marble. *Q.* How can it be eaten, if it is like a marble? *A.* Please sir, it is the kernel that we eat. *Q.* How are nuts produced? *A.* They grow on trees.

O.

Q. What letter is this? *A.* Letter O, for orange. *Q.* Of what colour is an orange? *A.* An orange is green at first, but afterwards becomes of a colour called orange-red. *Q.* Do they grow in the ground like potatoes? *A.* No, they grow on trees like apples. *Q.* Can you tell me anything in the shape of an orange? *A.* Yes, the earth on which we live is nearly of that shape. *Q.* On what part of the earth do we live? *A.* The surface. *Q.* What do you mean by the surface? *A.* The outside. *Q.* Who formed the earth, and preserves it in its proper motions? *A.* Almighty God.

* This answer was given by a child four years old; and immediately afterwards another child called out, "Please sir, if it were not for bugs, some people would not clean their bedsteads."

P.

Q. What letter is this ? *A.* Letter P, for pig, for plum-pudding, &c. *Q.* What is the use of the pig ? *A.* Its flesh is eaten, and is called pork. *Q.* What is the use of the hair or bristles ? *A.* To make brushes or brooms. *Q.* What is the use of a brush ? *A.* Some brushes are to brush the clothes, and others to brush the dirt out of the corners of the room. *Q.* Does a good servant ever leave the dirt in the corners ? *A.* No, never ; a good servant or any clean little girl would be ashamed of it.

Q.

Q. What letter is this ? *A.* Letter Q, for quill, &c. *Q.* How are quills produced ? *A.* From the wings of geese and other large birds. *Q.* What is the use of the quill ? *A.* To form into pens and many other things. *Q.* What is the use of the pen ? *A.* To dip into ink and write with it. *Q.* What do you write upon ? *A.* Paper. *Q.* What is paper made of ? *A.* Rags.

R.

Q. What letter is this ? *A.* Letter R, for rabbit, &c. *Q.* What is the use of the rabbit ? *A.* The flesh of the rabbit is eaten, and is very nice. *Q.* What does the rabbit eat ? *A.* Corn, grass, cabbage leaves, and many different herbs. *Q.* What is the use of the skin ? *A.* To make hats, and to trim boys' caps. *Q.* Are they very numerous? *A.* They are to be found in almost all countries.

S.

Q. What is this ? *A.* Letter S, for shoe, &c.
Q. What is the use of shoes ? *A.* To keep the feet
warm and dry. *Q.* Should children walk in the mud
or in the kennel ? *A.* No, because that would spoil
the shoes, and wear them out too soon. *Q.* And why
should little children be careful not to wear them out
any more than they can help ? *A.* Because our parents must work harder to buy us more.

T.

Q. What letter is this ? *A.* Letter T, for tea-
kettle. *Q.* What are tea-kettles made of ? *A.* Some
are make of tin, and some of copper, and some of
iron. *Q.* Why are they not made of wood ? *A.*
Because the wood would burn. *Q.* What thing is
that at the top ? *A.* The handle. *Q.* What is underneath the handle ? *A.* The lid. *Q.* What is in
the front of it ? *A.* The spout. *Q.* What is the
use of the spout ? *A.* For the water to come out.
Q. What is the use of the handle ? *A.* To take hold
of. *Q.* Why do they not take hold of the spout ?
A. Because it is the wrong way.

U.

Q. What letter is this ? *A.* Letter U, for umbrella, &c. *Q.* Is letter U a vowel or consonant ?
A. A vowel. *Q.* What is the use of the umbrella ?
A. To keep the rain off any body. *Q.* What are
umbrellas made of ? *A.* Some of silk and some of
cotton. *Q.* Which are the best ? *A.* Those that
are made of silk. *Q.* Is there any thing else in an

umbrella? *A.* Yes; whalebone. *Q.* Where does whalebone come from? *A.* Out of a large fish called a whale. *Q.* Who made the whale? *A.* Almighty God.

V.

Q. What letter is this? *A.* Letter V, for vine, &c. *Q.* What is a vine? *A.* A thing that grows against the wall and produces grapes. *Q.* Why does it not grow like another tree and support its own weight? *A.* Because it is not strong enough. *Q.* Then it cannot grow and become fruitful in this country without man's assistance? *A.* No; and, please sir, we cannot grow and become fruitful without the assistance of Almighty God.*

W.

Q. What letter is this? *A.* It is letter W, for wheel. *Q.* Spell wheel. *A.* W-h-e-e-l. *Q.* What is the use of wheels? *A.* To make it easier for horses to draw. *Q.* How do you know that? *A.* Please sir, I had a little cart full of stones, and the wheel came off; and, please sir, I found it much harder to draw. *Q.* Then if it was not for wheels the horse could not draw so great a weight? *A.* No, and, please sir, people could not go into the country so quick as they do. *Q.* What trade do they call the persons that make wheels? *A.* Wheel-wrights.

X.

Q. What letter is this? *A.* Letter X, for Xeno-

* This answer was given by a child five years of age.

phon, a man's name. *Q.* What was the particular character of Xenophon? *A.* He was very courageous. *Q.* What does courageous mean? *A.* To be afraid to do harm, but not to be afraid to do good or anything that is right. *Q.* What is the greatest courage? *A.* To conquer our own bad passions and bad inclinations. *Q.* Is he a courageous man that can conquer his bad passions? *A.* Yes; because they are the most difficult to conquer.

Y.

Q. What letter is this? *A.* Letter Y, for yoke, &c. *Q.* Is it a vowel or consonant? *A.* When it begins a word it is called a consonant, but if not, a vowel. *Q.* What is a yoke? *A.* Please sir, what the milk people carry the milk pails on. *Q.* What is the use of the yoke? *A.* To enable the people to carry the milk easier.

Z.

Q. What letter is this? *A.* Letter Z, for Zealander. *Q.* What is a Zealander? *A.* A man that lives on an island on the southern ocean, called Zealand. *Q.* How do they live? *A.* Principally by hunting and fishing. *Q.* What is hunting? *A.* Following animals to catch them. *Q.* Who made all the animals? *A.* Almighty God.

The method above described is adapted to the large room, where the children may be taught altogether; but it is necessary to change the scene even in this; for however novel and pleasing a thing may be at first, if it be not managed with prudence it will soon lose its effect. It is then to be observed, that the mode of teaching described is not practised every day, but only twice or thrice a week. The children will take care that the teacher does not altogether forget to teach them in any way that they have been accustomed to. After letting the above plan lie by for a day or two, some of the children will come to the teacher, and say, "Please sir, may we say the picture alphabet up in the gallery?" If the other children overhear the question, it will go through the school like lightning: "Oh yes—yes—yes, sir, if you please, do let us say the letters in the gallery." Thus a desire is created in the children's minds, and it is then especially that they may be taught with good effect.

Another plan which we adopt, is in practice almost every day; but it is better adapted to what is called the class-room: we have the alphabet printed in large letters, both in Roman and Italic characters, on one sheet of paper: this paper is pasted on a board, or on pasteboard, and placed against the wall; the whole class then stand around it, but instead of one of the monitors pointing to the letters, the master or mistress does it; so that the children not only obtain instruction from each other, but every child has a lesson from the master or mistress twice every day.

Before they go to the reading lessons, they have the sounds of all the words in spelling: thus the sound of a—ball, call, fall, wall; then the reading-lesson is full of words of the same sound. In like manner they proceed with other letters, as i—the sound of

R

which they learn from such words as five, drive, strive, until, by a series of lessons, they become acquainted with all the sounds, and are able to read any common book.

I have observed in some instances the most deplorable laxity in this particular. Cases have occurred in which children have been for two years at a school, and yet scarcely knew the whole alphabet; and I have known others to be four years in an Infant School, without being able to read. I hesitate not to say that the fault rests exclusively with the teachers, who, finding this department of their work more troublesome than others which are attractive to visitors, have sometimes neglected it, and even thrown it entirely aside, affirming that reading is not a part of the Infant System at all! Such a declaration is, however, only to be accounted for from the most lamentable ignorance, perverseness, or both. Had it been true, we should not have had a single Infant School in Scotland, and throughout that country the children read delightfully.

The great importance of full instruction in reading will be apparent from the following considerations.

1. If the parents do not find the children learn to read, they will discontinue sending them. This they consider essential, and nothing else will be deemed by them an adequate substitute.

2. Children cannot make desirable progress in other schools which they may enter, unless they obtain an ability to read at least simple lessons.

3. Neglect in this respect impedes the progress of the Infant System. Such an obstacle ought not to exist, and should at once be removed.

4. In manufacturing districts children go to work very soon ; if they are not able to read before, there is reason to fear they will not afterwards acquire the power; but if they have this, Sunday Schools may supply other deficiences.

5. Want of ability to read prevents, of course, a knowledge of the Word of God.

To prevent this evil, I have arranged a series, denominated "Developing Lessons," the great object of which is to induce children to think and reflect on what they see. They are thus formed : at the top is a coloured picture, or series of coloured pictures of insects, quadrupeds, and general objects. For instance, there is one containing the poplar, hawk-moth, and wasp. The lesson is as follows : " The wasp can sting and fly as well as the moth, which does not sting. I hope no wasp will sting me; he is small, but the hawk-moth is large. The moth eats leaves, but the wasp loves sweet things, and makes a round nest. If boys take the nest they may be stung: the fish like the wasp-grubs." On this questions are proposed: Which stings? Which is small and which large? Which eats leaves? Which makes a round nest? &c. &c.

To take another instance. There is a figure of an Italian, to which is appended the following: " The Italian has got a flask of oil and a fish in his hand, and something else in his hand which the little child who reads this must find out. Any child can tell who makes use of the sense of seeing. In Italy they make a good deal of wine; big grapes grow there that they make it with. Italians can sing very

vell, and so can little children when they are taught."
Questions are likewise proposed on this as before.

Of these lessons, however, there is a great variety.
All schools should possess them : they will effectually
prevent the evil alluded to, by checking the apathy of
children in learning to read, and calling the teacher's
powers into full exercise. They are equally adapted
to spelling and reading.

I will give two specimens of reading lessons in
natural history, each of which has a large, well-en-
graved and coloured plate at the top, copied from
nature.

THE EAGLE.

How glad some poor children would be if they
could read about the eagle. He is a big strong
bird, and has such great wings, and such long sharp
claws, that he can dig them into the lamb, hare,
rabbit, and other animals, and thus fly away with
them to feed his young ones, and to eat them himself.
Eagles make such a large nest on the side of some
high rock, where nobody can get at it. There used
to be eagles in Wales, and there are some now in
Scotland, but very few in England, for they do not
like to be where there are many people. *The Almighty gave man dominion over the birds of the air,* as
well as over the other animals, and as he gave man
power to *think,* if the eagles become troublesome,
men catch them, though they can fly so high; and
as the eagle knows this, he likes to keep out of our
way and go into parts of the world where there are

not so many people. There are many sorts of eagles : the black eagle, the sea eagle, the bald eagle, and others. They have all strong bills bent down in front, and strong claws. This bird is mentioned in the Bible.

Questions are proposed after this is read, and thus the examination proceeds :—" What is that ? An eagle. What sort of a bird is he ? He is big and strong. What are those ? His feathers. What else are they called ? His plumage," &c. &c.

THE CROCODILE.

I hope you will not put your dirty hands on this picture of the crocodile. The live ones have hard scales on their backs, and such a many teeth. They could bite a man's leg off, but there are none in our land, only young ones that sailors bring with them. The crocodile can run fast; those are best off who are out of his way. He lives by the water; he goes much in it; and he can swim well. Young ones come out of eggs, which the old one lays in the sand. Some beasts eat the eggs, or else there would be too many crocodiles. The crocodile can run fast if he runs straight, and those who wish to get out of his way run zigzag, and he takes some time to turn; the poor black men know this, and can get out of his way; but some of them can fight and kill him on the land or in the water. I think the crocodile is mentioned in *Scripture*. Ask your teacher what Scripture means. When you learn geography you will know where many of the places are that are mentioned in the Bible, and you will see where the

R 3

river Nile is. There are such a many crocodiles on the banks of that river that the people are afraid to go alone. What a many wonderful animals our great Creator has made! How humble and thankful we should be to see so many great wonder!

On this questions are asked as before.

The spelling lessons contain words capable of explanation, such as white, black, round, square; others are classed as fleet, ship, brig, sloop, &c.; and others are in contrast, as hot, cold, dark, light, wet, dry, &c.

In this department we use the tablet placed beneath the arithmeticon, the invention and improvement of which are described in the volume entitled " Early Discipline Illustrated, or the Infant System Successful and Progressing." A clear idea of the whole apparatus is given by the wood-cut on the opposite page, and it ought certainly to be found in every Infant School. The sense of sight is then brought into full action to aid the mind, and that with results which would not easily be conceived. We shall take another opportunity of explaining the use of the upper part of the apparatus, the lower demanding our present attention.

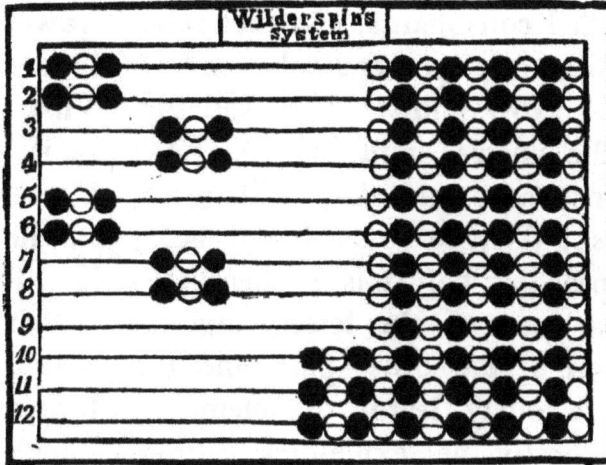

To use the *tablet*, let the following things be observed. It is supposed the children know well there

are twenty-six letters in the alphabet; that twenty
are called consonants, and that six are vowels. We
take first one perpendicular row of letters in the
figure. Now point to D, and say, What is that?
and the answer will be, D. Ask, Is it a vowel
or consonant, and they will reply, A consonant;
but ask, Why do you know it is D, and the answer
will probably be, It is so because it is. Hide the
circular part of the letter, and ask, What is the
position of the other part, and they will say, having previously learnt the elements of form which
will shortly be explained, A perpendicular line;
hide that, and ask them what the other part is,
telling them to bend one of their fore-fingers in the
same form, and they will say, A curve line. If they
are then asked how they may know it is D, they will
say, Because it is made of a perpendicular line and
has a curved line behind. Further information may
then be given. Turn the D letter up thus ⌒, and
say, I want to teach you the difference between concave and convex: the under part of the curve is
concave and the upper part of it is convex. Then
say, I shall now take the letter away, and wish you to
shew me concave and convex on one of your fingers;
when they will bend the fore-finger, and point them
both out on it. Go on with the other letters in
the same way: shew them the vowels after the
consonants and analyse each one. For example, A
is formed of two inclined lines and a horizontal line
to join them in the centre; and the top of that
letter is an acute angle, and were a line placed at
the bottom it would be a triangle. A brass letter
may be moreover shewn to be a substance: its

properties may be described as hard, smooth, bright, &c. and its coming from the mineral kingdom may be noticed, and thus the instruction may be indefinitely varied.

The *power* of letters may then be pointed out. Ask them to spell M R, and they will give you the sound of R, or something like it, and so in reference to other letters. But place the A against the M as it appears in the figure, and you may teach them to say A, M, AM; and thus all the way down the left side of the row of consonants. If then you carry the vowel down on the other side of them, you will change the lesson, and by such means go on almost *ad infinitum*. Double rows of consonants may be placed with a vowel between them, and when well practised in this, they will ask for the vowel to be omitted that they may supply it, which they will do very readily and with great pleasure, while there is a tasking of the mind which cannot but prove beneficial.

Again, turn the frame with the balls round, so that the wires are perpendicular instead of horizontal, raise a ball gently, and say, To ascend, ascending, ascended; let it fall gently, saying, to descend, descending, descended; with a little explanation these words will then be understood, and others may be taught in the same way. To fall, falling, fallen; to rise, rising, risen; to go, going, gone, will readily occur, and others will easily be supplied by the ingenuity of the instructor. The frame may also be applied to *grammar*.

It is to be used as follows :—Move one of the balls to a part of the frame distinct from the rest. The children will then repeat, "There *it* is, there *it* is." Apply your finger to the ball, and set it running round. The children will immediately change from saying, "There *it* is," to "There *it* goes, there *it* goes."

When they have repeated "There it goes" long enough to impress it on their memory, stop the ball; the children will probably say, "Now *it* stops, now *it* stops." When that is the case, move another ball to it, and then explain to the children the difference between singular and plural, desiring them to call out, "There *they* are, there *they* are;" and when they have done that as long as may be proper, set both balls moving, and it is likely they will call out, "There *they* go, there *they* go," &c. &c.

CHAPTER X*.

ARITHMETIC.

"In arithmetic, as in every other branch of education, the principal object should be to preserve the understanding from implicit belief, to invigorate its powers, and to induce the laudable ambition of progressive improvement."—*Edgeworth*.

THE advantage of a knowledge of arithmetic has never been disputed. Its universal application to the business of life renders it an important acquisition to all ranks and conditions of men. The practicability of imparting the rudiments of arithmetic to very young children, has been satisfactorily shewn by the Infant-school System; and it has been found, likewise, that it is the readiest and surest way of developing the thinking faculties of the infant mind. Since the most complicated and difficult questions of arithmetic, as well as the most simple, are all solvable by the same rules, and on the same principles, it is of the utmost importance to give children a clear insight into the primary principles of number.

For this purpose we take care to shew them, by visible objects, that all numbers are combinations of unity; and that all changes of number must arise, either from adding to or taking from a certain stated number. After this, or rather, perhaps I should say, in conjunction with this instruction, we exhibit to the children the *signs* of number, and make them acquainted with their various combinations; and, lastly, we bring them to the abstract consideration of number; or what may be termed *mental arithmetic*. If you reverse this, which has generally been the system of instruction pursued—if you set a child to learn its multiplication, pence, and other tables,—before you have shewn it by *realities*, the combinations of unity which these tables express in words—you are rendering the whole abstruse, difficult, and uninteresting; and, in short, are giving it knowledge which it is unable to apply.

As far as regards the general principles of numerical tuition, it may be sufficient to state, that we should begin with unity, and proceed very gradually, by slow and sure steps, through the simplest forms of combinations to the more comprehensive. Trace and retrace your first steps—the children can never be too thoroughly familiar with the first principles or facts of number.

We have various ways of teaching arithmetic in use in the schools; I shall speak of them all, beginning with a description of the arithmeticon, which is of great utility.

It will be seen, that on the twelve parallel wires there are 144 balls, alternately black and white. By these the elements of arithmetic may be taught as follows :—

Numeration.—Take one ball from the lowest wire, and say units, *one;* two from the next, and say tens, *two;* three from the third, and say hundreds, *three;* four from the fourth, and say thousands, *four;* five from the fifth, and say tens of thousands, *five;* six from the sixth, and say hundreds of thousands, *six;* seven from the seventh, and say millions, *seven;* eight from the eighth, and say tens of millions, *eight;* nine from the ninth, and say hundreds of millions, *nine;* ten from the tenth, and say thousands of millions, *ten;* eleven from the eleventh, and say tens of thousands of millions, *eleven;* twelve from the twelfth, and say hundreds of thousands of millions, *twelve.*

The tablet beneath the balls has six spaces for the insertion of brass letters and figures, a box of which accompanies the frame. Suppose then the only figure inserted is the 7 in the second space from the top : now were the children asked what it was, they would all say, without instruction, " It is one." If, however, you tell them that an object of such a form stands instead of seven ones, and place seven balls together on a wire, they will at once see the use and power of the number. Place a 3 next the 7, merely ask what it is, and they will reply, " We don't know ;" but if you put out three balls on a wire, they will say instantly, " O it is three ones, or three ;" and that they may have the proper name they may be told that they have before them *figure* 7 and *figure* 3. Put a nine to these figures, and their attention will be arrested: say, Do you think you can tell me what that is? and, while you are speaking, move the balls gently out, and, as soon as they see them, they will immediately cry out " Nine ;" and in this way they may acquire a knowledge of all the figures separately. Then you may proceed thus : Units 7, tens 3; place three balls on the top wire and seven on the second, and say, Thirty-seven, as you point to the figures, and thirty-seven as you point to the balls. Then go on, units 7, tens 3, hundreds 9, place nine balls on the top wire, three on the second, and seven on the third, and say, pointing to each, Nine hundred and thirty-seven. And so onwards.

To assist the understanding and exercise the judgment, slide a figure in the frame, and say, Figure 8. *Question.* What is this? *Answer.* No. 8. *Q.* If No. 1 be put on the left side of the 8, what will it be? *A.* 81. *Q.* If the 1 be put on the right side, then what will it be? *A.* 18. *Q.* If the figure 4 be put before the 1, then what will the number be? *A.* 418. *Q.* Shift the figure 4 and put it on the left side of the 8, then ask the children to tell the number, the answer is 184. The teacher can keep adding and shifting as he pleases, according to the capacity of his pupils, taking care to explain as he goes on, and to satisfy himself that his little flock perfectly understand him. Suppose figures 5476953821 are in the frame; then let the children begin at the left hand, saying, units, tens, hundreds, thousands, tens of thousands, hundreds of thousands, millions, tens of millions, hundreds of millions, thousands of millions. After which, begin at the right hand side, and they will say, Five thousand four hundred and seventy-six million, nine hundred and fifty-three thousand, eight hundred and twenty-one. If the children are practised in this way, they will soon learn numeration.

The frame was employed for this purpose, long before its application to others was perceived; but at length I found we might proceed to

Addition.—We proceed as follows :—1 and 2 are 3, and 3 are 6, and 4 are 10 and 5 are 15, and 6 are 21, and 7 are 28, and 8 are 36, and 9 are 45, and 10 are 55, and 11 are 66, and 12 are 78.

Then the master may exercise them backwards, saying, 12 and 11 are 23, and 10 are 33, and 9 are 42, and 8 are 50, and 7 are 57, and 6 are 63, and 5 are 68, and 4 are 72, and 3 are 75, and 2 are 77, and 1 is 78, and so on in great variety.

Again: place seven balls on one wire and two on the next, and ask them how many 7 and 2 are; to this they will soon answer, Nine: then put the brass figure 9 on the tablet beneath, and they will see how the amount is marked: then take eight balls and three, when they will see that eight and three are eleven. Explain to them that they cannot put underneath two figure ones which mean 11, but they must put 1 under the 8, and carry 1 to the 4, when you must place one ball under the four, and, asking them what that makes, they will say, Five. Proceed by saying, How much are five and nine? put out the proper number of balls, and they will say, Five and nine are fourteen. Put a four underneath, and tell them, as there is no figure to put the 1 under, it must be placed next it: hence they see that 937 added to 482, make a total of 1419.

Subtraction may be taught in as many ways by this instrument. Thus: take 1 from 1, nothing remains; moving the first ball at the same time to the other end of the frame. Then remove 1 from the second wire, and say, Take 1 from 2, the children will instantly perceive that only 1 remains; then 1 from 3, and 2 remain; 1 from 4, 3 remain; 1 from 5, 4 remain; 1 from 6, 5 remain; 1 from 7, 6 remain; 1 from 8, 7 remain; 1 from 9, 8 remain; 1 from 10, 9 remain; 1 from 11, 10 remain; 1 from 12, 11 remain.

Then the balls may be worked backwards, beginning at the wire containing 12 balls, saying, take 2 from 12, 10 remain; 2 from 11, 9 remain; 2 from 10, 8 remain; 2 from 9, 7 remain; 2 from 8, 6 remain; 2 from 7, 5 remain; 2 from 6, 4 remain; 2 from 5, 3 remain; 2 from 4, 2 remain; 2 from 3, 1 remain.

The brass figure should be used for the remainder in each case. Say then can you take 8 from 3 as you point to the figures, and they will say " Yes"; but shew them 3 balls on a wire and ask them to deduct 8 from them, when they will perceive their error. Explain that in such a case they must *borrow* one; then say take 8 from 13, placing 12 balls on the top wire, borrow one from the second, and take away eight and they will see the remainder is five; and so on through the sum, and others of the same kind.

In *Multiplication*, the lessons are performed as follows. The teacher moves the first ball, and immediately after the two balls on the second wire, placing them underneath the first, saying at the same time, twice one are two, which the children will readily perceive. We next remove the two balls on the second wire for a multiplier, and then remove two balls from the third wire, placing them exactly under the first two, which forms a square, and then say twice two are four, which every child will discern for himself, as he plainly perceives there are no more. We then move three on the third wire, and place three from the fourth wire underneath them saying, twice three are six. Remove the four on the fourth wire, and four on the fifth, place them as before and say, twice four are eight. Remove five from the fifth wire, and five from the sixth wire underneath them, saying, twice five are ten. Remove six from the sixth wire, and six from the seventh wire underneath them and say, twice six are twelve. Remove seven from the seventh wire, and seven from the eighth wire underneath them, saying, twice seven are fourteen. Remove eight from the eighth wire, and eight from the ninth, saying, twice eight are sixteen. Remove nine on the ninth wire, and nine on the tenth wire, saying, twice nine are eighteen. Remove ten on the tenth wire, and ten on the eleventh underneath them, saying, twice ten are twenty. Remove eleven on the eleventh wire, and eleven on the twelfth, saying, twice eleven are twenty-two. Remove one from the tenth wire to add to the eleven on the eleventh wire, afterwards the remaining ball on the twelfth wire, saying, twice twelve are twenty-four.

Next proceed backwards, saying, 12 times 2 are 24, 11 times 2 are 22, 10 times 2 are 20, &c.

For *Division*, suppose you take from the 144 balls gathered together at one end, one from each row, and place the 12 at the other end, thus making a perpendicular row of ones : then make four perpendicular rows of three each, and the children will see there are 4 3's in 12. Divide the 12 into six parcels, and they will see there are 6 2's in 12. Leave only two out, and they will see, at your direction, that 2 is the sixth part of 12. Take away one of these and they will see one is the twelfth part of 12, and that 12 1's are twelve.

To explain the state of the frame as it appears in the cut, we must first suppose that the twenty-four balls which appear in four lots, are gathered together at the *figured side :* when the children will see there are three perpendicular 8's, and as easily that there are eight horizontal 3's. If then the teacher wishes them to tell how many 6's there are in twenty-four, he moves them out as they appear in the cut, and they see there are four; and the same principle is acted on throughout.

The only remaining branch of numerical knowledge, which consists in an ability to comprehend the powers of numbers, without either visible objects or signs—is imparted as follows :

Addition.

One of the children ascends the rostrum or small pulpit, and repeats aloud, in a kind of chaunt, the whole of the school repeating after him ; One and one are two ; two and one are three ; three and one are four ; &c. up to twelve.

Two and two are four ; four and two are six ; six and two are eight, &c. to twenty-four.

Three and three are six ; six and three are nine ; nine and three are twelve, &c. to thirty-six.

Subtraction.

One from twelve leaves eleven; one from eleven leaves ten, &c.

Two from twenty-four leave twenty-two; two from twenty-two leave twenty, &c.

Multiplication.

Twice one are two; twice two are four; &c. &c.

Three times three are nine, three times four are twelve, &c. &c.

Twelve times two are twenty-four; eleven times two are twenty-two, &c. &c.

Twelve times three are thirty-six; eleven times three are thirty-three, &c. &c. until the whole of the multiplication table is gone through.

Division.

There are twelve twos in twenty-four.—There are eleven twos in twenty-two, &c. &c.

There are twelve threes in thirty-six, &c.

There are twelve fours in forty-eight, &c. &c.

Fractions.

Two are the half ($\frac{1}{2}$) of four.
———————— third ($\frac{1}{3}$) of six.
———————— fourth ($\frac{1}{4}$) of eight.
———————— fifth ($\frac{1}{5}$) of ten.
———————— sixth ($\frac{1}{6}$) of twelve.
——— —— seventh ($\frac{1}{7}$) of fourteen.
———————— twelfth ($\frac{1}{12}$) of twenty-four; two are the eleventh ($\frac{1}{11}$) of twenty-two, &c. &c.

Three are the half ($\frac{1}{2}$) of six.
———————— third ($\frac{1}{3}$) of nine.
———————— fourth ($\frac{1}{4}$) of twelve.

Three are the twelfth ($\frac{1}{12}$) of thirty-six; three are the eleventh ($\frac{1}{11}$) of thirty-three, &c. &c.

Four are the half ($\frac{1}{2}$) of eight, &c.

In twenty-three are four times five, and three-fifths ($\frac{3}{5}$) of five; in thirty-five are four times eight, and three-eighths ($\frac{3}{8}$) of eight.

In twenty-two are seven times three, and one-third ($\frac{1}{3}$) of three.

In thirty-four are four times eight, and one-fourth ($\frac{1}{4}$) of eight.

The tables subjoined are repeated by the same method, each section being a distinct lesson. To give an idea to the reader, the boy in the rostrum says ten shillings the half ($\frac{1}{2}$) of a pound; six shillings and eightpence one-third ($\frac{1}{3}$) of a pound, &c.

Sixpence the half ($\frac{1}{2}$) of a shilling, &c. Always remembering, that whatever the boy says in the rostrum, the other children must repeat after him, but not till the monitor has ended his sentence; and before the monitor delivers the second sentence, he waits till the children have concluded the first, they waiting for him, and he for them; this prevents confusion, and is the means of enabling persons to understand perfectly what is going on in the school.

In a book lately published, which is a compilation by two London masters, it is stated, in the preface, that they were at a loss for proper lessons : had they used those in existence I cannot help thinking they were enough for the capacity of children under six years of age.

Numeration, Addition, Subtraction, Multiplication, Division, and Pence Tables.

ADDITION AND SUBTRACTION TABLE.

1 &	2 &	3 &	4 &	5 &	6 &
1 are 2	1 are 3	1 are 4	1 are 5	1 are 6	1 are 7
2 — 3	2 — 4	2 — 5	2 — 6	2 — 7	2 — 8
3 — 4	3 — 5	3 — 6	3 — 7	3 — 8	3 — 9
4 — 5	4 — 6	4 — 7	4 — 8	4 — 9	4 — 10
5 — 6	5 — 7	5 — 8	5 — 9	5 — 10	5 — 11
6 — 7	6 — 8	6 — 9	6 — 10	6 — 11	6 — 12
7 — 8	7 — 9	7 — 10	7 — 11	7 — 12	7 — 13
8 — 9	8 — 10	8 — 11	8 — 12	8 — 13	8 — 14
9 — 10	9 — 11	9 — 12	9 — 13	9 — 14	9 — 15
10 — 11	10 — 12	10 — 13	10 — 14	10 — 15	10 — 16
11 — 12	11 — 13	11 — 14	11 — 15	11 — 16	11 — 17
12 — 13	12 — 14	12 — 15	12 — 16	12 — 17	12 — 18

7 &	8 &	9 &	10 &	11 &	12 &
1 are 8	1 are 9	1 are 10	1 are 11	1 are 12	1 are 13
2 — 9	2 — 10	2 — 11	2 — 12	2 — 13	2 — 14
3 — 10	3 — 11	3 — 12	3 — 13	3 — 14	3 — 15
4 — 11	4 — 12	4 — 13	4 — 14	4 — 15	4 — 16
5 — 12	5 — 13	5 — 14	5 — 15	5 — 16	5 — 17
6 — 13	6 — 14	6 — 15	6 — 16	6 — 17	6 — 18
7 — 14	7 — 15	7 — 16	7 — 17	7 — 18	7 — 19
8 — 15	8 — 16	8 — 17	8 — 18	8 — 19	8 — 20
9 — 16	9 — 17	9 — 18	9 — 19	9 — 20	9 — 21
10 — 17	10 — 18	10 — 19	10 — 20	10 — 21	10 — 22
11 — 18	11 — 19	11 — 20	11 — 21	11 — 22	11 — 23
12 — 19	12 — 20	12 — 21	12 — 22	12 — 23	12 — 24

MULTIPLICATION AND DIVISION TABLE.

2— 2 are 4	4— 5 are 20	6—12 are 72	
3 — 6	6 — 24	7— 7 — 49	
4 — 8	7 — 28	8 — 56	
5 — 10	8 — 32	9 — 63	
6 — 12	9 — 36	10 — 70	
7 — 14	10 — 40	11 — 77	
8 — 16	11 — 44	12 — 84	
9 — 18	12 — 48	8— 8 — 64	
10 — 20	5— 5 — 25	9 — 72	
11 — 22	6 — 30	10 — 80	
12 — 24	7 — 35	11 — 88	
3— 3 — 9	8 — 40	12 — 96	
4 — 12	9 — 45	9— 9 — 81	
5 — 15	10 — 50	10 — 90	
6 — 18	11 — 55	11 — 99	
7 — 21	12 — 60	12 — 108	
8 — 24	6— 6 — 36	10 10 — 100	
9 — 27	7 — 42	11 — 110	
10 — 30	8 — 48	12 — 120	
11 — 33	9 — 54	11 11 — 121	
12 — 36	10 — 60	12 — 132	
4— 4 — 16	11 — 66	12 12 — 144	

NUMERATION TABLE.

1	Units.
21	Tens.
321	Hundreds.
4,321	Thousands.
54,321	X of Thousands.
654,321	C of Thousands.
7,654,321	Millions.
87,654,321	X of Millions.
987,654,321	C of Thousands.

PENCE TABLE.

d.	s. d.	d.	s. d.
20 is 1 8		90 is 7 6	
30 — 2 6		100 — 8 4	
40 — 3 4		110 — 9 2	
50 — 4 2		120 —10 0	
60 — 5 0		130 —10 10	
70 — 5 10		140 —11 8	
80 — 6 8		144 —12 0	

Tables of Weights and Measures.

Shillings Table.

s.	l.	s.	s.	l.	s.
20 are	1	0	100 are	5	0
30 —	1	10	110 —	5	10
40 —	2	0	120 —	6	0
50 —	2	10	130 —	6	10
60 —	3	0	140 —	7	0
70 —	3	10	150 —	7	10
80 —	4	0	160 —	8	0
90 —	4	10	170 —	8	10

Practice Table.

Of a Pound.

s.	d.		
10	0	are	half
6	8	—	third
5	0	—	fourth
4	0	—	fifth
3	4	—	sixth
2	6	—	eighth
1	8	—	twelfth
1	0	—	twentieth

Of a Shilling.

6d. are		half
4	—	third
3	—	fourth
2	—	sixth
1	—	twelfth

Time.

60 seconds	1 minute
60 minutes	1 hour
24 hours	1 day
7 days	1 week
4 weeks	1 lunar month
12 cal. mon.	1 year

13 lunar months, 1 day, 6 hours, or 365 days, 6 hours, 1 year.

Thirty days hath September,
April, June, & November;
All the rest have thirty-one,
Save February, which alone
Hath twenty-eight, except Leap year,
And twenty-nine is then its share.

Troy Weight.

24 grains	1 pennywt.
20 pennywhts.	1 ounce
12 ounces	1 pound

Avoirdupoise Weight.

16 drams	1 ounce
16 ounces	1 pound
28 pounds	1 quarter
4 quarters	1 hund. wt.
20 hund. wt.	1 ton.

Apothecaries Weight.

20 grains	1 scruple
3 scruples	1 dram
8 drams	1 ounce
12 ounces	1 pound

Wool Weight.

7 pounds	1 clove
2 cloves	1 stone
2 stones	1 tod
6½ tods	1 wey
2 weys	1 sack
12 sacks	1 last

Wine Measure.

2 pints	1 quart
4 quarts	1 gallon
10 gallons	1 ank. bndy.
42 gallons	1 tierce
63 gallons	1 hogshead
84 gallons	1 puncheon
2 hogsheads	1 pipe
2 pipes	1 ton

Ale & Beer Measure.

2 pints	1 quart
4 quarts	1 gallon
8 gallons	1 firkin of ale
9 gallons	1 firk. of beer
2 firkins	1 kilderkin
2 kilderkins	1 barrel
1½ barrel	1 hogshead
2 barrels	1 puncheon
3 barrels	1 butt

Coal Measure.

4 pecks	1 bushel
9 bushels	1 vat or strike
3 bushels	1 sack
12 sacks	1 chaldron
21 chaldron	1 score

Dry Measure.

2 pints	1 quart
2 quarts	1 pottle
2 pottles	1 gallon
2 gallons	1 peck
4 pecks	1 bushel
2 bushels	1 strike
5 bushels	1 sack flour
8 bushels	1 quarter
5 quarters	1 wey or load
5 pecks	1 bshl. water measure
4 bushels	1 coom
10 cooms	1 wey
2 weys	1 last corn

Solid or Cubic Measure.

1728 inches	1 foot
27 feet	1 yard or ld.

Long Measure.

3 barleycorns	1 inch
12 inches	1 foot
3 feet	1 yard
6 feet	1 fathom
5½ yards	1 pole or rod
40 poles	1 furlong
8 furlongs	1 mile
3 miles	1 league
20 leagues	1 degree

Cloth Measure

2¼ inches	1 nail
4 nails	1 quarter
4 quarters	1 yard
5 quarters	1 English ell
3 quarters	1 Flemish ell
6 quarters	1 French ell

Land or Square Meas.

144 inches	1 foot
3 feet	1 yard
30¼ yards	1 pole
40 poles	1 rood
4 roods	1 acre
640 acres	1 mile

This includes length and breadth.

Hay.

36 pounds	1 trs. of straw
56 pounds	do. of old hay
60 pounds	1 do of new
36 trusses	1 load

MONEY.

Two farthings one halfpenny make,
A penny four of such will take ;
And to allow I am most willing
That twelve pence always make a shilling ;
And that five shillings make a crown,
Twenty a sovereign, the same as pound.
Some have no cash, some have to spare—
Some who have wealth for none will care.
Some through misfortune's hand brought low,
Their money gone, are filled with woe,
But I know better than to grieve ;
If I have none I will not thieve ;
I'll be content whate'er 's my lot,
Nor for misfortunes care a *groat*.
There is a Providence whose care,
And sovereign love I crave to share ;
His love is *gold without alloy* ;
Those who possess 't have *endless joy*.

TIME OR CHRONOLOGY.

Sixty seconds make a minute ;
    Time enough to tie my shoe :
Sixty minutes make an hour ;
    Shall it pass and nought to do ?

Twenty-four hours will make a day ;
    Too much time to spend in sleep,
Too much time to spend in play,
    For seven days will end the week.

Fifty and two such weeks will put
    Near an end to every year ;
Days three hundred sixty-five
    Are the whole that it can share.

Except in leap year, when one day
   Added is to gain lost time ;
May it not be spent in play,
   Nor in any evil crime.

Time is short, we often say ;
   Let us, then, improve it well ;
That eternally we may
   Live where happy angels dwell.

AVOIRDUPOISE WEIGHT.

Sixteen drachms are just an ounce,
   As you 'll find at any shop ;
Sixteen ounces make a pound,
   Should you want a mutton chop.

'l'wenty-eight pounds are the fourth
   Of an hundred weight call'd gross ;
Four such quarters are the whole
   Of an hundred weight at most.

    Oh! how delightful,
    Oh! how delightful,
    Oh! how delightful,
    To sing this rule.

Twenty hundred make a ton ;
   By this rule all things are sold
That have any waste or dross :
   And are bought so, too, I 'm told.

When we buy and when we sell
   We do it in our Maker's sight,
Whose laws command, you all know well,
   That we should practice what is right.

    Oh! how delightful,
      &c., &c., &c.

T

APOTHECARIES' WEIGHT.

Twenty grains make a scruple,—some scruple to take,
Though at times it is needful, just for our health's sake;
Three scruples one drachm, eight drachms make one ounce,
Twelve ounces one pound, for the pestle to pounce.
By this rule is all medicine mix'd, though I 'm told
By Avoirdupoise weight 'tis bought and 'tis sold.
But the best of all physic, if I may advise,
Is temperate living and good exercise.

DRY MEASURE.

Two pints will make one quart
   Of barley, oats, or rye;
Two quarts one pottle are, of wheat
   Or any thing that 's dry.

Two pottles do one gallon make,
   Two gallons one peck fair,
Four pecks one bushel, heap or brim,
   Eight bushels one quarter are.

If, when you sell, you give
   Good measure shaken down,
Through motives good, you will receive
   An everlasting crown.

ALE AND BEER MEASURE.

Two pints will make one quart,
   Four quarts one gallon, strong:—
Some drink but little, some too much,—
   To drink too much is wrong.

Eight gallons one firkin make,
   Of liquor that 's call'd ale:
Nine gallons one firkin of beer,
   Whether 'tis mild or stale.

With gallons fifty-four,
   A hogshead I can fill :
But hope I never shall drink much,
   Drink much whoever will.

WINE, OIL, AND SPIRIT MEASURE.

Two pints will make one quart
   Of any wine, I 'm told :
Four quarts one gallon are of port
   Or claret, new or old.

Forty-two gallons will
   A tierce fill to the bung :
And sixty-three 's a hogshead full
   Of brandy, oil, or rum.

Eighty-four gallons make
   One puncheon fill'd to brim
Two hogsheads make one pipe or butt,
   Two pipes will make one tun.

A little wine within
   Oft cheers the mind that 's sad ;
But too much brandy, rum, or gin,
   No doubt is very bad.

From all excess beware,
   Which sorrow must attend ;
Drunkards a life of woe must share,—
   When time with them shall end.

———

The arithmeticon, I would just remark, may be applied to *geometry*. Round, square, oblong, &c. &c., may be easily taught. It may also be used in teaching *geography*. The shape of the earth may be shewn by a ball, the surface by the outside, its revolution on its axis by turning it round, and the idea of day and night may be given. by a ball and a candle in a dark room.

As the construction and application of this instrument is the result of personal, long-continued, and anxious effort, and as I have rarely seen a pirated one made properly or understood, I may express a hope that whenever it is wanted either for schools or nurseries, application will be made for it to my depot.

I have only to add, that a board is placed at the back to keep the children from seeing the balls, except as they are put out; and that the brass figures at the side are intended to assist the master when he is called away, so that he may see, on returning to the frame, where he left off.

CHAPTER XI.

FORM, POSITION, AND SIZE.

———

" Geometry is eminently serviceable to improve and strengthen
the intellectual faculties."—*Jones.*

———

AMONG the novel features of the Infant School
system, that of geometrical lessons is the most
peculiar. How it happened that a mode of instruction so evidently calculated for the infant mind
was so long overlooked, I cannot imagine; and it
is still more surprising, that, having been once
thought of, there should be any doubt as to its
utility. Certain it is that the various forms of
bodies is one of the first items of natural education,
and we cannot err when treading in the steps of
Nature. It is undeniable that geometrical knowledge is of great service in many of the mechanic
arts, and, therefore, proper to be taught children who
are likely to be employed in some of those arts;
but, independently of this, we cannot adopt a better
method of exciting and strengthening their powers

T 3

of observation. I have seen a thousand instances, moreover, in the conduct of the children, which have assured me, that it is a very pleasing as well as useful branch of instruction. The children, being taught the first elements of form, and the terms used to express the various figures of bodies, find in its application to objects around them an inexhaustible source of amusement. Streets, houses, rooms, fields, ponds, plates, dishes, tables,—in short, every thing they see, calls for observation, and affords an opportunity for the application of their geometrical knowledge. Let it not, then, be said that it is beyond their capacity—for it is the simplest and most comprehensible to them of all knowledge;—let it not be said that it is useless, since its application to the useful arts is great and indisputable; nor let it be asserted that it is unpleasing to them, since it has been shewn to add greatly to their happiness.

It is essential in this, as in every other branch of education, to begin with the first principles, and proceed *slowly* to their application, and the complicated forms arising therefrom. The next thing is to promote that application of which we have before spoken, to the various objects around them. It is this, and this alone, which forms the distinction between a school lesson and practical knowledge; and so far will the children be found from being averse from this exertion, that it makes the acquirement of knowledge a pleasure instead of a task. With these prefatory remarks I shall introduce a description of the method I have pursued, and a few examples of geometrical lessons.

We will suppose that the whole of the children

are seated in the gallery, and that the teacher (provided with a brass instrument formed for the purpose, which is merely a series of joints like those to a counting-house candlestick, from which I borrowed the idea, and which may be altered as required, in a moment) points to a strait line, asking, What is this? *A.* A strait line. *Q.* Why did you not call it a crooked line? *A.* Because it is not crooked, but strait. *Q.* What are these? *A.* Curved lines. *Q.* What do curved lines mean? *A.* When they are bent or crooked. *Q.* What are these? *A.* Parallel strait lines. *Q.* What does parallel mean? *A.* Parallel means when they are equally distant from each other in every part. *Q.* If any of you children were reading a book that gave an account of some town which had twelve streets, and it said the streets were parallel, would you understand what it meant? *A.* Yes; it would mean that the streets were all the same way, side by side, like the lines which we now see. *Q.* What are those? *A.* Diverging or converging strait lines. *Q.* What is the difference between diverging and converging lines and parallel lines? *A.* Diverging or converging lines are not at an equal distance from each other, in every part, but parallel lines are. *Q.* What does diverge mean? *A.* Diverge means when they go from each other, and they diverge at one end and converge at the other.* *Q.* What does converge mean? *A.* Converge means when they come towards each other. *Q.* Suppose the lines were

---

* Desire the children to hold up two fingers, keeping them apart, and they will perceive they diverge at top and converge at bottom.

longer, what would be the consequence? *A.* Please sir, if they were longer, they would meet together at the end they converge. *Q.* What would they form by meeting together? *A.* By meeting together they would form an angle. *Q.* What kind of an angle? *A.* An acute angle? *Q.* Would they form an angle at the other end? *A.* No; they would go further from each other. *Q.* What is this? *A.* A perpendicular line. *Q.* What does perpendicular mean? *A.* A line up strait, like the stem of some trees. *Q.* If you look, you will see that one end of the line comes on the middle of another line; what does it form? *A.* The one which we now see forms two right angles. *Q.* I will make a strait line, and one end of it shall lean on another strait line, but instead of being upright like the perpendicular line, you see that it is sloping. What does it form? *A.* One side of it is an acute angle, and the other side is an obtuse angle. *Q.* Which side is the obtuse angle? *A.* That which is the most open. *Q.* And which is the acute angle? *A.* That which is the least open. *Q.* What does acute mean? *A.* When the angle is sharp. *Q.* What does obtuse mean? *A.* When the angle is less sharp than the right angle. *Q.* If I were to call any one of you an acute child, would you know what I meant? *A.* Yes, sir; one that looks out sharp, and tries to think, and pays attention to what is said to him; then you would say he was an acute child.

Equi-lateral Triangle.

Q. What is this? *A.* An equi-lateral triangle. *Q.* Why is it called equi-lateral? *A.* Because its sides are all equal. *Q.* How many sides has it? *A.* Three sides. *Q.* How many angles has it? *A.* Three angles. *Q.* What do you mean by angles? *A.* The space between two right lines, drawn gradually nearer to each other, till they meet in a point. *Q.* And what do you call the point where the two lines meet? *A.* The angular point. *Q.* Tell me why you call it a tri-angle? *A.* We call it a tri-angle, because it has three angles. *Q.* What do you mean by equal? *A.* When the three sides are of the same length. *Q.* Have you any thing else to observe upon this? *A.* Yes, all its angles are acute.

Isoceles Triangle.

Q. What is this? *A.* An acute-angled isoceles triangle. *Q.* What does acute mean? *A.* When the angles are sharp. *Q.* Why is it called an isoceles triangle? *A.* Because only two of its sides are equal. *Q.* How many sides has it? *A.* Three, the same as the other. *Q.* Are there any other kind of isoceles triangles? *A.* Yes, there are right angled and obtuse-angled.

[Here the other triangles are to be shewn, and the master must explain to the children the meaning of right-angled and obtuse-angled.]

Scalene Triangle.

Q. What is this? *A.* An acute-angled scalene triangle. *Q.* Why is it called an acute-angled scalene tri-angle? *A.* Because all its angles are acute, and its sides are not equal. *Q.* Why is it called scalene? *A.* Because it has all its sides *unequal*. *Q.* Are there any other kind of scalene triangles? *A.* Yes, there is a right-angled scalene triangle, which has one right angle. *Q.* What else? *A.* An obtuse-angled scalene triangle, which has one obtuse-angle. *Q.* Can an acute triangle be an equi-lateral triangle? *A.* Yes, it may be equi-lateral, isoceles, or scalene. *Q.* Can a right-angled tri-angle, or an obtuse-angled tri-angle, be an equilateral? *A.* No; it must either be an isoceles or a scalene tri-angle.

Square.

Q. What is this? *A.* A square. *Q.* Why is it called a square? *A.* Because all its angles are right angles, and its sides are equal. *Q.* How many angles has it? *A.* Four angles. *Q.* What would it make if we draw a line from one angle to the opposite one? *A.* Two right-angled isoceles triangles. *Q.* What would you call the line that we drew from one angle to the other? *A.* A diagonal. *Q.* Suppose we draw another line from the other two angles. *A.* Then it would make four triangles.

Pent-agon.

Q. What is this? *A.* A regular pentagon. *Q.* Why is it called a pentagon? *A.* Because it has five sides and five angles. *Q.* Why is it called regular? *A.* Because its sides and angles are equal. *Q.* What does pentagon mean? *A.* A five-sided figure. *Q.* Are there any other kinds of pentagons? *A.* Yes, irregular pentagons. *Q.* What does irregular mean? *A.* When the sides and angles are not equal.

Hex-agons.

Q. What is this? *A.* A hexagon. *Q.* Why is it

called a hexagon? *A.* Because it has six sides and six angles. *Q.* What does hexagon mean? *A.* A six-sided figure. *Q.* Are there more than one sort of hexagons? *A.* Yes, there are regular and irregular. *Q.* What is a regular hexagon? *A.* When the sides and angles are all equal. *Q.* What is an irregular hexagon? *A.* When the sides and angles are not equal.

Hepta-gon.

Q. What is this? *A.* A regular heptagon. *Q.* Why is it called an heptagon? *A.* Because it has seven sides and seven angles. *Q.* Why is it called a regular heptagon? *A.* Because its sides and angles are equal. *Q.* What does a heptagon mean? *A.* A seven-sided figure. *Q.* What is an irregular heptagon? *A.* A seven-sided figure, whose sides are not equal.

Octa-gon.

Q. What is this? *A.* A regular octagon. *Q.* Why is it called a regular octagon? *A.* Because it has eight sides and eight angles, and they are all equal. *Q.* What does an octagon mean? *A.* An eight-sided figure. *Q.* What is an irregular octagon? *A.* An eight-sided figure, whose sides and angles are not all equal. *Q.* What does an octave mean? *A.* Eight notes in music.

Nona-gon.

Q. What is this? *A.* A nonagon. *Q.* Why is it called a nonagon? *A.* Because it has nine sides and nine angles. *Q.* What does a nonagon mean?

A. A nine-sided figure. *Q.* What is an irregular no-nagon? *A.* A nine-sided figure whose sides and angles are not equal.

Deca-gon.

Q. What is this? *A.* A regular deca-gon. *Q.* What does a decagon mean? *A.* A ten-sided figure. *Q.* Why is it called a decagon? *A.* Because it has ten sides and ten angles, and there are both regular and irregular decagons.

Rect-angle or Oblong.

Q. What is this? *A.* A rectangle or oblong. *Q.* How many sides and angles has it? *A.* Four, the same as a square. *Q.* What is the difference between a rect-angle and a square? *A.* A rectangle has two long sides, and the other two are much shorter, but a square has its sides equal.

Rhomb.

Q. What is this? *A.* A rhomb. *Q.* What is the difference between a rhomb and a rectangle? *A.* The sides of the rhomb are equal, but the sides of the rectangle are not all equal. *Q.* Is there any other difference? *A.* Yes, the angles of the rectangle are equal, but the rhomb has only its opposite angles equal.

Rhomboid.

Q. What is this? *A.* A rhomboid. *Q.* What is the difference between a rhomb and a rhomboid. *A.* The sides of the rhomboid are not equal, nor yet its angles, but the sides of the rhomb are equal.

Trapezoid.

Q. What is this. *A.* A trapezoid. *Q.* How many sides has it? *A.* Four sides and four angles, but it has only two of its angles equal, which are opposite to each other.

Tetragon.

Q. What do we call these figures that have four sides. *A.* Tetragons, *tetra* meaning four. *Q.* Are they called by any other name? *A.* Yes, they are called quadri-laterals, or quadr-angles. *Q.* How many regular tetragons are among those we have mentioned? *A.* One, and that is the square, all the others are irregular tetragons, because their sides and angles are not all equal. *Q.* By what name would you call the whole of the figures on this board? *A.* Polygons; those that have their sides and angles equal we would call regular polygons. *Q.* What would you call those angles whose sides were not equal? *A.* Irregular polygons, and the smallest number of sides a polygon can have is three, and the number of corners are always equal to the number of sides.

Ellipse or Oval.

Q. What is this? *A.* An ellipse or an oval. *Q.* What shape is the top or crown of my hat? *A.* Circular. *Q.* What shape is that part which comes on my forehead and the back part of my head? *A.* Oval.

The other polygons are taught the children in rotation, in the same simple manner, all tending to please and edify them.

U

The following is sung :—

> Horizontal, perpendicular,
> Horizontal, perpendicular,
> Parallel, parallel,
> Parallel lines,
> Diverging, converging, diverging lines,
> Diverging, converging, diverging lines.
>
> Spreading wider, or expansion,
> Drawing nearer, or contraction,
> Falling, rising,
> Slanting, crossing,
> Convex, concave, curved lines,
> Convex, concave, curved lines.
>
> Here's a wave line, there's an angle,
> Here's a wave line, there's an angle;
> An ellipsis,
> Or an oval,
> A semicircle half way round,
> Then a circle wheeling round.

Some amusing circumstances have occurred from the knowledge of form thus acquired.

"D'ye ken, Mr. Wilderspin," said a child at Glasgow one day, "that we have an oblong table: it's made o' deal? four sides, four corners, twa lang sides, and twa short anes; corners mean angles, and angles mean corners. My brother ga'ed himsel sic a clink o' the eye against ane at hame; but ye ken there was nane that could tell the shape o' the thing that did it !"

A little boy was watching his mother making pancakes and wishing they were all done; when, after various observations as to their comparative goodness with and without sugar, he exclaimed, "I wonder which are best, *elliptical* pan-cakes or *circular* ones !" As this was Greek to the mother she turned round with "What d'ye say ?" When the child repeated the observation. "Bless the child!" said the astonished parent, "What odd things ye are always saying; what can you mean by liptical pan-cakes? Why, you little fool, don't you know they are made of flour and eggs, and did you not see me put the milk into the large pan and stir all up together ?" "Yes," said the little fellow, "I know what they are made of, and I know what bread is made of, but that is'nt the shape; indeed, indeed, mother, they are *elliptical pan-cakes,* because they are made in an *elliptical frying-pan.*" An old soldier who lodged in the house, was now called down by the mother, and he decided that the child was right, and far from being what, in her surprize and alarm, she took him to be.

On another occasion a little girl had been taken to market by her mother, where she was struck by the sight of the carcases of six sheep recently killed, and said, "Mother, what are these?" The reply was, "Dead sheep, dead sheep, don't bother." "They are suspended, perpendicular, and parallels," rejoined the child. "What? What?" was then the question. "Why, mother," was the child's answer, "don't you see they hang up, that's suspended ; they are straight up, that's perpendicular ; and they are at equal distances, that's parallel."

The idea of *size* is necessary to a correct apprehension of objects. To talk of yards, feet, or inches, to a child, unless they are shewn, is just as intelligible

as miles, leagues, or degrees.   Let there then be two
five-feet rods, a black foot and a white foot alternately, the bottom foot marked in inches, and let
there be a horizontal piece to slide up and down to
mark various heights.   Thus, when the height of a
lion, or elephant, &c. &c. is mentioned, it may be
shewn by the rod; while the girth may be exhibited
by a piece of *cord,* which should always be ready.
Long measure is taught as follows :

> Take barley-corns of mod'rate length,
>   And three you'll find will make an inch ;
> Twelve inches make a foot ;—if strength
>   Permit, I'll leap it and not flinch.
> Three feet's a yard, as understood
>   By those possessed with sense and soul ;
> Five feet and half will make a rood,
>   And also make a perch or pole.
> Oh how pretty, wonderously pretty,
>   Every rule
>   We learn at school
> Is wonderously pretty.
>
> Forty such poles a furlong make,
>   And eight such furlongs make a mile,
> O'er hedge, or ditch, or seas, or lake ;
>   O'er railing, fence, or gate, or stile.
> Three miles a league, by sea or land,
>   And twenty leagues are one degree ;
> Just four times ninety degrees a band
>   Will make to girt the earth and sea.
> Oh how pretty, &c.
>
> But what's the girth of hell or heav'n ?
>   (No natural thought or eye can see,)
> To neither girth or length is given ;
>   'Tis without space—Immensity.

Still shall the good and truly wise,
  The seat of heaven with safety find;
Because 'tis seen with inward eyes,
  And first resides within their mind.

Oh how pretty, &c.

Whatever can be shewn by the rod should be, and I entreat teachers not to neglect this part of their duty. If the tables be merely learnt, the children will be no wiser than before.

CHAPTER XII.

GEOGRAPHY.

" From sea to sea from realm to realm I rove."—*Tickell.*

GEOGRAPHY is to children a delightful study. We give some idea of it at an early period in Infant Schools, by singing, " London is the capital, the capital, the capital, London is the capital, the capital of England," and other capitals in the same way; and also by pictures of the costumes of the various people of the world. To teach the four quarters of the globe, we tell children the different points of the play-ground, and then send them to the eastern, western, northern, or southern quarters, as we please. A weathercock should also be placed at the top of the School, and every favourable day opportunities should be seized by the teachers to give practical instruction upon it.

Sacred geography is of great importance, and children are much pleased at finding out the spots visited by our Saviour, or the route of the apostle Paul.

THE EARTH.

The earth, on which we all now live,
Is call'd a globe—its shape I'll give;
If in your pocket you've a ball,
You have its shape,—but that's not all;
For land and water it contains,
And presently I'll give their names.
The quarters are called, Africa,
Europe, Asia, and America;
These contain straits, oceans, seas,
Continents, promontories.
Islands, rivers, gulfs, or bays,
Isthmuses, peninsulas.
Each divides or separates
Nations, kingdoms, cities, states,
Mountains, forests, hills, and dales,
Dreary deserts, rocks, and vales.

In forests, deserts, hills, and plains,
    Where feet have never trod,
There still in mighty power, he reigns,
    An ever-present God.

THE CARDINAL POINTS.

The *east* is where the sun doth rise
Each morning, in the glorious skies;
Full *west* he sets, or hides his head,
And points to us the time for bed.
He's in the *south* at dinner time;
The *north* is facing to a line.

CHAPTER XIII.

PICTURES AND CONVERSATION.

———

" The parents of Dr. Doddridge brought him up in the early knowledge of religion. Before he could read, his mother taught him the histories of the Old and New Testament, by the assistance of some Dutch tiles in the chimney of the room where they usually sat; and accompanied her instructions with such wise and pious reflections, as made strong and lasting impressions upon his heart."—*See his Life.*

———

To give the children general information, it has been found advisable to have recourse to pictures of natural history, such as of birds, beasts, fishes, flowers, insects, &c. all of which tend to shew the glory of God; and as colours attract the attention of children as soon as anything, they eagerly inquire what such a thing is, and this gives the teacher an opportunity of instructing them to great advantage; for when a child of his own free will eagerly desires to be informed, he is sure to profit by the information then imparted.

We use also pictures of public buildings, and of the different trades; by the former, the children acquire much information, from the explanations which are given to them of the use of the buildings, in what year they were built, &c.; whilst by the latter, we are enabled to find out the bias of a child's inclination. Some would like to be shoe-makers, others builders, others weavers, others brewers, &c.; in short it is both pleasing and edifying to hear the children give answers to the different questions. I remember one little boy, who said he should like to be a doctor; and when asked why he made choice of that profession in preference to any other, his answer was, "Because he should like to cure all the sick people." If parents did but study the inclinations of their children a little more, I humbly conceive, that there would be more eminent men in every profession than there are. It is great imprudence to determine what business children shall be of before their tempers and inclinations are well known. Every one is best in his own profession—and this should not be determined on rashly and carelessly.

But as it is possible that a person may be very clever in his business or profession, and yet not be a Christian, it has been thought necessary to direct the children's attention particularly to the Scriptures. Many difficulties lie in our way; the principal one arises not from their inability to read the Bible, nor from their inability to comprehend it, but from the apathy of the heart to its divine principles and precepts. Some parents, indeed, are quite delighted if their children can read a chapter or two in the Bible, and think that when they can do this, they have arrived at the summit of knowledge, without once considering whether they understand a single sentence of what they read, or whether if they understand it, they *feel* its truth and importance. And how can it be expected that they should do either, when no ground-work has been laid at the time when they received their first impressions and imbibed their first ideas? Every one comes into the world without ideas, yet with a capacity to receive knowledge of every kind, and is therefore capable, to a certain extent, of becoming intelligent and wise. An infant would take hold of the most poisonous reptile, that might sting him to death in an instant; or attempt to stroke the lion with as little fear as he would the lamb; in short, he is incapable of distinguishing a friend from a foe. And yet so wonderfully is man formed by his adorable Creator, that he is capable of increasing his knowledge, and advancing towards perfection to all eternity, without ever being able to arrive at it.

I am the ardent friend of *religious* education, but what I thus denominate I must proceed to explain; because of the errors that abound on this subject. Much that bears the name is altogether unworthy of it. Moral and religious sentiments may be written as copies; summaries of truth, admirable in themselves, may be deposited in the memory; chapter after chapter too may be repeated by rote, and yet, after all, the slightest salutary influence may not be exerted on the mind or the heart. These may resemble " the way-side " in the parable, on which the fowls of the air devoured the corn as soon as it was sown; and hence those plans should be devised and pursued from which we may anticipate a harvest of real good. On these, however, my limits will only allow a few hints.

As soon as possible, I would have a distinction made between the form and power of religion; between the grimaces and long-facedness so injurious to multitudes, and that principle of supreme love to God which he alone can implant in the heart. I would exhibit too that " good will to man " which the gospel urges and inspires, which regards the human race apart from all the circumstances of clime, colour, or grade; and which has a special reference to those who are most necessitous. And how can this be done more hopefully than by inculcating, in dependance on the divine blessing, the history, sermons, and parables of our Lord Jesus Christ; and by the simple, affectionate, and faithful illustration and enforcement of other parts of holy writ? The Infant System, therefore, includes a considerable number of scripture lessons, of which the following are specimens :—

Joseph and his Brethren.

The following method is adopted :—The picture being suspended against the wall, and one class of the children standing opposite to it, the master repeats the following passages : " And Joseph dreamed a dream, and he told it to his brethren; and they hated him yet the more. And he said unto them, Hear, I pray you, the dream which I have dreamed ; for behold, we were binding sheaves in the field, and lo ! my sheaf arose and also stood upright ; and behold, your sheaves stood round about, and made obeisance to my sheaf."

The teacher being provided with a pointer, will point to the picture, and put the following questions, or such as he may think better, to the children :—

Q. What is this ? A. Joseph's first dream. Q. What is a dream ? A. When you dream,. you see things during the time of sleep. Q. Did any of you ever dream any thing?

Here the children will repeat what they have dreamed ; perhaps something like the following :— Please sir, once I dreamed I was in a garden. Q. What did you see? A. I saw flowers and such nice apples. Q. How do you know it was a dream? A. Because, when I awoke, I found I was in bed.

During this recital the children will listen very attentively, for they are highly pleased to hear each other's relations. The master having satisfied himself that the children, in some measure, understand the nature of a dream, he may proceed as follows :—

Q. What did Joseph dream about first ? A. He dreamed that his brother's sheaves made obeisance to his sheaf. Q. What is a sheaf? A. A bundle of corn. Q. What do you understand by making obeisance ? A To bend your body, which we call making a bow. Q. What is binding sheaves ? A. To bind them, which they do with a band of twisted straw. Q. How many brothers had Joseph? A. Eleven. Q. What was Joseph's father's name ? A. Jacob, he is also sometimes called Israel.

Master.— And it is further written concerning Joseph, that he dreamed yet another dream, and told it to his brethren, and said, Behold, I have dreamed a dream more ; and behold the sun and the moon and the eleven stars made obeisance to me.

Q. What do you understand by the sun? A. The

sun is that bright object in the sky which shines in the day-time, and which gives us heat and light. *Q.* Who made the sun? *A.* Almighty God. *Q.* For what purpose did God make the sun? *A.* To warm and nourish the earth and every thing upon it. *Q.* What do you mean by the earth? *A.* The ground on which we walk, and on which the corn, trees, and flowers grow. *Q.* What is it that makes them grow? *A.* The heat and light of the sun. *Q.* Does it require any thing else to make them grow? *A.* Yes; rain, and the assistance of Almighty God. *Q.* What is the moon? *A.* That object which is placed in the sky, and shines in the night, and appears larger than the stars. *Q.* What do you mean by the stars? *A.* Those bright objects that appear in the sky at night. *Q.* What are they? *A.* Some of them are worlds, and others are suns to give them light. *Q.* Who placed them there? *A.* Almighty God. *Q.* Should we fear and love him for his goodness? *A.* Yes; and for his mercy towards us. *Q.* Do you think it wonderful that God should make all these things? *A.* Yes. *Q.* Are there any more things that are wonderful to you? *A.* Yes;—

> Where'er we turn our wondering eyes,
>   His power and skill we see;
> Wonders on wonders grandly rise,
>   And speak the Deity.

Q. Who is the Deity? *A.* Almighty God.

Nothing can be a greater error, than to allow the children to use the name of God on every trifling occasion: whenever it is necessary, it should, in my opinion, be commenced with Almighty first, both by teacher and scholars. I am convinced, from what

I have seen in many places, that the frequent repetition of his holy name has a very injurious effect.

Solomon's Wise Judgment.

Q. What is this? *A.* A picture of Solomon's wise judgment. *Q.* Describe what you mean? *A.* Two women stood before king Solomon. *Q.* Did the women say any thing to the king when they came before him? *A.* Yes; one woman said, O my Lord, I and this woman dwell in one house, and I had a child there, and this woman had a child also, and this woman's child died in the night. *Q.* To whom did the women speak when they said, O my Lord? *A.* To king Solomon. *Q.* What did the woman mean when she said, we dwell in one house? *A.* She meant that they both lived in it. *Q.* Did the woman say any thing more to the king? *A.* Yes; she said the other woman rose at midnight, and took her son from her. *Q.* What is meant by midnight? *A.* Twelve o'clock, or the middle of the night. *Q.* What did the other woman say in her defence? *A.* She said the live child was hers, and the other said it is mine; this they spake before the king. *Q.* When the king heard what the women had to say, what did he do? *A.* He said bring me a sword; and they brought a sword before the king. *Q.* Did the king do any thing with the sword? *A.* No; he said divide the child in two, and give half to the one, and half to the other. *Q.* What did the women say to that? *A.* One said, O my Lord, give her the living child, and in nowise slay it; but the other said, let it be neither mine nor thine, but divide it. *Q.* What took place next? *A.* The king answered and said,

Give her the living child, and in nowise slay it, she is the mother thereof. *Q.* What is meant by slaying? *A.* To kill any thing. *Q.* To which woman was the child given? *A.* To the woman that said do not hurt it. *Q.* What is the reason that it was called a wise judgment? *A.* Because Solomon took a wise method to find it out. *Q.* Did the people hear of it? *A.* Yes, all Israel heard of it, and they feared the king, for they saw that the wisdom of God was in him to do judgment. *Q.* What is meant by all Israel? *A.* All the people over whom Solomon was king. *Q.* If we want to know any more about Solomon where can we find it? *A.* In the third chapter of the first book of Kings.

Incidental conversation.—*Q.* Now my little children, as we have been talking about king Solomon, suppose we talk about our own king; so let me ask you his name? *A.* King William the Fourth. *Q.* Why is he called king? *A.* Because he is the head man, and the governor of the nation. *Q.* What does governor mean? *A.* One that governs the people, the same as you govern and manage us. *Q.* Why does the king wear a crown on his head? *A.* To denote that he governs from a principle of wisdom, proceeding from love. *Q.* Why does he hold a sceptre in his hand? *A.* To denote that he is powerful, and that he governs from a principle of truth. *Q.* What is a crown? *A.* A thing made of gold, ovelaid with a number of diamonds and precious stones, which are very scarce? *Q.* What is a sceptre? *A.* A thing made of gold, and something like an officer's staff. *Q.* What is an officer? *A.* A person who acts in the king's name; and there are various

x 2

sorts of officers, naval officers, military officers, and civil officers. *Q.* What is a naval officer? *A.* A person who governs the sailors and tells them what to do. *Q.* What is a military officer. *A.* A person who governs the soldiers and tells them what to do. *Q.* What does a naval officer and his sailors do. *A.* Defend us from our enemies on the sea. *Q.* What does a military officer and his soldiers do? *A.* Defend us from our enemies on land. *Q.* Who do you call enemies? *A.* Persons that wish to hurt us and do us harm. *Q.* What does a civil officer do? *A.* Defend us from our enemies at home. *Q.* What do you mean by enemies at home. *A.* Thieves, and all bad men and women. *Q.* Have we any other enemies besides these? *A.* Yes, the enemies of our own household, as we may read in the Bible, and they are the worst of all. *Q.* What do you mean by the enemies of our own household? *A.* Our bad thoughts and bad inclinations. *Q.* Who protects and defends us from these? *A.* Almighty God. *Q.* Are there any other kind of officers besides these we have mentioned? *A.* Yes, a great many more, such as the king's ministers, the noblemen and gentlemen in both houses of parliament, and the judges of the land. *Q.* What do the king's ministers do. *A.* Give the king advice when he wants it. *Q.* And what do the noblemen and gentlemen do in both houses of parliament? *A.* Make laws to govern us, protect us, and make us happy. *Q.* After they have made the laws, who do they take them to? *A.* To the king. *Q.* What do they take them to the king for? *A.* To ask him if he will be pleased to approve of them. *Q.* What are laws? *A.* Good rules for the people to go

by, the same as we have rules in our school to go by.
Q. Suppose the people break these good rules, what
is the consequence? *A.* They are taken before the
judges, and afterwards sent to prison. *Q.* Who
takes them before the judge? *A.* A constable, and
afterwards he takes them to prison, and there they
are locked up and punished. *Q.* Ought we to love
the king? *A.* Yes, and respect his officers. *Q.*
Do you suppose the king ever prays to God?
A. Yes, every day. *Q.* What does he pray for?
A. That God would be pleased to make him a wise
and good man, so that he may make all his people
happy. *Q.* What do the Scriptures say about the
king? *A.* They say that we are to fear God and
honour the king. *Q.* Who was the wisest king? *A.*
King Solomon. *Q.* How did he become the wisest
king? *A.* He asked God to give him wisdom to
govern his kingdom well; and God granted his request. *Q.* Will God give our king wisdom? *A.*
Yes, he will give him what is best for him. It says
in the Bible, if any man lack wisdom let him ask of
God, for he giveth to all men liberally, and upbraideth
not. *Q.* What is the best book to learn wisdom
from? *A.* The Bible. *Q.* Is the queen mentioned
in the Bible? *A.* Yes; it is said queens shall be
thy nursing mothers. *Q.* Who came to Solomon besides the two women? *A.* The queen of Sheba, she
came to ask him questions. *Q.* When he answered
her questions what happened? *A.* The queen was so
much delighted with his wisdom, that she gave him
a hundred and twenty talents of gold, and spices in
abundance. *Q.* How much is one talent of gold
worth? *A.* Five thousand, four hundred, and se-

venty-five sovereigns.   *Q.* Did she give him any thing more ?   *A.* Yes, she gave him precious stones. *Q.* What are precious stones ?   *A.* Diamonds, jasper, sapphire, chalcedony, emerald, sardonyx, sardius, chrysolite, beryl, topaz, chrysoprasus, jacinth, amethyst.   *Q.* Did king Solomon give the queen of Sheba any thing ?   *A.* Yes, he gave her whatsoever she desired, besides that which she brought with her. *Q.* Where did she go ?   *A.* She went away to her own land.   *Q.* What part of the Bible is this ?   *A.* The ninth chapter of the second book of Chronicles. *Master.* The queen is mentioned in other places in the Bible, and another day I will tell in what parts.

The Nativity of Jesus Christ.

The picture being suspended as the others, and a whole class being in the class-room, put the pointer into one of the children's hands, and desire the child to find out the Nativity of Jesus Christ.   The other children will be on the tip-toe of expectation, to see whether the child makes a mistake ; for, should this be the case, they know that one of them will have the same privilege of trying to find it ; should the child happen to touch the wrong picture, the teacher will have at least a dozen applicants, saying, " Please, sir, may I?   Please, sir, may I?"   The teacher having selected the child to make the next trial, say one of the youngest of the applicants, the child walks round the room with the pointer, and puts it on the right picture ; which will be always known by the other children calling out, " That is the right, that is the right."   To view the child's sparkling eyes, who has found the picture, and to see the pleasure beam-

ing forth in his countenance, you might imagine, that
he conceived he had performed one of the greatest
wonders of the age. The children will then proceed
to read what is printed on the picture, which is as
follows: "The Nativity of our Lord and Saviour
Jesus Christ;" which is printed at the top of the picture. At the bottom are the following words: "And
she brought forth her first-born son, and wrapped him
in swaddling clothes, and laid him in a manger, because there was no room for them in the inn."—We
then proceed to question them in the following manner:—

Q. What do you mean by the Nativity of Jesus
Christ? *A.* The time he was born. *Q.* Where was
he born? *A.* In Bethlehem of Judea. *Q.* Where
did they lay him? *A.* In a manger. *Q.* What is a
manger? *A.* A thing that horses feed out of. *Q.*
What was the reason they put him there? *A.* Because there was no room in the inn. *Q.* What is an
inn? *A.* A place where persons lodge who are travelling, and it is like a public house. *Q.* What do
you mean by travelling? *A.* When you go from one
place to another; from London into the country, or
from the country into London. *Q.* Is any thing else
to be understood by travelling? *A.* Yes, we are all
travelling. *Q.* What do you mean by being all travelling? *A.* We are all going in a good road or
else in a bad one. *Q.* What do you mean by a good
road? *A.* That which leads to heaven. *Q.* What will
lead us to heaven? *A.* Praying to God, and endeavouring to keep his commandments, and trying all we
can to be good children. *Q.* Can we make ourselves good? *A.* No; we can receive nothing, ex-

cept it be given us from heaven. *Q.* What is travelling in a bad road ? *A.* Being naughty children,
and not minding what is said to us ; and when we
say bad words, or steal any thing, or take God's
name in vain. *Q.* Where will this road lead to ?
A. To eternal misery.

Here we usually give a little advice according to
circumstances, taking care always to avoid long
speeches, that will tend to stupify the children. If
they appear tired, we stop, but if not, they repeat
the following hymn, which I shall insert in full, as
I believe there is nothing in it that any Christian
would object to.

> Hark ! the skies with music sound !
> Heav'nly glory beams around ;
> Christ is born ! the angels sing,
> Glory to the new-born King.
>
> Peace is come, good-will appears,
> Sinners, wipe away your tears ;
> God in human flesh to-day,
> Humbly in the manger lay.
>
> Shepherds tending flocks by night,
> Heard the song, and saw the light ;
> Took their reeds, and softest strains
> Echo'd through the happy plains.
>
> Mortals, hail the glorious King !
> Richest incense cheerful bring ;
> Praise and love Emanuel's name,
> And his boundless grace proclaim.

The hymn being concluded, we put the following
questions to the children:

Q. Who was the new-born king? *A.* Jesus Christ. *Q.* Who are sinners? *A.* We, and all men. *Q.* What are flocks? *A.* A number of sheep. *Q.* What are shepherds? Those who take care of the sheep. *Q.* What are plains? *A.* Where the sheep feed. *Q.* Who are mortals? *A.* We are mortals. *Q.* Who is the glorious king? *A.* Jesus Christ. *Q.* What is meant by Emanuel's name? *A.* Jesus Christ.

Here the teacher can inform the children, that Jesus Christ is called by a variety of names in the Bible, and can repeat them to the children if he thinks proper; for every correct idea respecting the Saviour which he can instil into their minds will serve as a foundation for other ideas, and he will find that the more ideas the children have, the more ready they will be in answering his questions; for man is a progressive being; his capacity for progression is his grand distinction above the brutes.

Lazarus raised from the Dead.

The picture being suspended as before described, we proceed thus:—

Q. What is this? *A.* Jesus Christ raising Lazarus from the dead. *Q.* Who was Lazarus? *A.* A man that lived in a town called Bethany, and a friend of Christ's. *Q.* What is a town? *A.* A place where there are a great number of houses, and persons living in them. *Q.* What do you mean by a friend? *A.* A person that loves you, and does all the good he can for you, to whom you ought to do the same in return. *Q.* Did Jesus love Lazarus? *A.* Yes, and his sisters, Martha and Mary. *Q.* Who was it that sent unto Jesus Christ, and told him that Lazarus was sick? *A.* Martha and Mary. *Q.* What did they say? *A.* They said, Lord, behold he whom thou lovest is sick. *Q.* What answer did Jesus make unto them? *A.* He said, this sickness is not unto death, but for the glory of God. *Q.* What did he mean by saying so? *A.* He meant that Lazarus should be raised again by the power of God, and that the people that stood by, should see it, and believe on him. *Q.* How many days did Jesus stop where he was when he found Lazarus was sick? *A.* Two days. *Q.* When Jesus Christ wanted to leave the place, what did he say to his disciples? *A.* He said let us go into Judea again. *Q.* What do you mean by Judea? *A.* A country where the Jews lived. *Q.* Did the disciples say any thing to Jesus Christ, when he expressed a wish to go into Judea again? *A.* Yes, they said, Master, the Jews of late sought to stone thee, and goest thou thither again? *Q.* What did Jesus Christ tell them? *A.* He told them a great many things, and at last told them plainly that Lazarus was dead. *Q.* How many days had Lazarus lain in the grave before he was raised up? *A.* Four. *Q.* Who went to meet Jesus Christ, when she heard that he was coming? *A.* Martha; but Mary sat still in the house. *Q.* Did Martha say any thing to Jesus when she met him? *A.* Yes, she said, Lord, if thou hadst been here my brother had not died. *Q.* Did Martha tell her sister that Jesus Christ was come? *A.* Yes; she said, the Master is come, and calleth for thee. *Q.* Did Mary go to meet Jesus Christ? *A.* Yes; and when she saw him, she fell down at his feet, and said, Lord, if thou hadst been here, my brother had not died. *Q.* Did Mary weep? *A.* Yes; and the Jews that were with her. *Q.* What is weeping? *A.* To cry. *Q.* Did Jesus weep? *A.* Yes; and the Jews said, Behold, how he loved him. *Q.* Did the Jews say anything else? *A.* Yes; they said, could not this man that opened the eyes of the blind, have caused that even this man should not have died? *Q.* What took place next? *A.* He went to the grave, and told the persons that stood by, to take away the stone. *Q.* And when they took away the stone, what did Jesus Christ do? *A.* He cried, with a loud voice, Lazarus, come forth; and he that was dead, came forth, bound hand and foot, with grave clothes, and his face was bound about with a napkin. —Jesus saith unto them, loose him, and let him go; and many of the Jews which came to Mary, and had seen these things which Jesus did, believed on him. *Q.* If we wanted any more information about Lazarus and his sisters, where should we find it? *A.* In the Bible. *Q.* What part? *A.* The eleventh and twelfth chapters of John.

I have had children at the early age of four years, ask me questions that I could not possibly answer; and among other things, the children have said, when being examined at this picture, "That if Jesus Christ had cried, softly, Lazarus, come forth, he would have come."—And when asked, Why they thought so, they have answered, "Because God can do anything;" which is a convincing proof, that children, at a very early age, have an idea of the Omnipotence of the Supreme Being. Oh, that men

would praise the Lord for his goodness to the
children of men!

Picture of the Last Supper.

Q. What is this? *A.* A picture of the Last
Supper.   *Q.* What do you mean by the last supper?
A. A sacrament instituted by Jesus Christ himself.
Q. What do you understand by a sacrament?   *A.*
There are two sacraments, baptism and the holy
supper, and they are both observed by true Christians
Q. We will speak about baptism presently, but as we
have the picture of the holy supper before us, let me
ask if it is called by any other name?   *A.* Yes; it is
said that Jesus kept the passover with his disciples,
and when the even was come he sat down with them,
and as they did eat, Jesus took bread, and blessed it,
and brake it, and gave to his disciples, saying, Take,
eat, this is my body.   *Q.* What took place next?   *A.*
He took the cup, and when he had given thanks, he
gave it them, saying, this is my blood, the blood of
the New Testament, which is shed for many.   *Q.*
Did Jesus command this ordinance to be observed by
his people?   *A.* Yes; he said in another place,
This do in remembrance of me (Luke xxii. 19).   *Q.*
What ought those persons to remember who do this?
A. They should remember that Jesus Christ died on
the cross to save sinners.   A. Is any thing else to be
understood by the sacrament of the Lord's supper?
A. Yes, a great deal more.   *Q.* Explain some of
it?   *A.* When they drink the wine they should recollect that they ought to receive the truth of God into
their understandings.   *Q.* What will be the effect

of receiving the truth of God into our understanding?
A. It will expel or drive out all falsehood. *Q.* What
ought they to recollect when they eat the bread? *A.*
They should recollect that they receive the love of
God into their will and affections. *Q.* What will be
the effect of this? *A.* It will drive out all bad
passions and evil desires; for it is said, he that
eateth my flesh and drinketh my blood, dwelleth in
me and I in him (John vi. 27). *Q.* Is any thing
more to be understood by these things? *A.* Much
more, which we must endeavour to learn when we
get older. *Q.* How will you learn this? *A.* By
reading the Bible and going to a place of worship.

———

Allow such things as these to be brought before the
infant mind: let the feelings of the heart, as well as
the powers of the understanding, be called into exercise; let babes have "the pure milk of the Word"
before "the strong meat;" let as little stress as possible be laid on "the mere letter," and as much as
possible on "the spirit" of "the truth;" let it be
shewn, that piety is not merely rational, but in the
highest degree practicable; let all this be done with
diligence, faith, and prayer, and I hesitate not to say,
that we shall have an increase of the religion of the
heart.

Religious instruction may be given in other ways.
Let the teacher take a flower or an insect, and ask the
children if they could make such a one; and I never
found one who would answer, "Yes." A microscope
will increase the knowledge of its wonders. The

Y

teacher may then make a needle the subject of remark; the children will admit that it is smooth, very
smooth; let him tell them it is the work of man, and
as such will appear imperfect in proportion as it is
examined; and shewing them it through the microscope, they will perceive it is rough and full of holes.
As a contrast, let him take a bee, obtain their observations on it as it is, give them a short history of it,
and they will acknowledge its superiority over the
needle. But on viewing it through the microscope,
astonishment will be increased, and I have heard many
say at such a time; "O Sir, how good (meaning
great) God must be!" The sting may then be pointed
out, as *unlike* the needle, and perfectly smooth; and
thus truth may be imparted in a manner the most
interesting and delightful.

The influence of such considerations on *character* is
obvious. When the *greatness* of God is spoken of,
allusion may be made to our pride, and to the importance of humility; his *goodness* may suggest the evil
of unkindness, and the importance of benevolence;
and his *truth* may lead to remarks on its necessity,
and the sin of falsehood.

A small plot of ground may moreover be appro-
priated to the children; some grains of wheat, barley, or rye may be sown, and they may be told
that, at a certain time, they will spring forth. Often
will they go, and anxiously watch for this; and at
length, they will say perhaps, "Please, sir, such a
thing has come up; we know it is so, for it is just
what you said it would be." Week after week the
progress of vegetation will be observed, and the fulfil-
ment of the master's promise will greatly tend to in-

crease *his* influence. So great will *he* appear, that his words and commands will be more regarded; while it will be his object to trace the wonders which he predicted to their divine Source. I have frequently observed, on such occasions, what I should term an act of infant worship. Often has the question been put to me, "Please, sir, is it wicked to play?" As if the spirit were awed, and transgression against God were regarded with dread. Caution has been also discovered in the use of the divine name; and I have listened with delight to such remarks as these: "Please, sir, when we sing a hymn, we may say God, or if we talk about the sun, we may say God made it; and it is'nt taking his name in vain, is it? But when we talk of God as boys do in the street, that is very wicked!"

The following facts will illustrate the benefit of scriptural instruction.

———

A little boy, about four years and a half old, belonging to an Infant School, went to see his cousin, a little girl about his own age. At bed-time, the little boy, to his great surprise, saw her get into bed without having said her prayers. The little fellow immediately went up to the side of the bed, and put this question to her: "Which would you rather go to, heaven or hell?" The little girl said, "I don't know!" "Not know!" said the boy; "Why, wicked people go to hell, and the good go to heaven, a happy place." The little girl then said, "Why, I should like to go to heaven." "Ah!" but replied the little fellow again, " You did not say your prayers; and all that go to heaven pray to God." She then said, " Will you teach me to pray your prayer ?" "If I lived with you," said he, " I would : but if you go to the Infant School, they will teach you to say your prayers, and sing hymns too."

One day, while the teacher of an Infant School was speaking to his little children, from the conversation of our Lord with the woman of Samaria at the well, a gentleman present asked the following questions : " Where should we go to worship God ?" When a little boy answered, " To a throne of grace." " And where is a throne of grace ?" "Any where," answered the boy; " for where we kneel down, and pray to God with our hearts, we are *then* at a throne of grace."

There are times when the children are in a better state to receive religious instruction than others. A teacher of observation will soon perceive this, and act accordingly; if, however, the thing is overdone, which it may be, and which I have seen, then the effect is fatal. Hypocrisy will take the place of sincerity, and the heart will remain unaffected and unimproved.

A little boy, the subject of the following anecdote, being six years of age, and forward in his learning, I considered him fit to be sent to another school; and informed the parents accordingly. The father came immediately, and said, he hoped I would keep him till he was seven years of age; adding, that he had many reasons for making the request. I told him, that the design of the Institution was to take such children as no other school would admit; and as his child had arrived at the age of six, he would be received into the National School; moreover, as we had a number of applications for the admission of children much younger, I could not grant his request. He then said, "I understand that you make use of pictures in the school, and I have good reason to approve of them; for," said he, "you must know that I have a large Bible in the house, Matthew Henry's, which was left me by my deceased mother; like many more, I never looked into it, but kept it merely for show. The child, of course, was forbidden to open it, for fear of its being spoiled: but still he was continually asking me to read in it, and I as continually denied him : indeed, I had imbibed many unfavourable impressions concerning this book, and had no inclination to read it, and was not very anxious that the child should. However, the child was not to be put off, although several times I gave him a box on the ear for worrying me; for, notwithstanding this usage, the child would frequently ask me to read it, when he thought I was in a good humour; and at last I complied with his wishes. 'Please, father,' said the child, 'will you read about Solomon's wise judgment.' 'I don't know where to find it,' was the reply. 'Then,' says the child, 'I will tell you; it is in the third chapter of the first book of Kings.' I looked as the child directed, and, finding it, I read it to him. Having done so, I was about to shut up the book; which the child perceiving, said, 'Now, please father, will you read about Lazarus raised from the dead ?' which was done; and, in short," said the father, "he kept me at it for at least two hours that night, and completely tired me out, for there was no getting rid of him. The next night he renewed the application, with 'Please, father, will you read about Joseph and his brethren?' and he could always tell me where these stories were to be found. Indeed, he was not contented with my reading it, but would get me into many difficulties, by asking me to explain that which I knew nothing about; and if I said I could not tell him, he would tell me that I ought to go to church, for his master had told him, that that was the place to learn more about it; adding, 'and I will go with you, father.' In short, he told me every picture you had in your school, and kept me so well at it, that I at last got into the habit of *reading for myself,* with some degree of delight; this, therefore, is one reason why I wish the child to remain in the school." A short time afterwards, the mother called on me, and told me, that no one could be happier than she was, for there was so much alteration in her husband for the better, that she could scarcely believe him to be the same man. Instead of being in the skittle-ground, in the evening, spending his money and getting tipsy, he was reading at home to her and his children; and the money that used to go for gambling, was now going to buy books, with which, in conjunction with the Bible, they were greatly delighted, and afforded both him and them a great deal of pleasure and profit.

Here we see a whole family were made comfortable, and called to a sense of religion and duty, by the instrumentality of a child of six years of age. I subsequently made inquiries, and found that the whole family attended a place of worship, and that their character would bear the strictest investigation.

The following anecdote will also shew how early impressions are made on the infant mind, and the effects such impressions may have in the dying moments of a child. A little boy, between the age of five and six years, being extremely ill, prevailed on his mother to ask me to come and see him. The mother called, and stated, that her little boy said he wanted to see his master so bad, that he would give anything if he could see him. The mother likewise said, she should herself be very much obliged to me if I would come; conceiving that the child would get better after he had seen me. I accordingly went; and on seeing the child considered that he could not recover. The moment I entered the room, the child attempted to rise, but could not. "Well, my little man," said I, "did you want to see me?" "Yes sir, I wanted to see you very much," answered the child. "Tell me what you wanted me for." "I wanted to tell you that I cannot come to school again, because I shall die." "Don't say that," said the mother, "you will get better, and then you can go to school again." "No," answered the child, "I shall not get better, I am sure; and I wanted to ask master to let my class sing a hymn over my body, when they put it in the pit-hole." The child, having made me promise that this should be done, observed, "You told me, master, when we used to say the pictures, that the souls of children never die; and do you think I shall go to God?" "You ask me a difficult question, my little boy," said I. "Is it, sir?" said the child, "I am not afraid to die, and I know I shall die." "Well, child, I should not be afraid to change states with you; for if such as you do not go to

God, I do not know what will become of such as myself; and from what I know of you, I firmly believe that you will, and all like you; but you know what I used to tell you at school." "Yes, sir, I do; you used to tell me that I should pray to God to assist me to do to others as I would that they should do to me, as the hymn says; and mother knows that I always said my prayers, night and morning; and I used to pray for father and mother, master and governess, and every body else." "Yes, my little man, this is part of our duty; we should pray for every one; and, I think, if God sees it needful, he will answer our prayers, especially when they come from the heart." Here the child attempted to speak, but could not, but waved his hand, in token of gratitude for my having called; and I can truly say, that I never saw so much confidence, resignation, and true dependence on the divine will, manifested by any grown person, on a death-bed, much less by a child under the tender age of seven years. I bade the child adieu, and was much impressed with what I had seen. The next day the mother called on me, and informed me that the child had quitted his tenement of clay; and that just before his departure, had said to her, and those around him, that the souls of children never die; it was only the body that died; that he had been told at school, while they were saying the pictures, that the soul went to God, who gave it. The mother said that these were the last words the child was known to utter. She then repeated the request about the children singing a hymn over his grave, and named the hymn she wished to have sung. The time arrived for the funeral, and the parents of the children who were to sing the hymn, made them very neat and clean, and sent them to school. I sent them to the house whence the funeral was to proceed, and the undertaker sent word that he could not be troubled with such little creatures, and that unless I attended myself the children could not go. I told him that I was confident that the children would be no trouble to him, if he only told them to follow the mourners two and two, and that it was unnecessary for any one to interfere with them further than shewing them the way back to the school. I thought, however, that I would attend to see how the children behaved, but did not let them see me, until the corpse had arrived at the ground. As soon as I had got to the ground, some of the children saw me, and whispered, "There's master;" when several of them stepped out of the ranks to favour me with a bow. When the corpse was put into the ground, the children were arranged round the grave, not one of whom was more than six years of age. One of them gave out the hymn, in the usual way, and then it was sung by the whole of them; and, according to the opinions of the by-standers, very well. The novelty of the thing caused a great number of persons to collect together; and yet, to their credit, while the children were singing, there was not a whisper to be heard; and when they had finished the hymn, the poor people made a collection for the children, on the ground. The minister himself rewarded one or two of them, and they returned well stored with money, cakes, &c. This simple thing was the means of making the school more known; for I could hear persons inquiring, "Where do these children come from ?" "Why, don't you know ?" replied others, "from the Infant School." "Well," answered a third, "I will try to get my children into it ; for I should like them to be there of all things. When do they take them in, and how do they get them in ?" "Why, you must apply on Monday mornings," answered another ; and the following Monday I had no less than forty-nine applications, all of which I was obliged to refuse, because the school was full.

Natural History.

When teachers are conversing with their children, they should always take care to watch their countenances, and the moment they appear tired, to stop. An hour's instruction when the children's minds and hearts are engaged, is better than many hours' effort, when they are thinking of something else. In addition to thirty-four pictures of Scripture history, we have sixty of natural history, each picture having a variety of quadrupeds, birds, fishes, and flowers. The first thing we do is to teach the children the names of the different things; then to distinguish them by their forms ; and lastly, they are questioned on them as follows :—If the animal is a horse, we put the pointer to it, and say—

What is this ? *A.* A picture of a horse. *Q.* What is the use of the horse ? *A.* To draw carts, coaches, waggons, drays, fire-engines, caravans, the plough and harrow, boats on the canals, and any thing that their masters want them. *Q.* Will they carry as well as draw ? *A.* Yes, they will carry a lady or gentleman on their backs, a sack of corn, or paniers, or even little children, but they must not hit them hard, if they do, they will fall off their backs; besides, it is very cruel to beat them. *Q.* What is the difference between carrying and drawing? *A.* To carry is when they have the whole weight on their backs, but to draw is when they pull any thing along. *Q.* Is there any difference between those horses that carry, and those horses that draw ? *A.* Yes; the horses that draw carts, drays, coal-waggons, stage-waggons, and other heavy things, are stouter and much larger, and stronger than those that carry on the saddle, and are called draught horses. *Q.* Where do the draught horses come from ? *A.* The largest come from Leicestershire, and some come from Suffolk, which are very strong, and are called Suffolk punches. *Q.* Where do the best saddle-horses come from ? *A.* They came at first from Arabia, the place in which the camel is so useful ; but now it is considered that those are as good which are bred in England. *Q.* What do they call a horse when he is young? *A.* A foal, or a young colt. *Q.* Will he carry and draw while he is young ? *A.* Not until he is taught, which is called breaking of him in. *Q.* And when he is broke in, is he very useful? *A.* Yes; and please, sir, we hope to be more useful when we are properly taught. *Q.* What do you mean by being properly taught? *A.* When we have as much trouble taken with us as the horses and dogs have taken with them. *Q.* Why, you give me a great deal of trouble, and yet I endeavour to teach you. *A.* Yes, sir, but before Infant Schools were established, little children like us were running the streets.* *Q.* But you ought to be good children if you do run the streets. *A.* Please sir, there is nobody to tell us how†, and if the man did not teach the horse, he would not know how to do his work.

Here we observe to the children, that as this animal is so useful to mankind, it should be treated with kindness. And having questioned them as to the difference between a cart and a coach, and satisfied ourselves that they understand the things that are mentioned, we close, by asking them what is the use of the horse after he is dead, to which the children reply, that its flesh is eaten by other animals (naming them), and that its skin is put into pits with oak bark, whch is called tanning ; and that when it is tanned it is called leather ; and leather is made into shoes to keep the feet warm and dry, and that we are indebted to the animals for many things that we both eat and wear, and above all to the great God for every thing that we possess. I cannot help thinking that if this plan were more generally adopted, in all schools, we should not have so many persons ascribing every thing to blind chance, when all nature exhibits a God, who guides, protects, and continually preserves the whole.

We also examine the children concerning that ill-treated animal, the ass, and contrast it with the beautiful external appearance of the zebra ; taking care to warn the children not to judge of things by their outward appearance, which the world in general are too apt to do, but to judge of things by their uses,

---

* This answer was given by a child five years of age.

† This answer was given by a child six years of age.

and of men by their general character and conduct. After having examined the children concerning the animals that are most familiar to us, such as the sheep, the cow, the dog, and others of a similar kind, we proceed to foreign animals, such as the camel, the elephant, the tiger, the lion, &c. &c. In describing the use of the camel and the elephant, there is a fine field to open the understandings of the children, by stating how useful the camel is in the deserts of Arabia; how much it can carry; how long it can go without water; and the reason it can go without water longer than most other animals; how much the elephant can carry; what use it makes of its trunk, &c. All these things will assist the thinking powers of children, and enlarge their understandings, if managed carefully. We also contrast the beautiful appearance of the tiger with its cruel and blood-thirsty disposition, and endeavour to shew these men and women in miniature, that it is a dangerous plan to judge of things by outward appearances, but that there is a more correct way of judging, which forms a part of the business of education.

The children are highly delighted with these pictures, and, of their own accord, require an explanation of the subjects. Nay, they will even ask questions that will puzzle the teacher to answer; and although there is in some minds such a natural barrenness, that, like the sands of Arabia, they are never to be cultivated or improved, yet I can safely say, that I never knew a child who did not like the pictures; and as soon as I had done explaining one, it was always, "Please sir, may we learn this?" "Please teacher, may we learn that?" In short, I find that

I am generally tired before the children; instead of having to apply any magisterial severity, they are petitioning to learn; and this mode of teaching possesses an advantage over every other, because it does not interfere with any religious opinion, there being no body of Christians that I know, or ever heard of, who would object to the facts recorded in the Bible, being thus elucidated by pictures. Thus a ground-work may be laid, not only of natural history, but of sacred history also; for the objects being before the children's eyes, they can, in some degree, comprehend them, and store them in their memories. Indeed, there is such attraction in pictures, that you can scarcely pass a picture-shop in London, without seeing a number of grown persons around the windows gazing at them. When pictures were first introduced into the school, the children told their parents; many of whom came and asked permission to see them; and although the plates are very common, I observed a degree of attention and reverence in the parents, scarcely to be expected, and especially from those who could not read.

It is generally the case, that what we have always with us, becomes so familiar, that we set little store by it; but on being deprived of it for a time, we then set a greater value on it: and I have found this to be the case with the children. If the pictures we make use of in our schools be exposed all at once, and at all times, then there would be such a multiplicity of objects before the eyes of the children, that their attention would not be fixed by any of them; they would look at them all, at first, with wonder and surprise, but in a short time the pictures would cease to attract notice, and, consequently, the children would think no more of them than they would of the paper that covers the room. To prevent this, and to excite a desire for information, it is always necessary to keep some behind, and to let very few objects appear at one time. When the children understand, in some measure, the subjects before them, these may be replaced by others, and so on successively, until the whole have been seen.

CHAPTER XIV.

ON TEACHING BY OBJECTS.

———

" The eyes will greatly aid the ears."

———

As I have before said that it is our object to teach the children from objects in preference to books, I will mention a method we adopt for the accomplishment of this purpose. It consists of a number of boards, of which, and of their use, the following description will convey an accurate idea.

The boards are about sixteen inches square, and a quarter of an inch thick : wainscot is the best, as it does not warp. These will go into the groove of the lesson post : there should be about twenty articles on each board, or twenty-five, just as it suits the conductors of the school ; there should be the same quantity of things on each board, in order that all the children may finish at one time ; this will not be the case, if there be more objects on one board than another. I will give an account of a few of our boards, and that must suffice, or I shall exceed the limits I have prescribed to myself.

The first board contains a small piece of gold in its rough state, a piece of gold in its manufactured state, a piece of silver in both states, a piece of copper in both states, a piece of brass in both states, a piece of iron in both states, a piece of steel in both states, a piece of tinfoil, a piece of solder, a screw, a clasp nail, a clout nail, a hob nail, a spike nail, a sparable, and a tack.

These articles are all on one board, and the monitor puts his pointer to each article, and tells his little pupils their names, and encourages them to repeat the names after him. When they finish at one post they go to the next.

The next board may contain a piece of hemp, a piece of rope, a piece of string, a piece of bagging, a piece of sacking, a piece of canvass, a piece of hessian, a piece of Scotch sheeting, a piece of unbleached linen, a piece of bleached linen, a piece of diaper linen, a piece of dyed linen, a piece of flax, a piece of thread, a piece of yarn, a piece of ticking, a piece of raw silk, a piece of twisted silk, a piece of wove silk, figured, a piece of white plain silk, and a piece of dyed silk, a piece of ribbon, a piece of silk cord, a piece of silk velvet, &c.

The next may contain raw cotton, cotton yarn, sewing cotton, unbleached calico, bleached calico, dimity, jean, fustian, velveteen, gause, nankeen, gingham, bed furniture, printed calico, marseilles, flannel, baise, stuff, woollen cloth and wool, worsted, white, black, and mixed.

The next may contain milled board, paste board, Bristol card, brown paper, white paper of various sorts, white sheep skin, yellow sheep, tanned sheep, purple sheep, glazed sheep, red sheep, calf skin, cow hide, goat skin, kid, seal, pig leather, seal skin, wash leather, beaver, &c.

The next may contain about twenty-five of those wood animals which are imported into this country, and are to be had at the foreign toy warehouses; some of them are carved exceedingly well, and appear very like the real animals.

The next may contain mahogany, and the various kinds of wood.

The next may contain prunings of the various fruit trees.

The next may contain the different small articles of ironmongery, needles, pins, cutlery, small tools, and every other object that can be obtained small enough for the purpose.

The lessons are to be put in the lesson post the same as the picture lessons; and the articles are either glued or fastened on the boards with screws or waxed thread.

I would have dried leaves provided, such as an oak leaf, an elm leaf, an ash leaf, &c. &c. The leaves of ever-greens should be kept separate. These will enable a judicious instructor to communicate a great variety of valuable information.

On some things connected with such instruction I find I arrived at the same conclusions as Pestalozzi, though I have never read his works, and for some years after my first efforts, did not know that such a person existed. I mean, however, to give my views on teaching by objects more fully in a work I hope soon to prepare, to be entitled " The Infant Teacher in the Nursery and the School."

The utility of this mode of teaching must be obvious, for if the children meet with any of those terms in a book which they are reading, they *understand them immediately*, which would not be the case unless they had seen the *object*. The most intellectual person would not be able to call things by their *proper names*, much less describe them, unless he had been taught, or heard some other person call them by their right names ; and we generally learn more by mixing with society, than ever we could do at school; these sorts of lessons persons can make themselves, and they will last for many years, and help to lay a foundation for things of more importance.

CHAPTER XV.

"Would you make infants happy, give them variety, for novelty
has charms that our minds can hardly withstand."

As an Infant School may be regarded in the light of
a combination of the school and nursery, the *art of
pleasing*, forms a prominent part in the system; and
as little children are very apt to be fretful, it becomes
expedient to divert as well as teach them. If children
of two years old and under are not diverted, they will
naturally cry for their mothers; and to have ten or
twelve children crying in the school, it is very obvious
would put every thing into confusion. But it is
possible to have two hundred, or even three hundred
children assembled together, the eldest not more than
six years of age, and yet not to hear one of them crying for a whole day. Indeed I may appeal to the numerous and respectable persons who have visited
Infant Schools, for the truth of this assertion; many
of whom have declared, in my hearing, that they
could not have conceived it possible, that such a

number of little children could be assembled together, and all be so happy as they had found them, the greater part of them being so very young. I can assure the reader, that many of the children who have cried heartily on being sent to school the first day or two, have cried as much on being kept at home, after they have been in the school but a very short time: and I am of opinion that when children are absent, it is generally the fault of the parents. I have had children come to school without their breakfast, because it has not been ready; others have come to school without shoes, because they would not be kept at home while their shoes were mending; and I have had others come to school half-dressed, whose parents have been either at work or gossipping; and who, when they have returned home, have thought that their children were lost; but to their great surprise and joy, when they have applied at the school, they have found them there.

Need any thing more be advanced than these facts, to prove, that it is not school, or the acquirement of knowledge, that is disagreeable to children, but the system of injudicious instruction there pursued. Children are anxious to acquire knowledge, and nothing can be more congenial to their taste than association with those of their own age; but we ought not to wonder that little children should dislike to go to school, when, as in most of the dames' schools, forty or fifty, or perhaps more, are assembled together in one room, scarcely large enough for one third of that number, and are not allowed to speak to, or scarcely look at each other. In those places, I firmly believe, many, for the want of proper exercise

become cripples, or have their health much injured, by
being kept sitting so many hours ; but as children's
health is of the greatest consequence, it becomes
necessary to remedy this evil by letting them have
proper exercise, combined, as much as possible, with
instruction ; to accomplish which many measures
have been tried, but I have found the following to be
the most successful.

The children are desired to sit on their seats, with
their feet out straight, and to shut each hand; and then
ordered to count a hundred, or as many as may be
thought proper, lifting up each hand every time they
count one, and bringing each hand down again on
their knees when they count another. The children
have given this the name of blacksmith, and when
asked why they called it blacksmith, they answered,
because they hammered their knees with their fists, in
the same way as the blacksmith hammers his irons
with a hammer. When they have arrived at a
hundred (which they never fail to let you know by
giving an extra shout,) they may be ordered to
stand up, and bring into action the joints of the
knees and thighs. They are desired to add up one
hundred, two at a time, which they do by lifting
up each foot alternately, all the children counting at
one time, saying, two, four, six, eight, ten, twelve,
and so on. By this means, every part of the body is
put in motion; and it likewise has this advantage,
that by lifting up each foot every time, they keep
good time, a thing very necessary, as unless this was
the case, all must be confusion. They also add
up three at a time, by the same method, thus, three,
six, nine, twelve, fifteen, eighteen, and so on ; but

care must be taken not to keep them too long at one
thing, or too long in one position, thus exercising
the elbow joints, by pushing them out and drawing
them back as far as possible.

> Come here, my dear boy, look at baby's two hands,
> And his two little feet upon which baby stands;
> Two thumbs and eight fingers together make ten;
> Five toes on each foot the same number again.
>
> Two arms and two shoulders, two elbows, two wrists,
> Now bind up your knuckles, make two little fists;
> Two legs and two ancles, two knees, and two hips.
> His fingers and toes have all nails on their tips.
>
> With his hands and his feet he can run, jump, and crawl,
> He can dance, walk, or caper, or play with his ball;
> Take your hoop or your cart, and have a good race,
> And that will soon give you a fine rosy face.
>
> Oh! what would my boy do without his two hands;
> And his two little feet, upon which baby stands!
> They 're the gift of kind heaven for you to enjoy,
> Then be thankful to heaven, my dear little boy.

Having done a lesson or two this way, they are
desired to put their arms out straight, and to say, one
and one are two, two and one are three, three and
one are four, four and one are five, five and one are
six, six and two are eight; and in this way they go
on until they are desired to stop.

It should be observed, that all *graceful* actions may
be adopted. I am sorry to find, from visits to various
schools, that the movements of the children have de-
generated into buffoonery; they have been allowed to

put themselves into the most ridiculous postures, and have thus raised objections which would not otherwise have been urged. As, however, the whole Infant System is designed to make the *children think*, I would urge the *teachers* to guard against being automatons. Let them mark every impropriety with promptitude, and correct it with judgment.

I have specified these methods not as being the only ones practicable, or fit to be adopted, but merely as hints to the judicious teacher, who will doubtless think of many others, conducive to the same end: and the more he can diversify them the better. It is the combination of amusement with instruction, which, in my opinion, renders the system so successful; and unimportant or improper even as it may appear to some, is of more real service in the management of young children, than all the methods of restraint and coercion, which have been hitherto but too generally pursued.

The children may also learn the pence and multiplication tables, by forming themselves into circles around a number of young trees, where such are planted in the play-ground. For the sake of order, each class should have its own particular tree; that when they are ordered to the trees, every child may know which tree to go to; as soon as they are assembled around the trees, they are to join hands and walk round, every child saying the multiplication table, until they have finished it; they then let go hands, and put them behind, and, for variety's sake, sing the pence table, the alphabet, hymns, &c. &c.: thus the children are gradually improved and delighted, for they

they call it play, and it is of little consequence what they call it, so long as they are edified, exercised, and made happy.

This plan is calculated to impress the lessons on their memories, and is adapted for fine weather, when they can go out to play, as it is called. But as in wet, or snowy weather, they cannot go out of the school, we then have recourse to the mode previously mentioned. Besides it is necessary that children should have exercise in winter as well as in summer, in wet as well as in dry weather; for this purpose we have several swings in the school-room, made of cord only, on which the children are allowed to swing, two at a time. The time that they are permitted to be on the swing, is according to what they have to repeat. If it is the pence-table, they say—

Twenty pence are one and eightpence,
　That we can't afford to lose;
Thirty pence are two and sixpence,
　That will buy a pair of shoes,

Forty pence are three and fourpence,
　That is paid for certain fees;
Fifty pence are four and twopence,
　That will buy five pounds of cheese.

Sixty pence will make five shillings,
　Which, we learn, is just a crown;
Seventy pence are five and tenpence,
　This is known throughout the town.

Eighty pence are six and eightpence,
　I'll always try to think of that;
Ninety pence are seven and sixpence,
　This will buy a beaver hat.

A A

A hundred pence are eight and fourpence,
Which is taught in th' Infant School;
Eight pence more make just nine shillings,
So we end this pretty rule.

As soon as the table is thus gone through, the children who are on the swings get off, and others supply their places, until, probably, the pence table has been said twenty times; then we go on with the multiplication table, until the children have repeated as far as six times six are thirty-six; when the children on the swings get off, and are succeeded by two more on each swing; they then commence the other part of the table, beginning at six times seven are forty-two, until they have finished the table. During this time, it should be borne in mind, all the children are learning, not only those on the swings, but those who are sitting in the school; and it is surprising to see with what alacrity the children will despatch their other lessons, when it is a wet day, in order to get to the swings. In addition to the knowledge acquired by this method, it is admirably calculated to try their courage. Many little boys and girls, who at first are afraid to get on the swings, will soon swing standing on one leg, and perform other feats with the greatest dexterity, at once shewing their increased courage and greater activity. We generally let four or five children come to a swing, and those that can seat themselves first, are entitled to the first turn, for they are never lifted on. In the anxiety to get on the swing, some of them will perhaps get out of temper, especially those who are not disciplined; but when this is detected they are not allowed to swing that day, which soon makes them goodnatured to each other, and very cautious not to get into a passion. Thus, in some degree, their bad tempers are corrected, which is very desirable. It is a current remark, that bad workmen find fault with the tools ; and lazy teachers find fault with the swings, because they must perpetually watch the children. We are so tinctured with the old plan of *rivetting* the children *to seats*, that I despair of ever seeing the opposite plan become general in my time. As soon as two children are seated on each swing, to preserve order, the others retire (generally speaking) in the greatest good humour to their seats.

Some will, I know, be apt to exclaim, surely this is encouraging and fostering bad feelings—creating enmity and ill-will amongst the children; but I say, No,—it is teaching them to feel a spirit of generous emulation, as distinguishable from that of ill-nature or envy.

Beside the swings, in many schools they have a very useful addition to the play-ground. I mean the gymnastic pole.

Although it is most proper for the master in the play-ground to relax altogether the brow of magisterial severity, yet there is no occasion for him to withdraw the influence of love. He will not prove a check to the enjoyment of the children, if, entering into the spirit of their innocent pastimes, he endeavours to heighten their pleasures by a judicious direction of their sports.

Among other amusements, which his ingenuity may suggest, I would mention a geometrical amusement, which is very practicable. First, let a certain number of children stand in a row. Opposite to these let one or more children be placed as directors to order the change of figure. A straight line, we will suppose is the first thing shewn by the position of the children; the next thing to be formed is a *curve*, by the advancement of each end; then a half-circle,—a circle, by joining hands in a ring;—two equal parallel lines, by the division of the number in action; next a square, —triangle, &c. &c. These changes may either be made at the command of the master, or, as we before proposed, of one or more children acting as officers to direct these geometrical movements.

CHAPTER XVI.

MUSIC.

" Music hath charms."

MUSIC has been found a most important means of *mental* and *moral* improvement. Its application took place from my finding a great difficulty in teaching some children, especially the younger ones, to sound their letters ; and hence I determined to set the alphabet to a simple tune. I sang it frequently to the children when they were low or dispirited, and although none attempted the same sounds at first, I had the satisfaction of observing unusual attention. My next effort was very injudicious ; for I urged on them the imitation of these sounds before they were actually capable of so doing; and hence, as more reflection would have shewn, only discordance arose. Having told them then to listen *only*, as they did at first, I soon discovered, that having learned the tune through the proper organ—the ear, they were able to imitate it with the voice. We then by the same means marked the distinction between vowels and consonants with a tune that was longer and rather more difficult. As the monitor always pointed out the letters in succession while the children were singing, attention was excited and secured, and error effectually prevented, as correct time and tune could not be kept unless every child sung the right letter.

Success as to the alphabet led to the adoption of music in the teaching of arithmetic. This was available in two ways, first by combining with it physical exercise, and then by tasking the faculties of observation. The former was effected as follows: the children sang one is the half of two, two is the half of four, three is the half of six, &c. &c. and then brought one hand down on the other alternately, without however making too much noise, so as to interrupt the time; the latter was accomplished by the arithmeticon, which has already been explained. A few specimens of the ditties thus used, shall now be given.

THE CREATION.

God first created heaven and earth,
　　With light to cheer the way;
To day and night he then gave birth,—
　　Which ended the first day.

The firmament God next creates,
　　Now decked in glad array;
The waters, too, he separates,—
　　Then clos'd the second day.

He drain'd the earth; form'd rich display
　　Of herbs, and plants, and trees,
And clos'd his work on this third day,
　　By forming lakes and seas.

The fourth day saw the glorious sun
    Commence his bright career;
The moon, stars, planets, then begun
    The midnight gloom to cheer.

The little birds, with lively song,
    This fifth day quickly sweep
The air, in journies short or long;
    Fish swim the mighty deep.

The sixth day, insects, reptiles, too,
    With beasts both wild and tame;
And man, in God's own image view;
    Alas! not now the same.

God then his six days' work reviewed,
    Pronounced them all the best,
And said, the seventh ever should
    Remain a hallow'd rest.

RELIANCE ON GOD.

If all my earthly friends should die,
    And leave me mourning here
Since God regards the orphan's cry,
    O what have I to fear?

If I am rich, he'll guard my heart,
    Temptations to withstand!
And make me willing to impart
    The bounties of his hand.

If I am poor, He can supply,
    Who *has* my table spread;
Who feeds the ravens when they cry,
    And fills his poor with bread.

And, Lord, whatever grief or ill
  For me may be in store,
Make me submissive to thy will,
  And I would ask no more.

Then still, as seasons hasten by,
  I will for heaven prepare ;
That God may take me when I die,
  To dwell for ever there.

OBEDIENCE TO TEACHERS.

Little children must obey,
Every thing their teachers say;
God is watching all day long,
Whether they do right or wrong.

And wherever they may be,
Every action he can see ;
At home, at school, by day, by night,
Children still are in his sight.

When children do not as they're bid,
And for their naughty ways are chid,
He from the heavens is looking down,
And sees their conduct with a frown.

But when good children strive to please
Their teachers, God their conduct sees;
He marks their actions, and the while
Is looking on them with a smile.

Then little children, all of you,
Do as God would have you do ;
And always think, where'er you be,
Whate'er you 're doing—God can see.

THE BIBLE.

This is a precious book indeed,
Happy the child that loves to read!
'Tis God's own word, which he has given
To shew our souls the way to heaven.

It tells us how the world was made;
And how good men the Lord obeyed;
Here his commands are written, too,
To teach us what we ought to do.

It bids us all from sin to fly,
Because our souls can never die;
It points to heaven where angels dwell,
And warns us to escape from hell.

Be thankful, children, that you may
Read this good Bible every day:
'Tis God's own word, which he has given,
To shew your souls the way to heaven.

ENCOURAGEMENT FOR LITTLE CHILDREN.

God is so good that he will hear
  Whenever children humbly pray;
He always lends a gracious ear
  To what the youngest child can say.

His own most holy book declares
  He loves good little children still;
And that he answers all their prayers,
  Just as a tender father will.

He will not scorn an infant tongue
  That thanks him for his mercies given;
And when by babes his praise is sung,
  Their cheerful songs ascend to heaven.

Come,then, dear children, trust his word,
  And seek him for your friend and guide ;
Your little voices will be heard,
  And you shall never be denied.

THE GOODNESS OF GOD.

The God who reigns above the sky
  Sees all that children do ;
We cannot from his presence fly ;
  And he can hear us too.

'Tis God who ev'ry blessing sends
  That little children need,
And finds for them so many friends
  Who teach them how to read.

They teach us likewise how to pray,
  And sing his praises thus;
Then let us do so, that he may
  Bless both those friends and us.

FOUR SEASONS OF HUMAN LIFE.

Our days four seasons are at most,
  And Infancy's the time of Spring;
Oh! with what trouble, care, and cost,
  Must we be taught to pray and sing.

In Summer as our growth proceeds,
  Good fruit should hang on every branch;
Our roots be cleared from evil weeds,
  As into knowledge we advance.

Our Autumn is the season, when
  Temptations do our minds assail :
Our fruits are proved in manhood; then
  Let not sin, death, and hell prevail.

For Winter brings old age and death,
   If we've good fruits laid up in store;
Soon as we gasp our latest *breath*,
   We land on a *triumphant shore*.

FOUR SEASONS OF THE YEAR.

On March the twenty-first is Spring,
When little birds begin to sing ;
Begin to build and hatch their brood,
And carefully provide them food.

Summer 's the twenty-first of June,
The cuckoo changes then his tune ;
All nature smiles, the fields look gay,
The weather's fair to make the hay.

September, on the twenty-third,
When sportsmen mark at ev'ry bird,
Autumn comes in ; the fields are shorn,
The fruits are ripe ; so is the corn.

Winter's cold frosts and northern blasts,
The season is we mention last ;
The date of which in *truth* we must
Fix for December — twenty-first.

FIVE SENSES.

All human beings must (with birds and beasts)
To be complete, five senses have at least,
The sense of hearing to the ear 's confined ;
The eye, we know, for seeing is designed.

The nose to smell an odour sweet or ill,
The tongue to taste what will the belly fill.
The sense of feeling is in every part
While life gives motion to a beating heart.

THE MASTER'S DAILY ADVICE TO HIS SCHOOL.

If you'd in wisdom's ways proceed,
You intellectual knowledge need.
Let science be your guiding star,
Or from its path you'll wander far.

'Tis science that directs the mind,
The path of happiness to find.
If *goodness* added is to *truth*,
Twill bring reward to every youth.

THE GOOD CHILDREN'S MONEY-BOX.

All pence by the gen'rous deposited here,
When holidays come, I will equally share
Among all good children attending this school,
I should wish not to find a dunce or a fool.
Then listen, all you, who a prize hope to gain,
Attend to your books, and you'll not hope in vain.

THE MASTER.

THE COW.

Come, children, listen to me now,
And you shall here about the cow;
You'll find her useful, live or dead,
Whether she's black, or white, or red.

When milk-maids milk her morn and night,
She gives them milk so fresh and white;
And this, we little children think,
Is very nice for us to drink.

The curdled milk they press and squeeze,
And so they make it into cheese;
The cream they skim and shake in churns,
And then it soon to butter turns.

And when she 's dead, her flesh is good,
For *beef* is our true English food;
But though 'twill make us brave and strong,
To eat too much, we know, is wrong.

Her skin, with lime and bark together,
The tanner tans, and makes it leather;
And without *that* what should we do
For soles to every boot and shoe?

The shoemaker cuts it with his knife,
And bound the tops are by his wife,
And then he nails it to the last,
And after sews it tight and fast.

The hair that grows upon her back
Is taken whether white or black,
And mixed with mortar, short or long,
Which makes it very firm and strong.

The plast'rer spreads it with a tool,
And this you 'll find is just the rule,
And when he 's spread it tight and fast,
I'm sure it many years will last.

And last of all, if cut with care,
Her horns make combs to comb our hair;
And so we learn—thanks to our teachers,
That cows are good and useful creatures.

THE SHEEP.

Hark now to me, and silence keep,
And we will talk about the sheep;
For sheep are harmless, and we know
That on their backs the wool does grow.

The sheep are taken once a year,
And plunged in water clean and clear;
And there they swim, but never bite,
While men do wash them clean and white.

And then they take them, fat or lean,
Clip off the wool, both short and clean,
And this is called, we understand,
Shearing the sheep, throughout the land.

And then they take the wool so white,
And pack it up in bags quite tight;
And then they take those bags so full,
And sell to men that deal in wool.

The wool is washed and comb'd with hand,
Then it is spun with wheel and band;
And then with shuttle very soon,
Wove into cloth within the loom.

The cloth is first sent to be dyed;
Then it is washed, and press'd, and dried:
The tailor then cuts out with care
The clothes that men and boys do wear.

THE HORSE.

Come, children, let us now discourse
About the pretty noble horse;
And then you soon will plainly see
How very useful he must be.

He draws the coach so fine and smart,
And likewise drags the loaded cart,
Along the road or up the hill,
Though then his task is harder still.

Upon his back men ride with ease,
He carries them just where they please;
And though it should be many a mile,
He gets there in a little while.

With saddle on his back they sit,
And manage him with reins and bit,
The whip and spur they use also,
When they would have him faster go.

And be the weather cold or hot,
As they may wish he'll walk or trot;
Or if to make more haste they need,
Will gallop with the greatest speed.

When dead his shining skin they use,
As leather for our boots and shoes;
Alive or dead, then, thus we see
How useful still the horse must be.

THE DOG.

The Cow, the Sheep, the Horse, have long,
Been made the subject of our song;
But there are many creatures yet,
Whose merits we must not forget.

And first the dog, so good to guard
His master's cottage, house, or yard,—
Dishonest men away to keep,
And guard us safely while we sleep.

For if at midnight, still and dark,
Strange steps he hears, with angry bark,
He bids his master wake and see,
If thieves or honest folks they be.

At home, abroad, obedient still,
His only guide his master's will;
Before his steps, or by his side,
He runs or walks with joy and pride.

He runs to fetch the stick or ball,
Returns obedient to the call;
Content and pleas'd if he but gains
A single pat for all his pains.

But whilst his merits thus we praise,
Pleas'd with his character and ways,
This let us learn, as well we may,
To love our teachers and obey.

MORAL LESSON.*

THE TWO HALVES.

" What nice plum-cakes," said JAMES to JOHN,
Our mother sends ! Is your's all gone? "

" It is," JOHN answer'd; " is not thine?"

" No, JOHN, I've saved one half of mine;

* The following tale, though not adapted for the younger children of an Infant School, and too long to be committed to memory by the older ones, might be read to such by the master, and would serve as an admirable theme for conversation. It is likewise well adapted as a tale for family circles.

It was so large, as well as nice,
I thought that it should serve for twice.
Had I eat all to-day, to-morrow,
I might have mourn'd such haste in sorrow;
So half my cake I wisely took,
And, seated in my favourite nook,
Enjoyed alone, the *double pleasure*,
Of present and of future treasure."

" I, too," said JOHN, " made up my mind
This morning, when our mother kind
Sent down the cakes so nice and sweet,
That I but half to-day would eat,
And half I ate; the other half—"

JAMES stopped his brother with a laugh;
" I know what you 're about to say,—
The other half you gave away.
Now, brother, pray explain to me,
The charms which you in *giving* see.
Shew me how *feasting* foes or friends
Can for your *fasting* make amends."

" A poor old man," said JOHN, " came by,
Whose looks implor'd for charity.
His eyes, bedimmed with starting tears,
His body bowed by length of years,
His feeble limbs, his hoary hairs,
Were to my heart as silent prayers.
I saw, too, he was hungry, though
His lips had not informed me so.
To this poor creature, JAMES, I gave
The half which I had meant to save.
The lingering tears, with sudden start,
    Ran down the furrows of his cheek,
I knew he thank'd me in his heart,
    Although he strove in vain to speak.
The joy that from such acts we gain
I'll try for your sake to explain.

First, God is pleased, who, as you know,
  Marks every action that we do;
That God ' from whom all blessings flow,'
  So many, JAMES, to me and you.
Our mother, next, had she but seen
  Her gift of kindness so employ'd,
Would *she* not, JAMES, well pleased have been,
  And all my feelings then enjoyed?
The poor old man, was *he* not pleas'd?
  Must not his load of sorrow be,
Though but for one short moment, eas'd,
  To think, ' Then some one feels for me.'
But still you ask, of all this pleasure,
  How much will to *the giver* fall?
The whole, rich, undiminished treasure,—
  He feels, *he* shares the joy of *all*.

We eat the cake, and it is gone;
What have we left to think upon?
Who 's pleas'd by what we then have done?
How many pray, JAMES, more than one?
The joys by sympathy supplied
Are many, great, and dignified.
But do not on my word rely,
Whilst you, dear JAMES, the fact may try;
And if you do not find it true,
I'll next time eat *both halves* with you!"

————

It is desirable that the master should add instrumental to vocal music. He should be able to play
on the violin, flute, or clarionet, but, as he must speak
much, the former is to be preferred. Such is the influence of the weather that children are almost always
dull on dull days, and then a little music is of great
advantage. On wet days, when they cannot go into
the play-ground, it assists them in keeping the step

when they march, it cheers and animates their spirits, and, in some measure, compensates for their privations. It will also aid various evolutions.

Music may be employed, moreover, to soften the feelings, curb the passions, and improve the temper, and it is strange that it should not have been employed till the operation of the Infant System to which it is absolutely indispensable. When, for instance, after a trial by jury, as explained in a former page, the children have been disposed to harshness and severity, a soft and plaintive melody has produced a different decision. To recite one case; when I was organizing the Dry-gate school in Glasgow, a little girl in the gallery had lost one of her ear-rings (which, by the way, like beads, is a very improper appendage, and ought by all means to be discouraged), and on discovering the fact, commenced a most piteous lamentation. I made inquiry for it immediately, while the children were seated in the gallery, but in vain ; and I subsequently found it in the hands of a little girl at the bottom, who was attentively examining it, and who gave it me the moment it was demanded. On asking the children what was to be done in this case, they said she should have a pat of the hand. I then shewed, that had she intended to steal it, she would have secreted it, which she did not, and that her attention was so absorbed by it, that she had not heard my inquiry; but one little boy was not satisfied: he said, " She kenned right weel it was nae her ain;" but after singing a simple and touching air, I was pleased to find his opinion changed; "Perhaps, sir," he said, " ye may as weel forgie her this ance as she is but a wee thing."

CHAPTER XVII.

GRAMMAR.

" A few months ago, Mr. —— gave his little daughter, H——,
a child of five years old, her first lesson in English Grammar; but
no alarming book of grammar was produced on the occasion,
nor did the father put on an unpropitious gravity of countenance.
He explained to the smiling child the nature of a verb, a pronoun,
and a substantive."—*Edgeworth.*

IT has been well observed, " that grammar is the first
thing taught, and the last learnt." Now, though it is
not my purpose to pretend that I can so far simplify
grammar, as to make all its rules comprehensible to
children so young as those found in Infant Schools,
I do think that enough may be imparted to them to
render the matter more comprehensible to them than
it is usually found to be in after years.

The great mystery of grammar results, in my
opinion, from not making the children acquainted
with the things of which the words used are the
signs, and moreover, from the use of a number of

hard words, which the children repeat without understanding. For instance, in the classification of words, or the parts of speech, as they are called, *nouns, substantives,* and *adjectives,* convey, as terms, no idea to the minds of children; and, in spite of the definitions by which their import is explained, remain to them as unintelligible as the language of magical incantation. That the children can easily comprehend the difference between words which express the names of things, and those which express their qualities, and between words which express actions, and those which express the nature of those actions, is undeniable: and this is just what should be taught in an Infant School. In the first place, let the children be accustomed to repeat the names of things, not of any certain number of things set down on a lesson card, or in a book, but of any thing, and every thing, in the school-room, play-ground, &c.:—next let them be exercised in telling something relating to those things—*their qualities;* as for instance, the school-room is *large, clean,* &c. —the children are *quiet, good, attentive,* &c.—the pictures are *pretty;* the play-ground is *pleasant,* &c. Having accustomed the children, in this manner, first to give you the *names* of things, and then to observe and repeat something respecting them—you have gained two ends; you have, first, taught the children to be observant and discriminative; and, secondly, you have taught them to distinguish two distinct classes of words,—or *names* and *qualities;* and you may now, if you please, give them terms by which to distinguish these respective classes,—viz. *substantives* and *adjectives.* They will no longer be mysterious words, " signifying nothing," but recognized signs, by which the children will understand and express definite ideas. The next thing you have to teach them, is, the distinction betwixt singular and plural, and, if you think proper, masculine and feminine: but before you talk to the children about *plural number* and *masculine gender,* &c. let them be made acquainted with the realities of which these hard-sounding words are the signs.

Having made the classification of words clear and comprehensible, you next proceed to the second grand class of words, the *verbs,* and their adjuncts, the *adverbs.* With these you will proceed as with the former; let action be distinguished by words;—the children *walk, play, read, eat, run;* master *laughs, frowns, speaks, sings;* and so on; letting the children find their own examples; then comes the demand from the master for words expressing the manner of action. How do the children *walk ?—slowly, quickly, orderly.* How do they *read, eat, run?* How does the master *laugh, speak, sing?* The children now find you ADVERBS, and it will be quite time enough to give them terms for the classification they thus intuitively make, when they have a clear idea of what they are doing. When this end is attained, your children have some ideas of grammar, and those clear ones. There is no occasion to stop here. Proceed, but slowly, and in the same method. The tenses of the verbs, and the subdivision into active, passive, and neuter, will require the greatest care and attention which the teacher can use, to simplify them sufficiently for the children's comprehension; as it will likewise enable them to understand the nature and office of the other classes of words. As, however, it is not my intention to write a grammar here, but merely to through out a few hints on the subject, I shall leave the further development of the plan to the ingenuity of those who may think fit to adopt its principles, as above laid down.

English Grammar doth us teach,
That it hath nine parts of speech;—
Article, adjective, and noun,
Verb, conjunction, and pronoun,
With preposition, and adverb,
And interjection, as I've heard.
The letters are just twenty-six,
These form all words when rightly mix'd.
The vowels are a, e, o, i,
With u, and sometimes w and y.
Without the little vowels' aid,
No word or syllable is made;
But consonants the rest we call,
And so of these we've mention'd all.
Three little words we often see,
Are articles,—*a*, *an*, and *the*.
A noun 's the name of any thing—
As *school*, or *garden*, *hoop*, or *swing*.
Adjectives tell the kind of noun—
As *great*, *small*, *pretty*, *white*, or *brown*.
Instead of nouns the pronouns stand—
John's head, *his* face, *my* arm, *your* hand.
Verbs tell of something being done—
To *read*, *write*, *count*, *sing*, *jump*, or *run*.
How things are done the adverbs tell—
As *slowly*, *quickly*, *ill* or *well*.
Conjunctions join the nouns together—
As men *and* children, wind *or* weather.
A preposition stands before
A noun, as *in* or *through* a door.

The interjection shows surprise—
As *oh!* how pretty, *ah!* how wise.
The whole are called nine parts of speech,
Which reading, writing, speaking teach.

THE ARTICLES.

Three little words we hear and see
In frequent use, *a, an,* and *the;*
These words so useful, though so small,
Are those which articles we call.

The first two, *a* and *an,* we use
When speaking of one thing alone;
For instance, we might wish to say
An *oak,* a *man,* a *dog,* a *bone.*

The speaks of either one or more,—
The cow, the cows, the pig, the pigs,
The plum, the plums (you like a score),
The pear, the pears, the fig, the figs.

An oak, a man, means *any* oak,
Or *any* man of all mankind;
A dog, a bone, means *any* dog,
Or *any* bone a dog may find.

This article we only use
Whenever it may be our wish
To speak of some determin'd thing,
As thus;—*the* bird, *the* ox, *the* fish.

By which we mean not *any* bird,
That flying in the air may be,
Or *any* ox amongst the herd,
Or *any* fish in stream or sea.

But some one certain bird or ox,
Or fish (let it be which it may)
Of which we're speaking, or of which
We something mean to write or say.

Remember these things when you see
The little words, a, an, and thee.
These words so useful, though so small
Are those which articles we call.

CHAPTER XVIII.

THE ELLIPTICAL PLAN OF TEACHING.

" He tried each art."— *Goldsmith.*

ALL persons acquainted with children are aware of
the torpor of some minds, and of the occasional
apathy of others, and to this it is necessary to provide
some counteraction. This is done effectually by what
is called the elliptical plan, according to which, words
are omitted in a narrative or poem repeated by the
teacher, for the purpose of being supplied by the
children.

These exercises are very agreeable to the children,
and by them some features of the mental character
become conspicuous. Children are usually sensible of
their need of instruction, but if they can make it appear that any of their statements are original, their
delight is especially manifest. There seems, too, a
dislike at first, to take any trouble to arrive at the
truth ; careless children will therefore guess several
times ; but an observant teacher will at once perceive

that there is no effort of the understanding, point it out to the child, and thus prevent its recurrence.

Dr. Gilchrist observes, in a letter sent to me, "You have now the whole method before you, and I shall boldly stake all my hard-earned fame, as a practical orientalist, on the salutary consequences that will spring from the adoption of short elliptical tales at your interesting institution."

My usual practice with respect to the elliptical method of teaching, is, to deliver some appropriate, simple, extemporaneous tale, leaving out but few words at first, and those such as must obviously strike the children; as they get used to the plan, I make the omissions more frequent, and of words less obvious. The following specimens will render the whole plain to the understandings of my readers.

A gardener's youngest[a]   was walking among the fruit[b]   of his father's[c]   , he saw a little[d]   fly up and sit on one of the[e]   of the trees; the[f]   lifted a stone, and was going to[g]   it at the poor[h]   which seemed to[i] most sweetly thus:

" My[k]   is   of moss and hair,
   The[m]   are[n]   and sheltered there;
   When[o]   soon shall my young[p]   fly
   Far from the[q]   school[r]   eye."

The[s]   eldest[t]   who understood the[u] of birds came up at that moment, and[v]

[a] Son [b] trees [c] garden [d] bird [e] branches [f] boy [g] throw
[h] bird [i] sing [k] nest [l] built [m] eggs [n] laid [o] hatched [p] ones
[q] roaming [r] boy's. [s] gardener's [t] son [u] notes [v] called

out, throw down the[w]   , you hard-hearted[x]
         , and don't[y]   the innocent[z]   in the
middle of his song; are you not[aa]   with his
swelling red-breast, his beautiful sharp eye, and above
all with the[bb]   of his notes, and the familiar[cc]
         he assumes, even in the[dd]   of a[ee]
         like you ? Ask your youngest[ff]   here
if she remembers the[gg]   which her good[hh]
read to her yesterday of a very[ii]   boy, who
was very[kk]   kind to a harmless green[ll]
which he caught[mm]   for hunger, among the[nn]
in the[oo]   of winter.

———

The following little verses upon the same principle
have been found to answer extremely well, by putting
one child in the rostrum, and desiring him purposely
to leave out those words that are marked, the other
children will fill them up as he goes on.

I must pray
Both   and day.

Before eat	I'll my bread
I must intreat,	From to door,
That would bless	Rather steal
To me meat.	My neighbour's store.

[w] stone [x] rogue or boy [y] disturb or hurt [z] bird [aa] pleased or
delighted [bb] sweetness or melody [cc] air [dd] presence [ee] naughty
boy [ff] sister [gg] story [hh] mother, aunt, &c. [ii] naughty or
good [kk] cruel or kind [ll] finch or linnet [mm] perishing or dying [nn] snow [oo] depth or middle.

I must not play
On God's own day,
But I must hear
His word with fear.

It is a sin
To steal a pin,
Much more to steal
A greater thing.

I must work,
And I must pray,
That God will feed
Me day by day.

All honest labour,
God will bless;
Let me not live
In idleness.

I will not be
Or rude or wild,
I must not be
A naughty child.

I will not speak
Of others ill,
But ever bear
To all good-will.

I'd rather die
Than tell a lie,
Lest I be lost
Eternally.

I must not kill
A little fly;
It is an act
Of cruelty.

I must not lie,
I must not feign,
I must not take
God's name in vain.

Nor may my tongue
Say what is wrong;
I will not sin
A world to win.

In my Bible
I am to read,
And trust in God
In all my need.

For Christ alone
My soul can save,
And raise my body
From the grave.

Oh! blessed Saviour,
Take my heart
And let not me
From thee depart.

Lord, grant that I
In faith may die,
And live with thee
Above the sky.

CREATION.

God made the   that looks so blue,
 God made the   so green,
God made the   that smell so sweet,
 In   colours seen.

God made the   that shines so bright,
 And gladdens all I see;
It comes to give us   and light,
 How   should we be!

God made the   bird to fly,
 How has she sung;
And though she   so very high,
 She won't her young.

God made the   to give nice milk,
 The horse for to use;
I'll treat them   for his sake,
 Nor dare his gifts abuse.

God made the   for my drink,
 God made the   to swim,
God made the   to bear nice fruit,
Which does my   so nicely suit;
 O how should I him!

"O Lord, how manifest are thy works; in wisdom hast thou made them all!"—*Psalm* civ. 24.

I subjoin, as an exercise for teachers themselves, the following hymn,—as one calculated to induce reflections on the scenes of nature, and direct the mind to that Being, who is the Source of all excellence!—

1 Hast   beheld   glorious
   Through all   skies his circuit run,
   At rising morn,   closing day,
   And when he beam'd his noontide

2 Say, didst   e'er attentive
   The evening cloud,   morning dew?
   Or, after   , the watery bow
   Rise in the   a beauteous   ?

3 When darkness had o'erspread the
   Hast thou e'er seen the   arise,
   And with a mild and placid
   Shed lustre o'er the face of night?

4 Hast   e'er wander'd o'er the plain,
   And view'd the fields and waving
   The flowery mead,   leafy grove,
   Where all   harmony   love.

5 Hast thou e'er trod the sandy
   And   the restless   roar,
   When rous'd by some tremendous
   It's billows rose   dreadful form?

6 Hast thou beheld the   stream
   Thro' nights dark gloom,   sudden gleam,
   While the bellowing thunder's
   Roll'd rattling   the heaven's profound?

7 Hast thou e'er   the cutting gale,
   The sleeting shower,   biting hail;
   Beheld   snow o'erspread the
   The water bound   icy chains?

8 Hast thou the various beings
  That sport   the valley green,
  That   warble on the spray,
  Or wanton in the sunny   ?

9 That shoot along   briny deep,
  Or   ground their dwellings keep;
  That thro' the   forest range,
  Or frightful wilds   deserts strange?

10 Hast   the wondrous scenes survey'd,
   That all around thee   display'd?
   And hast   never rais'd thine
   To Him   bade these scenes arise?

11 'Twas GOD who form'd the concave
   And all the glorious orbs   high;
       gave the various beings birth,
   That people all the spacious

12 'Tis   that bids the tempests
   And rolls the   thro'   skies :
   His voice the elements
   Thro' all the   extends His sway.

13 His goodness   His creatures share,
   But Man is His peculiar
   Then, while they all proclaim   praise,
   Let   his   the loudest

CHAPTER XIX.

REMARKS ON NATIONAL, BRITISH AND FOREIGN SOCIETY'S, AND SUNDAY SCHOOLS.

"Is it then fitting that one soul should pine
    For want of culture in this favoured land?
That spirits of capacity divine
    Perish, like seeds upon the desert sand?
That needful knowledge, in this age of light,
Should not by birth be every Briton's right?"

Southey.

ALTHOUGH it has been the special design of the present work to speak of the first efforts of *art* in assisting the proper development of the mental and moral faculties, I shall take the liberty of indulging in a few remarks on the methods at present adopted in the more advanced stages of education, as seen in our National and Sunday Schools. I need, I am sure, offer no other apology for so doing, than the fact, that it is in these institutions, the infant poor must complete their education—it is in these schools, the budding faculties must either ripen or perish—and the moral principles become confirmed or weakened.

Certain I am, that it is the wish of all concerned in these praiseworthy institutions *to do their best* for the attainment of this object—the welfare and improvement of the rising generation of the poor classes; and therefore I the less reluctantly offer a few thoughts on the subject, which it is my humble opinion may not be altogether useless.

With regard to National Schools, I must say, there is too much form, and too little of the spirit of instruction, to be found in their management: the minor faculties are attended to in preference to the higher ones; it is the memory alone which is called into action; the understanding is suffered to lie in a state of torpid inactivity. Their lessons, their plan of using them, and their discipline altogether, are of that monotonous nature, that the children always seem to me to be dosing over them. I know it will be pleaded that the number to be taught at once, renders this defect unavoidable; that it is impossible to teach a large body of children, in such a way as to secure the attention and activity of the whole. And it is so far true, as to its being impossible to detect and reform every idle pupil, who finds an opportunity of indulging his idleness in the divided attention of his teacher;—but I do think, if it be impossible to cure the evil, it may be in a great degree prevented. Make your system interesting, lively, and inspiriting, and your scholars will neither be able nor willing to slumber over it. Every one knows what an effect is produced on the physical faculties, by a succession of the same sound—for instance, by the long continued chiming of a single bell; it induces a drowsiness which we find it impossible to resist, except by turning our attention to another thing; but let a number of bells strike out into a merry peal—how quickly we are aroused—how lively we become—whilst their various *changes* secure the attention and interest, which their pleasing and spirited tones first excited. And just so it is with the mind in the matters of education; you must give a variety of tones, a newness of aspect to your lessons, or you will never be able to keep up a lively attention in your scholars. For this purpose I would particularly recommend to the attention of all concerned, the chapters in this volume on geometry, conversation, pictures, and likewise that on the elliptical method. By adopting the plan recommended in these chapters, the children will have something to do,—and to do that something they must be *active.* The first object of the teacher is to excite a thirst for knowledge; not to pour unwelcome information into the mind.

It will probably be said, that however well adapted the plan recommended may be for the infantine scholars for whom it was designed, yet, it does not follow that it may be equally advantageous for those of a more advanced age; and if by this it is meant, that the very same lessons, &c. are not equally applicable in both cases, I perfectly agree with the truth of the objection; but it is the *principle* of education that I recommend, and would affirm to be as applicable to children of the most advanced age, as to those of the youngest. And I may further add that unless this is done, these schools will not be in a proper state to receive our children, so as to carry on the cultivation of all the faculties, instead of the memory only. It is not sufficient to store the memory, we must give employment to the understanding. It is not sufficient to talk to the children of piety and of goodness; we must present them with a living example of both, and secure, as far as possible, an imitation of such example.

As applicable to Sunday Schools, I would particularly recommend the use of picture lessons on scripture subjects, for the use of the junior classes, to be used as a sort of text for conversation, suited to the state of their mental faculties. I am convinced that the knowledge acquired by this method is likely to make a deeper and more lasting impression, than that imparted in a less interesting mode. Nor should the lessons on natural history be neglected, in my humble opinion, in the system of Sunday School instruction; inasmuch as the more the children know of the wonders of creation, the greater must be their reverence of the Almighty Creator; in addition to which it will enable the teachers to supply variety, a thing so agreeable, and, indeed, indispensable, in the instruction of children. For these reasons, I think it could not justly be considered as either a mis-employment or profanation of the Sabbath-day. For the elder children, moreover, it would be advisable to have occasional class lectures, simplified for the occasion, on astronomy, natural history, &c.; and although it might be unadvisable to occupy the hours of the Sabbath-day with the delivery of them, they might be given, on some week-day evening, and should be made the medium of reward to good behaviour; such children as had misbehaved themselves being proscribed from attending. When thus seen in the light of a privilege, they would not fail to be interesting to the little auditors, as well as conducive to good behaviour.

Sunday Schools should not be too large, nor should children remain in them too long. I have observed some instances, when this has been neglected, of choices being made, and examples formed, which must be often very prejudicial.

It is with some degree of reluctance and apprehension, I touch upon another topic—that of religious doctrine. As schools for gratuitous instruction have been established by most of the religious sects extant, it is obvious that some dissimilarity of sentiment on religious subjects must exist, as imparted in such schools. Let it not be supposed, that I would cast a censure on any religious body, for establishing a school devoted to such a blessed purpose. On the contrary, I rejoice to see, that however various their theories may be, their opinion of Christian practice, as evinced in such actions, is the same. But one thing I would say, to each and to all, let a prominence be given to those fundamental truths of love and goodness which Christianity inculcates. Let the first sounds of religion which salute the ears of infancy, be that heavenly proclamation which astonished and enraptured the ears of the wakeful shepherds, "Peace on earth and good-will towards men." It was the herald-cry by which salvation was ushered into the world, and surely no other can be so proper for introducing it into the minds of children. I must candidly own, that I have occasionally witnessed a greater desire to teach particular doctrines, than the simple and beautiful truths which form the spirit of religion;

D D

and it is against this practice I have presumed to raise a dissentient voice.

The conductors of schools, in connexion with the British and Foreign School Society, have generally spoken more highly of the Infant System than others, and this is certainly to be attributed to more congeniality, since in them the mental powers are more fully exercised, and there is a greater variety in the instruction given. The only objection I can discover to them, is one that lies equally against the National Schools—I mean the opportunities afforded for monitorial oppression; but this may be obviated in both cases, by the judgment and vigilance of the teachers. It should be added, that schools of both kinds demand occasional inspection from those intimately acquainted with the systems avowedly adopted, as they appear very different in different places. I will only mention further on this topic, that many schools are too large. No Infant School, I conceive, should exceed 200, nor should a National or British and Foreign School exceed 400, when under the care of one master.

In conclusion, I would observe, that as the foregoing remarks have been kindly made, in such a man- it is my hope they will all be received.

CHAPTER XX.

HINTS ON NURSERY EDUCATION.

" 'Tis on his mother's bosom the babe learns his first lessons;
from her smile he catches the glow of affection; and by her frown,
or her gentle sigh, is he persuaded to give up what his ignorance
or selfishness prompt him with pertinacity to retain. Happy
where this sweet, this powerful influence is well directed; where
the mother's judgment guide's her affectionate feelings."— *Taylor.*

MANY persons, eminent by their charitable acts,
and who express themselves generally desirous of
aiding in any plan which may contribute to the improvement and happiness of the poorer classes, have,
nevertheless, been unwilling to assist in the establishment of Infant Schools, fearful that the superior
method pursued in these schools, should render the
children educated therein, much better informed than
the children of the richer classes, who might thus be
supplanted in numerous lucrative and honourable
situations in after-life.

From this circumstance one of the two following
conclusions must be drawn; either that the system

of education pursued in the higher schools is very
faulty and imperfect, or that the fears of those persons
are entirely groundless.

If the first be true, then it cannot be denied that
the consequences feared by the richer classes must
necessarily take place, if, either from prejudice or
apathy, they continue the same faulty and imperfect
method of education, which, by the expression of
these fears, they positively declare is usually pursued
in the higher schools; but the remedy is easy. Let
the same good principles of tuition be introduced into
nurseries, and into those schools to which the children
of the rich are sent—and the latter will not fail to
maintain their patrimonial ranks in society. They
need then have no fear lest the poorer classes should
become too intellectual, but, on the contrary, they
will soon find that their own welfare, security, and
happiness will not only be insured, but will increase in proportion as the poorer classes gain knowledge; for by the method of instruction pursued in
the *Infant Schools*, the knowledge there acquired, is
necessarily accompanied by the practice of industry,
sobriety, honesty, benevolence, and mutual kindness;
in fine, by all the moral and religious virtues.

That the system of instruction recommended in the
foregoing pages is equally applicable to the children
of the rich as to those of the poor, there can be no
doubt; and it might be adopted either in schools
established on its principles or in the nursery. It is,
indeed, obvious that it might be carried to a much
greater extent, where the means of so doing would
not be wanting. Many things might be taught,
which it is neither advisable nor practicable to teach

in the schools established for the instsuction of poor children.

Whilst the elements of number, form, and language, may be taught by the means and after the manner recommended in the preceding chapter on the respective subjects, there are other branches of knowledge which might enter into the scope of nursery instruction with great advantage to the children.

As an introduction to *botany*, I would make the children acquainted with the progress of vegetation, *not from words, but from observation*. I would have three or four garden-pots filled with mould, introduced into the nursery at a proper season of the year; the children should be asked, what is in the pots.— " Dirt," or " mould," will of course be the reply. They should then be shewn the seeds which are to be deposited in the mould, and assuming in the eyes of the children a prophetic character, the mother or governess should inform them of the process of vegetation, and that about a certain time a pretty flower will make its appearance in the pots; the seeds should then be deposited in the mould, and the pots placed in a proper situation. It would not be improper to let the children themselves sow the seed; thus convincing them of their power of being useful, and becoming the instrument of so great a wonder, as the transformation of a seed into a flower. During the time the seed is lying unperceived beneath the mould, the children should frequently be sent to look " if the pretty flower has come up,"—or questioned as to what they were told concerning it. At length the green shoot will make its appearance, just peeping

above the mould, to the no small surprise and gratification of the little observers. They will mark with
attentive eagerness the progress of its growth, the
appearance of the bud, and the gradual development
of "the pretty flower"—till they are fully convinced
of the wisdom of the parent or teacher who foretold
all which has happened, and made acquainted with
the process of vegetation, not from words, but from
observation. Certain it is, that such a lesson could
not be wholly useless. In the first place it might be
made the means of impressing them with ideas of the
Almighty power, highly conducive to piety; secondly,
it would beget a habit of observation; thirdly, it
would be likely to produce a love of flowers and the
vegetable world, favourable to their future pursuits in
the science of botany; and, lastly, it would inspire
their little breasts with a love and respect for the
parents or teachers who were wise and kind enough
to teach them so many true and wonderful things.

As an efficient and amusing introduction to *natural
history*, I would have every nursery provided with a
microscope, by means of which the minds of the
children might be excited to wonder and admiration,
at the amazing beauty and perfection of the insect
world, and the astonishing construction of various
substances, as seen through this instrument. So far
would this be from begetting habits of cruelty, that it
would be very likely to check them. Many children
who would be loath to torture a large animal, such as
a cat, a dog, or a bird, feel no compunction at ill-
using a fly, because it appears to them so insignificant
an animal; but had they once witnessed, by means

of a microscope, the wonderful and perfect conform-
ation of the insect, I am persuaded they would be less
inclined to make the distinction.

Various devices might be made use of to teach the
first truths of *astronomy.* So simple a device as an
apple, with a wire run through its centre, turned round
before a candle, might serve to explain the phenomena
of day and night, whilst the orrery, with the accom-
paniment of a simple and familiar lecture—(it should
be much more so, indeed, than any I have heard or
read)—would make them acquainted with those stu-
pendous facts which strike us with astonishment and
awe. It has been well observed by Dr. Young, with
respect to the wonders of astronomy—

" In little things we search out God—in great
" He seizes us."

One thing I would here notice—that it should be a
constant practice to remind the children, that in the
apple and the orrery, they see only a resemblance to
the earth and the heavenly bodies—that *they* are vast
in size and distance, beyond their comprehension ;
at the same time leading them to an actual observation
of the heavens by means of a telescope. This would
be a high treat to the children, and productive of
correct notions, which are but too apt to be lost where
we are under the necessity of teaching by signs so
infinitely unlike, in size and nature, as the candle and
the apple, and the brass balls and wires of the orrery
to the earth and the heavenly orbs.

For giving the children their first lessons in *geography,* I would have a floor-cloth in every nursery,
painted like a map, but of course not filled up so
perfectly as maps for adults necessarily are. It should

contain a correct delineation of the position of a certain space of the globe, we will say for instance of England; let the children then be told to proceed from a certain spot, to go through certain counties, towns, &c. and to fetch a piece of cloth from Yorkshire, or a knife from Sheffield, cheese from Cheshire, butter from Dorset, or lace from Huntingdonshire, &c. &c. The lessons thus given would be at once amusing and instructive both to the governess and children. If preferred, these maps might be painted of a less size, to cover a table. No difficulty would be found to get a set of such table-covers or floor-cloths painted, if the public would once encourage the plan.

I would also have an oblong tray made to hold water, large enough to cover a table. In this I would fasten pieces of cork, cut out in the shape of land, according to the best maps, while other small bits of cork should represent the mountains and hills on the surface of the respective islands. By application to the toy-makers, a sufficient number of animals might be got to stock the respective islands, &c. with their appropriate inhabitants; whilst the manufactures, and many of the natural products of the different places, might be readily supplied by the ingenuity of the parent or governess. A little boat should then be provided, and a voyage to a given part undertaken; various islands might be touched at, and various commodities taken on board or exchanged, according to the mercantile instructions the children should receive; whilst brief accounts might at first be read or given of the climate, productions, and inhabitants of the respective places, till the little scholar should be able to conduct the voyage, purchase or exchange commodities, and give an account of the various countries and their inhabitants, &c. by himself. Certain I am, that more might be acquired, by this method, of geographical knowledge, in one week, than by the old method in a twelvemonth : and what the children did learn they would always remember.* I might extend these suggestions to the size of a small volume, had I

* This might be done on a larger scale, with a pond and a *real* boat; the pond to be called some part of the ocean; for example, England might be in the centre, and a voyage might be undertaken from the Thames to Yarmouth; here should be models of shipping lying in the Roads, some of the crews might be spoken with, and inquiries made as to what is on board,—the guns, the officers, the captain, &c.; and orders might be given to look out for the sunklight, and other objects of interest. Next day a voyage might be undertaken to Shields, Sunderland, &c.: here some colliers should be lying, the quantity of the coal should be ascertained, &c. &c. In this voyage the chart should be examined, dangers should be marked out, the Newarp light should be looked for, the coast noticed where the Dudge light is, the vessel should lay off Flamborough Head, where there should be a few stuffed sea-fowl, an account of Scarborough should be given, the Humber and the Tees should be sailed up, and so on. Another voyage might be taken to Swansea; here there should be some dolls dressed like females, in the Welch costume, *small* wooden horses and cattle should be in the fields, and a house or two with the balls of culm made of clay and small coal, in the fire-place; iron and copper ore should be taken in at Neath, and lessons given upon them. Such questions as these might be proposed—What bay are we in? What channel is this? On which side of the coast are we? How many leagues are we from Waterford? How many from Dublin? &c. &c.

After having sailed round the island, and taken in various commodities in miniature, the children might go to France; here the French language should be spoken, some French articles taken on board, exchanged, &c.

space to do so; but the limits of the present one forbid; at a future period, should my active employments permit, I may resume the subject of *nursery hints* in an extended and separate form.

There are, indeed, many excellent works already published on the subject; but as by the suggestions and contributions of many, every plan is likely to be perfected, no one is justified in withholding any thing likely to promote the desired object.

A due improvement of these advantages will make the progress of the higher classes more than commensurate with that of the lower. It is obvious, that the former have resources which cannot be obtained by the latter. They have the means too of availing themselves of all improvements in education, of engaging the most intelligent and efficient instructors, and of frequently changing the scene for their children, and consequently the objects which come under their observation. Which, I ask, is the more honourable course,—to object, as some do, to the education of the infant poor, lest they should learn too much, or to improve, then, the opportunities they have, by which they and their children may surpass all others?

———

Having now concluded all that I have to say on Infant Schools, I would, in conclusion, breathe forth a sincere petition to the throne of Divine Truth and Goodness, for the prosperity and spread of the system, in which I am sure I shall be joined by all

who have been convinced of its beneficial effects in
promoting the present and everlasting welfare of
human beings.

Mysterious are thy ways, O God; yet who was
ever disappointed that asked of thee in a right
spirit? Prosper then thy work which is begun in
the world, we beseech thee, O Lord; may thy gracious providence so encircle and protect the rising
generation, that there may be no more complaining
in our streets. Protect them, O Lord, from the
many dangers that surround them, as soon as they
draw their breath in this vale of tears, and put into
the hearts of those who have the means to consider
the state of the infant poor, to give them the assistance they need. Grant that thy blessed example
may be followed by many, for thou didst desire
that children should come unto thee, and not be
forbidden, and thou didst take them up in thine
arms and bless them, declaring, that of such is the
kingdom of heaven. May thy creatures, therefore,
not be ashamed to notice little children, but co-
operate, hand and heart with each other, and endeavour to teach them all good. May difference of
sentiment and opinion be laid aside and forgotten;
and may all join hand and heart in endeavouring
to rescue the infant race from danger; that so these
tender plants may be nurtured with the dew of thy
divine blessing, and be thus made fit subjects for
thy heavenly kingdom, where the wicked cease from
troubling, and the weary are at rest. May thy
divine influence descend abundantly upon all those
who have hitherto turned their attention to infant

children; may they feel great pleasure in doing good; may they receive thy grace and protection abundantly; and when their days of probation are ended, may they find a place in thy heavenly mansions, and there glorify thee throughout the boundless ages of eternity.   Amen.

THE END.

LONDON:
J. S. Hodson, Printer, Cross Street, Hatton Garden.

*9 7 8 1 5 3 5 8 0 5 6 1 2 *